INTRODUCTION TO PSYCHOLOGICAL RESEARCH

INTRODUCTION TO PSYCHOLOGICAL RESEARCH

Mary J. Allen
California State University, Bakersfield

F.E. Peacock Publishers, Inc.
Itasca, Illinois

To my family, Carey, David, Micah, and Brittanie Allen,
and in loving memory of my father, Ferdinand Marcus Jockl

Contents in Brief

Contents

References   254

Index   261

Boxes, Figures, Sidebars, and Tables

SIDEBARS

TABLES

Preface

Introduction to Psychological Research offers broad coverage of research strategies and an introduction to research planning, data collection, data analysis, and research interpretation. Four other aspects characterize this book: attention to ethical principles, coverage of statistical and measurement principles related to research, an introduction to technical writing, and conclusions that students can understand.

Our society is increasingly driven by information and the challenge to make sense of it. The principles emphasized in this book should be valuable to students regardless of whether they enter research careers, because they will be faced with decisions that require judgments based on the same logical framework that underlies the scientific method. I hope they will adopt an empirical, critical, and open-minded approach in assessing proposed solutions to individual and social problems and that they will approach new questions with an enthusiasm for uncovering the truth. I also hope this book will give them the confidence to create their own research hypotheses and to design basic research studies that yield valid information.

This book will be both easy and hard for students. I have done my best not to insult them by offering lists of undefended rules. This means that some difficult concepts must be introduced and explained. I have attempted to give accurate technical information but phrased it in ways that non-specialists can understand. The logic of research and statistical analysis is difficult at first, but it becomes second nature once it is understood. I want students to understand the rationale for my suggestions and to balance it with their own perspectives.

I assume that readers have some background in psychology, including a course in elementary statistics. In my experience, however, many students leave the elementary statistics course without a foundation in the logic of statistical analysis. This topic is covered in Chapter 5, and in later chapters I discuss the relationship between statistics and research design. Computational formulas are not provided; most computations are easily done on computers. Statistical planning and interpretation, though, remain in human hands. Several advanced procedures, such as meta-analysis and factor analysis, are described to give beginners exposure to them, but without so much technical detail that novices are scared off. Students tell me that these overviews give them sufficient background to understand why such procedures are used, enabling them to read the literature without skipping technical sections.

I offer strong thanks for the reviews and support of my husband, Carey Allen, my colleagues, Steve Suter and Beth Rienzi, and the following reviewers who examined earlier drafts of this book: Ed Borgatta, University of Washington; Brad J. Bushman, Iowa State University; Laree Huntsman, San Jose State University; Cynthia A. Laurie, Otterbein College; Joel Warm, University of Cincinnati. In addition, Janet Tilden's outstanding editorial work on the final drafts is acknowledged with gratitude. The final product has been enriched by their suggestions, and all remaining errors are my own.

1

The Scientific Method

Psychologists conduct research in order to understand human and animal behavior. Topics of studies are wide-ranging, from sensory information processing to infants' language development, employee management models, and social patterns in chimpanzees. If research findings are to be meaningful, researchers must adhere to the scientific method, a set of principles that govern how research is planned, conducted, and interpreted. In this text, we will describe the scientific method, examining the major research strategies and assessing their strengths and weaknesses. We shall see how psychologists operate—how they convert their questions into testable hypotheses, select subjects, collect data, and evaluate their findings.

Specialists in any field have their own vocabulary, and a major aspect of understanding their field is to become fluent in their jargon. A few words can summarize difficult and important concepts. Imagine a psychoanalyst who did not have words like ego, repression, and catharsis. Research psychologists also have a specialized vocabulary. Much of this book is devoted to introducing this vocabulary and its associated conceptual framework. You will learn to conceptualize studies and research questions like an expert, using appropriate concepts. Don't despair if you feel as though you're studying a foreign language. You *are*, and soon you'll be fluent in it.

Each new vocabulary word is highlighted in boldface type, and once defined, concepts are used throughout the book. Master each concept as it is introduced, because concepts introduced later in the book build on those developed in earlier chapters.

WAYS OF ESTABLISHING KNOWLEDGE

How do we know the shape of the earth, our birthday, or the fact that Columbus sailed in 1492? How can we be sure of anything? In our childhood we probably believed in Santa Claus, but as we grew older we abandoned this belief as we began to develop our own sense of reality. The process of gaining knowledge about truth is known in philosophy as **epistemology**. Humans have multiple ways for establishing truths, including faith, common sense, logic, and the scientific method.

Faith, Common Sense, and Logic

We establish many truths on **faith**, which can be defined as belief based on authority. We accept experts' judgments about how to bake bread, fix cars, and prescribe medicines. Many of our beliefs are based on faith in the accuracy of parents, teachers, religious leaders, doctors, friends, newspapers, encyclopedias, and textbooks. Accepting facts from authorities allows us to spend our energies testing other beliefs, with a basic core of beliefs free from question. Experts can be wrong, however. Authorities once taught that the sun revolved around the earth, and people accepted this "fact" through faith. The history of civilization is marked by a series of disproven "facts" about the world. Psychologists, too, have discarded facts, such as phrenologists' position that bumps on people's heads provide information about their personalities. Psychologists, as scientists, do not base their "facts" on faith and are skeptical about concepts "proven" by the testimony of experts. They require a different type of evidence.

Common sense is what we believe based on the totality of our experiences. From these experiences we make conclusions about what is reasonable and what is unreasonable. We save for a rainy day, eat our meals before we eat dessert, and use umbrellas in the rain because such behaviors are sensible. The success of advice columnists such as Ann Landers and Abigail Van Buren rests largely on their common sense (and occasional use of faith when they consult experts). Two intelligent, sensible people may, however, be equally convinced that the other lacks common sense. For example, "common sense" about drinking and driving may be quite different for people who have been in accidents involving intoxicated drivers and people who have safely driven home after a beer or two. Common-sense conclusions may be wrong. For example, observations of the sun's apparent movement from east to west can lead to the common-sense notion that the sun revolves around the earth, rather than the other way around.

Logic consists of formal, self-evident rules leading to conclusions that must be true if premises are true. Given the premises that A is larger than B and that B is larger than C, logic dictates that A must be larger than C. The logical conclusion must be true. We do not have to accept the conclusion based on faith or personal experience in order to accept it as true. Nevertheless, some logical conclusions are inaccurate because the premises are wrong. Aristotle logically reasoned that heavier objects fall faster than lighter objects, based on the premise that heavier objects accelerate faster. Although Aristotle's conclusion logically followed from his premise, Galileo's application of the scientific method led to a rethinking of the concept of gravity. Other things being equal (such as air resistance or wind currents), all objects fall at the same rate.

Psychologists, as scientists, are not willing to accept facts on faith. They want observable evidence. Common sense can lead to inaccurate conclusions, such as the belief that the earth is flat; and logical deductions are not trusted until they are examined and checked for accuracy. Psychologists use the scientific method to establish facts.

The Scientific Method

The **scientific method** is a set of empirical, analytical, self-critical techniques for establishing facts. Let us examine each of the adjectives in this definition: empirical, analytical, and self-critical.

Empirical means based on observations. Scientists systematically observe and measure what they investigate; they do not simply speculate about the world. For example, a researcher interested in gender differences in assertiveness would measure the assertiveness of a group of men and women, then compare these empirically established scores. Psychologists, as empirical scientists, observe the world in order to evaluate their theories and hypotheses. These observations may be conducted in the field, as by watching how people behave on public streets; or they may be made under very carefully controlled laboratory conditions, as by measuring brain waves of individuals in soundproofed rooms.

Analytical means that topics of interest are broken into basic parts. For example, a psychologist may be interested in measuring intelligence. We all have a common-sense notion of what intelligence is. The scientist breaks down intelligence into its component parts and systematically includes these elements in intelligence measurement. Intelligence tests commonly measure knowledge, memory, and problem solving. Psychologists also analyze the causes of behavior. For example, a researcher interested in understanding the **etiology** (cause) of rape may analyze possible causes of this crime (such as psychopathology of the rapist, socio-cultural patterns of violence, and local sexual standards) and will systematically research each possible cause.

Scientists are **self-critical**: they look for flaws in their procedures and mistakes in their conclusions, and they publish their findings in scientific journals for public scrutiny and criticism. They are skeptical about claims unsubstantiated by empirical evidence, and they attempt to be open-minded and objective when reaching conclusions and when considering alternative explanations. Scientific facts are established through **consensual validation**, agreement based on review and analysis by peers. No single study can fully establish facts. "Facts" become more acceptable when supported by replications. A study is **replicated** when it is repeated in an independent investigation. Replications use different subjects and often use modified procedures. Results **generalize** if they hold true for new subjects and procedures.

An important aspect of the scientific method is that it is self-correcting. Hypotheses are empirically examined, alternative interpretations are offered, and further studies are conducted to evaluate competing theories.

Theories are not *proven* by research; they are supported or refuted. Positive results do not prove that a theory is correct. For example, a researcher notices that his previously injured knee aches before rainstorms; and he, not being particularly wise, theorizes that his knee causes the rain. Research results may be consistent with his theory: when his knee aches, the rain follows. Of course, an alternative explanation is more valid. Changes in humidity and temperature cause both his pain and the rain. Research cannot be used to prove a theory because it is possible that alternative theories more accurately describe reality. On the other hand, results inconsistent with the theory can be used to demonstrate that the theory is inadequate. Such results falsify a theory. **Falsification** occurs when theories are found wrong because results are not consistent with them. For example, the researcher's knee may ache after playing volleyball at a picnic; in this case the knee pain is not followed by rain. This evidence falsifies his theory. Research cannot prove a theory, but it can lend it support or falsify it.

WHY IS RESEARCH CONDUCTED?

Purposes of Research

Psychologists generally conduct research to explore, to describe, to uncover relationships, or to explain some phenomenon. Research also is conducted for practical reasons, such as to determine the most effective computer keyboard layout or to evaluate the effectiveness of a drug treatment program. Many studies have more than one purpose. They may be designed to explore some aspects of a phenomenon, including the development of an accurate description, the identification of related variables, and the examination of possible causal links.

Exploratory research targets the development of knowledge about some area. For example, the first research team to study people's notions of life after death might interview a number of people or conduct a survey to develop a better understanding of this concept. They are not testing a theory; they are conducting preliminary work to better define and understand the topic of interest. They may conduct exploratory research to develop instrumentation or to highlight possible variables to be examined in further research.

Descriptive research is aimed at describing some phenomenon. A descriptive study may target gang behavior in New York City, people's attitudes toward legalizing marijuana, or mating rituals among gorillas in the wild. The goal is to accurately describe a particular phenomenon in a particular setting.

Relational research is conducted to uncover variables that are related to a phenomenon of interest. Relational research does not necessarily uncover causes, and the relationships need not be explained by an overall theory. For example, we can establish that high school grades are related to college grades. We do not conclude that high school grades cause college grades. Both probably reflect a set of similar causal variables, such as intelligence, motivation, and study time. The goal of relational research may be to establish relationships that will allow us to make predictions, or its goal may be to better understand relationships among variables. For example, we might conduct relational research to uncover variables that predict delinquent behavior or to document relationships among a set of cognitive tasks.

Explanatory research is designed to explain phenomena, rather than to describe them. Causal variables are systematically examined in order to develop or to evaluate theories. For example, in the 1880s Hermann Ebbinghaus conducted classic studies on memory by systematically manipulating materials to be remembered. His goal was to understand the causes of good and faulty memory.

Studies can have a basic or applied focus. **Basic research** is conducted to test, to evaluate, or to develop theories. For example, we could postulate a theory that frustration causes aggression. To obtain empirical evidence for this theory, we would need to define variables and to design studies to test our hypotheses. For example, we could observe hockey players, recording for each player a frustration measure (e.g., the number of missed goal shots) and an aggression measure (e.g., the number of times each player hits a player on the other team). This study would be relational and explanatory because it would examine the relationship between two variables in order to evaluate a theory. Our theory would be supported if players who were more frustrated exhibited more aggression than players who were less frustrated. We also could design experiments to serve as explanatory studies. For example, we could deliberately frustrate children by taking away their favorite toys, then observe their aggressiveness (perhaps defined as hitting other children).

Applied research is designed to meet practical needs. For example, some psychologists conduct human factors research. **Human factors research** is used to investigate strategies that optimize interactions between people and technology. A human factors researcher may design and test a work station that is comfortable, convenient, and efficient. Other specializations of applied psychology exist. For example, educational psychologists create and evaluate assessment and treatment programs for children with reading difficulties. Some applied psychologists conduct **evaluation research**, applied research that provides information on needs and how effectively programs meet these needs. For example, a consultant may conduct an assessment study to evaluate community needs for the treatment of alcoholism and evaluate community treatment centers' effectiveness in reducing alcohol dependency.

Theory-Based and Issue-Based Research

Basic research is theory-based, and applied research is designed to meet practical needs. Sometimes research focuses on issues, such as racial prejudice or sexual assault. Issue-based research can have aspects of basic and applied research. Theories may play a major or minor role, and information that is discovered may or may not have immediate real-world applications.

Theory-based research is designed to test hypotheses generated under a specific theory. The purpose of the research is to support or to falsify the theory. The setting and subjects of such studies are less important than having a well-designed study that allows the theory to be tested. Such studies frequently are conducted in laboratories under carefully controlled conditions, so that additional variables cannot influence the "pure" effects of the theoretical variables.

The theory of positive reinforcement specifies that positively reinforced behaviors are likely to be repeated. We can form many hypotheses from this theory, and each hypothesis can be evaluated empirically. We could hypothesize that pigeons rewarded for pecking a lever would peck it more frequently than pigeons that were not rewarded, that prisoners rewarded for good behavior would behave better than prisoners whose good behavior was ignored, and that clients rewarded for introspection would talk about their feelings more than clients who were not rewarded for introspection. Once we had formed these hypotheses, we would develop measures of relevant variables (e.g., a rating scheme for classifying clients' comments as introspective or not). After collecting data, we would analyze our specific hypothesis and reach conclusions about the validity of the theory. The actual subjects studied and the variables measured are less important than the evaluation of our theory. A valid theory should be applicable in any setting and with any group of subjects. If the theory is not supported by the research, results suggest that the theory should be discarded or modified. For example, a theory may hold true for adults but not for children. Information from theory-based research studies allows us to determine the accuracy and limits of our theories.

Issue-based research is designed to examine a particular issue, rather than a particular theory. Generally this issue is a complex phenomenon. The nature of the subjects and settings for such studies are important because results should be directly relevant to the issue of interest in the real world.

A research team may be interested in understanding why adolescent girls become pregnant. Based on personal experiences and a review of the literature, they may isolate a few variables they think are important, such as religious beliefs, the extent of available sex education, and attitudes toward unprotected sex and early pregnancies. Alternatively, they may conduct an exploratory study by interviewing a sample of teenagers or school counselors. After selecting relevant variables, they design ways to measure them. They may create a survey that systematically reveals attitudes toward unprotected premarital sex, or they may examine school records to determine grades in sex education classes. They have ideas about how their variables are related, but they may not have formal theories. They may hypothesize that girls who view adolescent motherhood as a sign of maturity are more likely to become pregnant than girls who view adolescent motherhood as a sign of irresponsibility, and they can test this hypothesis by conducting research.

When conducting issue-based research, the primary focus is on the development of understanding about a crucial issue (e.g., adolescent pregnancy), and researchers are interested in finding results that generalize to a population of interest. Uncovering relationships that are true only for girls in one school or community would be of little interest to researchers who are primarily interested in developing a general understanding of some phenomenon. On the other hand, if they are specifically interested in applying results within a particular school or community, they are more concerned about results that generalize to this limited population than to a broader population.

Theory-based and issue-based research involve applying the scientific method, and they are judged on the accuracy of conclusions. Both types of research are important, and one is not necessarily superior to the other. It is important to develop accurate theories and to develop useful understandings of important issues. Theories should allow us to explain and predict real-world phenomena; and issue-based research should lead to theoretical understandings. Both types of studies use the same techniques and can examine causal variables, and each type of study can offer information or ideas relevant to the other. Issue-based researchers develop theories about causal variables, and these theories can be investigated in theory-based studies. Theory-based researchers isolate causal relationships, and issue-based studies can test the applicability of these theories to important issues. Researchers frequently conduct both types of research, and they may combine them in single studies or integrate them in research programs. For example, Elizabeth Loftus (1992) conducts theory-based research on human memory and issue-based research on eyewitness testimony. Her research program represents a blending of theory-based and issue-based research.

Ideographic and Nomothetic Approaches to Research

Studies of particular individuals generally represent the **ideographic approach** (emphasizing unique aspects of individuals), and studies designed to uncover general

---

CHARACTERISTICS OF IDEOGRAPHIC AND NOMOTHETIC RESEARCH

Ideographic Research

- The goal is to thoroughly understand and be able to predict behavior in one individual.
- Research involves an extensive, thorough analysis of one individual over a long period of time.
- Research is conducted in natural settings, reflecting the day-to-day life of the individual.
- Each individual is assumed to be unique and uniquely interesting.
- Subjects are encouraged to provide information in their own style and to describe their unique ways of viewing the world.
- Researchers use unstructured data collection techniques, such as interviews and projective tests (e.g., the Rorschach Inkblot Test); they examine personal documents, such as diaries and photo albums; and they interview others to learn more about the individual.

Nomothetic Research

- The goal is to establish general, causal laws of individual behavior and social phenomena.
- Research involves data collection in large, random samples of subjects.
- Research is conducted in laboratories or other highly structured environments.
- Variables are systematically manipulated or measured.
- Statistical analyses are used to generalize from samples to populations.
- Differences between individuals are considered "errors" that are eliminated through pooling data and statistical analysis.

Adapted from Denzin (1984).

principles represent the **nomothetic approach** (emphasizing general laws). The ideographic approach has a long and continuing history in psychological research, but the nomothetic approach is more useful for the evaluation of general psychological principles and theories. The approaches complement each other. For example, we have learned much about depression from nomothetic studies, but ideographic studies may allow us to learn why some depressed individuals recover more quickly than others. The "errors" of individual differences found in nomothetic studies are the substance of ideographic studies. Some research, such as studies of psychological diagnosis and treatment, may combine aspects of both approaches.

Both approaches attempt to define causal relationships, but their goals are different. Researchers using the ideographic approach attempt to develop explanations of the behavior of one individual. Generally, many causal factors are suggested and examined. The nomothetic approach yields theories that explain phenomena within a broad population, and fewer causal factors generally are postulated and examined. The nomothetic approach sacrifices precision for generality. Those who use it recognize that predictions made from their theories will not be precisely accurate, and they expect exceptions, people who are not predicted accurately. Researchers using a nomothetic approach may predict literacy from the presence of reading materials in the home; but this prediction may be inaccurate for homes in which adults merely look at pictures in magazines. These adults are exceptions to the general rule that people who accumulate reading materials are literate. The ideographic researcher, though, would be more interested in understanding the literacy of adults in one home, and would take into account more variables, such as educational attainment, occupational level, and literacy in more than one language.

THEORIES AND PARADIGMS

Theories

Much psychological research is devoted to the development and evaluation of theories. **Theories** describe relationships between variables and the nature of such relationships. We invent theories to explain regularities or patterns in psychological phenomena. Theories define concepts (theoretical constructs), such as extinction and spontaneous recovery, and explain causal connections among those concepts (e.g., spontaneous recovery causes an extinguished response to reappear). **Theoretical constructs** are abstract ideas that apply to a class of similar phenomena. Psychologists have created and researched many theoretical constructs, such as neurosis, imprinting, cognitive dissonance, need for affiliation, and short-term memory.

When we develop theories, we assume that the world functions in a regular, systematic way and that we can understand it. We believe there are **laws** or principles under which the universe operates. Theories offer tentative statements about laws, and we conduct research to examine the validity of our theories. Theories that have survived extensive, empirical evaluation may eventually be treated as laws, such as the law of gravity or Weber's law. As Faust (1984) points out, the theoretical constructs and theories that psychologists develop may not accurately describe the laws that govern behavior. Theories interpret the world in concepts that we can understand. Scientists are faced with a complex reality, and they construct concepts and theories in attempts to deal with it. Scientists, like artists, interpret the world; and like artists, they admire the beauty of an elegant interpretation. The id, ego, and superego may not be real, but these concepts are part of a theoretical model that allows us to understand and predict some aspects of behavior.

The Importance of Theories

Why are theories so important? Theories have four useful properties: they are efficient and they have intellectual, predictive, and heuristic value.

Theories are **efficient** because they organize masses of information succinctly. For example, the theory of positive reinforcement specifies that rewarded behaviors are more likely to be repeated than behaviors that are not rewarded. This one principle efficiently summarizes thousands of observations by researchers, parents, and animal trainers. Theories have **intellectual value** because they satisfy intellectual curiosity. We need to understand our world. We create theories that allow us to understand, control, and predict events in our lives. The theory of positive reinforcement has intellectual value because it offers considerable insight into human and animal behavior. Theories have **predictive value** because they allow psychologists to make predictions. For example, a behavior therapist predicts that children who are rewarded for good behavior are more likely than unrewarded children to repeat this behavior in the future. Finally, theories have **heuristic value**; that is, they inspire researchers toward further

---

WEBER'S LAW

Weber's law specifies that the percentage change in stimulation required for detection is a constant. For example, people can detect changes in loudness that are about 15% of the original stimulus's loudness. Weber and others demonstrated that this law applies to a variety of sensory stimuli, including brightness, pitch, color, smell, and skin pressure. Research has also demonstrated that Weber's law breaks down at extremely low or high levels of stimulation. Larger percentage changes are required for detections at these extreme levels. For example, a 15% change in loudness will not be detected when the original stimulus is extremely quiet or loud (Robinson, 1984).

---

research in systematic directions with specific hypotheses. The theory of positive reinforcement could inspire a researcher to develop and test a school curriculum based on positive reinforcement principles.

Many theories are proposed, and not all of them are good. Here are some questions that can be asked to evaluate a theory:

1. Is it logically consistent with known facts?

2. Is it testable? (Can evidence be provided to support it or to falsify it?)

3. Is it elegant? (Does it have intellectual value? Do you feel satisfied with its explanations? Are you "proud" to use it?)

4. Is it useful? (Does it have predictive value in a variety of situations?)

5. Does it lead to further, testable predictions? (Does it have heuristic value?)

6. Is it parsimonious? (The principle of **parsimony** dictates that we select the least complicated theory that fits the facts.)

These questions require relatively subjective answers, so it is not surprising that psychologists do not always agree about the value of proposed theories. Conferences, journals, and books provide forums for psychologists to debate and to examine their theories by applying the scientific method: using empirical, analytical, and self-critical techniques in an open debate in an attempt to achieve consensual validation.

Paradigms

Theories are embedded in **paradigms**, broad models of how to view the world. For example, Babbie (1983) describes three paradigms for understanding juvenile delinquency: interactionism, functionalism, and conflict theory. Those who subscribe to an interactionism paradigm attempt to understand delinquency by focusing on the interactions between juveniles and others in their world (e.g., family members, peers, teachers, legal personnel). They may study the formation of juvenile gangs and relationships among gang members. Those who apply the functionalist paradigm examine major organizational structures, such as educational institutions and the overall legal system. Rather than focusing on interactions between individuals, functionalists examine larger social forces, such as the effect of sentencing strategies on delinquent behavior. The conflict paradigm involves viewing people and groups as being in competition for resources, with conflicts expressed in behavior such as class warfare or turf battles between rival gangs. Delinquency may be seen as a natural consequence of competition for limited resources. The three paradigms may examine some similar constructs (such as social class), but from different perspectives.

The different social sciences represent major paradigms. Economists tend to explain phenomena with economic factors (e.g., balance of trade, income); sociologists emphasize sociological factors (e.g., roles, norms); political scientists emphasize political factors (e.g., democratic principles, power coalitions); and psychologists emphasize psychological factors (e.g., learning, perception, and motivation). These paradigms affect the theories and variables that are explored. For example, researchers using different social science paradigms might vary considerably in their explanations of a riot. An economist might examine unemployment rates, a political scientist might focus on the use of power by the police and courts, a sociologist might explore the social roles and norms within the community, and a psychologist might look at personality variables related to riot participation. Different researchers may be interested in explaining different aspects of the riot. Psychologists may be more interested in understanding the behavior of individual citizens, but researchers in other disciplines may be more interested in explaining the behaviors of groups of people (e.g., homeowners) or the entire community. Each discipline represents a paradigm for understanding the world; and each offers insight into relevant causal variables.

Psychologists have a variety of paradigms; these paradigms influence what is studied, how it is studied, and which causal variables are analyzed. Behaviorists emphasize observable stimuli and responses; social learning theorists emphasize reinforcement, punishment, and imitation; neuropsychologists emphasize chemical properties of the central nervous system; cognitive psychologists emphasize how information is acquired, stored, and processed; psychoanalysts emphasize unconscious internal dynamics and the influence of unresolved issues from childhood; and humanistic psychologists emphasize the uniqueness of individuals and their potential for growth. Psychologists also tend to specialize in particular areas of psychology. Developmental psychologists examine how people change with age; social psychologists examine interpersonal and group dynamics; and clinical psychologists examine mental illness. These paradigms have heuristic value, but they may limit the range of behaviors and causal variables that are considered.

CAUSALITY

Soft Determinism

Scientists especially desire to uncover cause-and-effect relationships. The concept of causality has been debated by philosophers for centuries. Scientists generally believe that A **causes** B if changes in A result in predictable changes in B. The theory that frustration causes aggression implies that people will become aggressive after their goals are blocked. Psychologists usually deal with **probabilistic causality**, in which a change in A affects the probabilities associated with B. For example, people who were battered as children are more likely to become battering adults than people who were not battered, but not all battered children become battering adults. This type of rela-

---

IS PSYCHOLOGY A "REAL" SCIENCE?

Some people are dismayed that psychologists discuss probabilistic causality, or soft determinism, rather than the hard determinism of the physical sciences. But is the difference so great?

Predictions can be made about individuals or groups, and accuracy is higher when group predictions are made. For example, we can predict that a given school will contain several hundred children at 10 A.M. on a Monday morning, but we are less confident that a specific child will be present at that time. Similarly, pollsters can predict overall election results, but they cannot accurately predict the vote of a specific citizen.

The same phenomenon holds for the physical sciences. Physicists cannot predict exactly when a specific atom of uranium will decay, but they can state with confidence that half the material will decay over a specific period (the half-life). Similarly, meteorologists can accurately predict rain in the midwest but are less able to predict the weather for a parade at noon in Iowa City. The physicist and meteorologist, like the psychologist, are more accurate in making predictions about thousands of objects than a single, specific object.

Psychology, like all sciences, deals with probabilities. Unlike other scientists, psychologists more often are asked to make predictions about individuals, so the fallibility of our predictions is more prominent. Clinical psychologists frequently must answer questions such as, "Is this person dangerous to himself or others?" or "Will this criminal revert to unlawful behavior if released from prison?". We probably are at least as accurate as a geophysicist who is asked, "When will the next earthquake strike San Francisco?", but the geophysicist works in the physical sciences and is less often criticized for dealing with soft probabilities.

Much of the difficulty in making predictions about humans resides in the complexity of the human brain and of human society. Recent mathematical developments in chaos theory demonstrate that very small changes in complex systems can create drastically different outcomes (Bak & Chen, 1991). As an exaggeration, a kitten sneezing in Bolivia might produce a hurricane in Miami because the sneeze sets off a complicated chain of events. Similarly, a chance meeting may lead to a marriage, a lawsuit, or the invention of a new theory. Research in chaos theory demonstrates that complex systems are inherently unpredictable at times. This explains the unpredicted thunderstorm, the unpredicted heart attack, and the unpredicted spark of creativity. Although scientists may not be able to predict perfectly, they can develop techniques to predict accurately much of the time, and they recognize that occasionally an unpredictable, chaotic event will occur.

---

tionship is sometimes known as **soft determinism**, versus the **hard determinism** of absolute causality (the notion that A always causes B), because the causation is probabilistic, rather than absolute.

Psychologists usually deal with complex, probabilistic relationships. For example, frustration may lead to aggression, but it sometimes leads to rationalization (e.g., "I didn't want it anyway"). Researchers must carefully describe the situations in which causal relationships are uncovered, and they are wary of generalizing results to different situations without additional empirical support established through research.

Necessary and Sufficient Causes

Causes may be necessary or sufficient for creating an effect. A cause is **necessary** if the effect can only occur when the cause has occurred. For example, a woman cannot become pregnant without a fertilized egg. The fertilized egg is a necessary cause of pregnancy. By contrast, a **sufficient** cause can produce the effect, but it is not the only possible cause. Rubella during pregnancy can cause deafness in the child; but people also may develop deafness from postnatal infections or injuries. Rubella in the pregnancy is a sufficient cause of deafness, but it is not a necessary cause. By accumulating a list of all sufficient causes, researchers may develop a more general concept of the necessary cause—deafness is caused by damage to or malformation of the nerves that transmit or process auditory information.

Determinism and Free Will

Theories specify the causal links between variables. By assuming these regularities, psychologists are adopting a **deterministic model for behavior**: given some set of causal variables, behavior becomes determined. We wear clothes, go to school, and care for friends because preceding causal events occurred. Psychologists deal with soft determinism, but they believe their predictions are probabilistic only because they are unable to include all predictive variables. Researchers using the nomothetic approach recognize they are losing precision when they apply general theories to individuals. Soft determinism is not a surprise to nomothetic researchers; it is expected. How can we predict a specific child's reaction to a spider unless we know all relevant information about that child's personal history and present mental state?

Deterministic models are in contrast to models of **free will**: people choose their own behaviors. Although most of us are willing to accept deterministic models of physical phenomena (e.g., gravity *causes* objects to fall), we may be uncomfortable with deterministic models of psychological phenomena. Even in our day-to-day lives, however, we assume deterministic models. For example, we may conclude that Lucy is late because she's rude, that Jesse is smart because his parents are smart, and that Will is unfriendly because he is shy. These causal explanations postulate critical explanatory variables (rudeness, inheritance of parental characteristics, and shyness) that cause our observations.

Causes are complicated when explaining human behavior. For example, why is Lucy rude, why are Jesse's parents smart, and why is Will shy? We might specify more links in a causal chain, e.g., Lucy is rude because her parents didn't teach her good manners, her parents didn't teach her good manners because Lucy was a sickly child, she was a sickly child because she was born with fetal alcohol syndrome, she was born with fetal alcohol syndrome because her mother is an alcoholic, her mother is an alcoholic because her parents abandoned her, and so on. The point here is that we believe there are regular patterns in human behavior and laws that govern them. We create theories to explain those patterns, and as scientists, we conduct research to test the validity of our theories.

A complicated causal chain was postulated for Lucy's rudeness. We have all heard that "a chain is only as strong as its weakest link." Maybe you objected to one or more links in the postulated chain. "Wait a minute," you might have thought, "I've known sickly children who have been taught good manners; that link in the causal chain is wrong." You may be right. I only postulated a theory that sickly children are not taught good manners. I offered no evidence for this theory except my own experience with spoiled, sickly children. Apparently my experiences did not correspond to yours. That's why psychologists are not willing to rely on common-sense explanations. We require proof, and the proof that we are willing to accept is evidence collected with the scientific method.

Perhaps, through research, we will discover that parents with sickly children are less likely to enforce good manners, *unless* the parents are concerned about the long-term interpersonal adjustment of their children. My theory can be modified to improve its predictive and explanatory accuracy. When faced with predicting the rudeness of some other person who was a sickly child, we would first have to determine the parents' concern about long-term interpersonal adjustment. Of course, another possibility is that my whole theory will be falsified by the evidence. This would force us to pursue alternative theories that are more accurate. Notice that my theory was first postulated to explain Lucy's behavior, but I generalized it to explain rudeness within the whole population. I began with the ideographic approach, then moved into the nomothetic approach, and I used the scientific method to amend my theory to account for exceptions to the general rule.

CHAPTER SUMMARY

Humans establish truths in a number of ways, including faith, common sense, and logic. Psychologists are not willing to accept these types of evidence; they use the scientific method, a set of empirical, analytical, self-critical techniques. Facts are established through consensual validation and by replicating studies to see if results generalize. Science is self-correcting because competing theories are examined empirically. Theories are not proven by research; they are either supported or falsified.

Research can be conducted to explore, to describe, to uncover relationships, or to explain some phenomenon. Studies can be classified in a number of ways. Basic research examines theories, and applied research examines practical questions. Studies can be theory-based or issue-based, and some studies and research programs combine these models. Researchers may apply an ideographic or nomothetic approach.

Much research is devoted to theories, which are descriptions of relationships between theoretical constructs. Theories attempt to describe laws, which are principles under which the universe operates. Theories are important because they are efficient, and they have intellectual, predictive, and heuristic value. Good theories also are testable, and they satisfy the principle of parsimony.

Theories are embedded in paradigms, broad models of how to view the world. The different social sciences represent paradigms; they focus on different types of variables and explanations. Psychologists apply a number of different paradigms, such as social learning and psychoanalytic perspectives.

Psychologists study probabilistic causality, or soft determinism, rather than hard determinism. Causes may be necessary or sufficient. By accumulating a list of sufficient causes, theorists may develop general concepts of causal variables. Psychologists assume a deterministic model for behavior, rather than a model of free will. Their predictions have soft determinism because they rarely are able to identify all relevant causal variables.

Key Concepts

analytical	human factors research
applied research	ideographic approach
basic research	intellectual value
causation	issue-based research
common sense	law
consensual validation	logic
descriptive research	necessary cause
deterministic model	nomothetic approach
efficient theory	paradigm
empirical	parsimony
epistemology	predictive value
etiology	probabilistic causality
evaluation research	relational research
explanatory research	replication
exploratory research	scientific method
faith	self-critical
falsification	soft determinism
free will	sufficient cause
generalization	theoretical construct
hard determinism	theory
heuristic value	theory-based research

Review Questions

1. Did American astronauts walk on the moon? Did George Washington ever tell a lie? Do people learn arithmetic before they learn algebra? Did you use faith, common sense, logic, or the scientific method to answer these questions? Explain.

2. The scientific method is a set of empirical, analytical, self-critical techniques for uncovering facts. Explain each of the adjectives in this definition and illustrate each with an original example. Why is science self-correcting?

3. John argues that dogs are smarter than cats. Describe a study that will allow him to support or to falsify this hypothesis.

4. Shirley finds results consistent with her hypothesis, and she concludes that her theory has been proven. Why can't she make this conclusion?

5. Isabel is interested in studying memories for faces. Why are some faces easier to remember than others? Describe an exploratory study, a descriptive study, a relational study, and an explanatory study that Isabel could conduct.

6. Describe a study that has both basic and applied functions. Explain your answer.

7. How do theory-based and issue-based researchers differ in their selection of research subjects?

8. A research team is interested in studying creativity. How could they do this using the ideographic approach? How could they do this using the nomothetic approach?

9. Marcus accuses you of ignoring him. His theory is that you don't like him any more. (In fact, you like Marcus, but you are too busy studying to spend more time with him.) Evaluate his theory using the criteria described in this chapter.

10. How are theories related to laws? Is "Weber's law" a theory or a law?

11. Psychologists have theorized that positive reinforcement increases the likelihood that rewarded behaviors will be repeated. What type of paradigm is being applied?

12. Explain, in your own words, what soft determinism is and how it differs from hard determinism. Give an original example illustrating each type of determinism.

13. Some people commit crimes because of poverty. Is poverty a necessary or sufficient cause of crime? Explain your answer.

14. A chemistry major tells you that psychology is not a "real" science. How would you respond to her?

15. Scientists believe in determinism, rather than free will. Ralph argues that he has free will; his behaviors aren't determined. To prove his point, Ralph stands on his head, arguing that he chose to do this. Explain some possible causes of Ralph's behavior, so he can understand how it is determined.

The Research Process

Psychologists conduct research using the scientific method. This process relies on two types of reasoning: inductive and deductive reasoning.

SCIENTIFIC REASONING

Inductive and deductive reasoning provide the vehicles for moving between the world of theory and the world of empirical research. **Inductive reasoning** goes from the specific to the general, and **deductive reasoning** goes from the general to the specific. Inductive reasoning is used to infer general principles and theories from observations of specific behaviors. For example, a child hits her brother after he takes her toy. Watching such interactions might lead to the general conclusion (by inductive reasoning) that frustration causes aggression. Deductive reasoning is used to form research hypotheses from general theories. **Research hypotheses** are explicit statements about expected results for a specific study. From the theory that frustration causes aggression, one could predict that frustrated hockey players become more aggressive (a deduction). Such hypotheses are explored in research studies, then inductive reasoning is used to relate results back to the general theory.

Research involves a series of alternating inductive and deductive conclusions that gradually sculpt a complex theory, with general rules and exceptions that have been empirically established. Sometimes researchers begin with a theory. Suppose a research team decides to test the theory that haste makes waste. They use deductive reasoning to form a research hypothesis: People will make more typing errors when forced to type quickly. Results might show that inexperienced typists make more errors, but professional typists do not make more errors when they work quickly. The researchers use inductive reasoning to generalize from these results. They adjust their theory: Haste makes waste, unless the person is very skillful on the task being examined.

Sometimes researchers begin by noticing a pattern among empirical results. Imagine that three facts have been empirically established: self-employed people are happier than employees of fast-food restaurants, mothers of older children are happier than mothers of infants, and generals are happier than privates. Using inductive reasoning, researchers might develop the theory that being in control of day-to-day activities causes people to be happier than being subject to control by other people. Alternatively, they might notice that happier people are older and develop the theory that maturity causes happiness.

The two theoretical explanations can be examined in an experiment. Researchers could take a group of younger people and a group of older people and assign each subject to one of two conditions. Subjects either are ordered to complete a task by carefully following a set of rigid procedures or are told to complete a task by designing their own procedures. After completing the task, all subjects rate their level of happiness. Figure 2.1a shows the pattern of results predicted by the first theory, Figure 2.1b shows the pattern of results predicted by the second theory, and Figure 2.1c shows the pattern of results if both theories are accurate. These predictions are based on deductive logic. After the study's results are known, the researchers make an inference about the relative merit of the two theories. If results resemble Figure 2.1a, they infer that self-direction causes happiness; if results are closer to Figure 2.1b, they infer that maturity causes happiness; and if results match Figure 2.1c, they infer that both factors cause happiness. These inferences are based on inductive reasoning.

VARIABLES IN PSYCHOLOGICAL RESEARCH

Psychologists study **variables**, characteristics that differ for people or groups. (Variables vary; constants stay the same. In a typical study, the number of eyes for each subject is a constant, but the number of hairs on each subject's head is a variable.) Some variables are relatively easy to measure (such as gender and eye color), and others are much harder to determine (such as intelligence, ego strength, and motivation).

To assess complex theoretical constructs, researchers employ **reductionism**, reducing variables to simpler units that can be measured and analyzed. For example, researchers might ask what makes people commit suicide. On a broad level, they might conclude that the cause is depression, but they reduce depression to more refined levels, such as hormone production, brain transmitter levels, or behavioral indicators.

After choosing the appropriate levels for analysis, researchers create **operational definitions**, clear-cut statements of how variables are measured, so that others can understand how each variable was defined. For example, achievement motivation could be operationally defined as the number of elected offices a person has attempted to obtain, the number of ambitious stories told when describing a set of pictures, or the number of affirmative responses to statements such as "I always try to do my best."

Frequently, psychologists are interested in the effect of one variable (the independent variable) on another variable (the dependent variable). Researchers manipulate or measure independent variables, then examine their influence on dependent variables. **Independent variables** are factors the researcher is interested in studying. Their influence on dependent variables is systematically examined. **Dependent variables** are factors that are measured to see the effects of changes in independent variables. Dependent variables are expected to depend on preceding independent variables. An investigator could manipulate the amount of time subjects are allowed to practice

---

FIGURE 2.1 AVERAGE HAPPINESS RATINGS

(a) Average happiness ratings for each condition if self-direction causes happiness

	Age	
	Younger	Older
Experimenter-directed	Low	Low
Self-directed	High	High

(b) Average happiness ratings for each condition if maturity causes happiness

	Age	
	Younger	Older
Experimenter-directed	Low	High
Self-directed	Low	High

(c) Average happiness ratings for each condition if both self-direction and maturity cause happiness

	Age	
	Younger	Older
Experimenter-directed	Low	Medium
Self-directed	Medium	High

---

some task, then examine how well subjects perform the task. The researcher is examining the effect of practice (the independent variable) on performance (the dependent variable).

Independent variables have two or more **levels** (possible scores). Researchers comparing the numerical reasoning skills of women and men examine the effect of gender (the independent variable) on numerical reasoning (the dependent variable). Gender has two levels (men and women). Researchers comparing three study techniques (cramming, daily self-study, and daily group-study) on student learning

EXAMPLE OF A STUDY WITH TWO INDEPENDENT VARIABLES **TABLE 2.1**		
	TEACHING METHOD	
	Rote	Conceptual
Low IQ	75	24
High IQ	98	98

examine the effect of study technique (the independent variable) on learning (the dependent variable). Study technique has three levels (cramming, daily self-study, and daily group-study).

Researchers **manipulate** the independent variable when they control each subject's level, and they **measure** the independent variable when they do not control each subject's level. In the above example, gender is a measured independent variable because the researcher cannot assign subjects to gender categories. Study technique is measured if students select their own study technique, but is manipulated if the researcher assigns each student to one of the three levels. Gender, by its nature, cannot be a manipulated independent variable; study technique, by contrast, can be manipulated or measured. As will be discussed more fully later, researchers are more confident about making causal conclusions when they study manipulated independent variables.

Researchers frequently compare results from experimental and control groups. Subjects in **control groups** are treated exactly like other subjects, with the exception of the independent variable. In a study of the effect of a new pill on sleep, subjects are in the **experimental group** (that receives the manipulated treatment, the sleeping pill) or in the control group (that receives the same treatment, minus the sleeping pill). Control subjects generally are given a **placebo**, an inert pill or innocuous treatment that is known not to affect behavior. Differences in the amount of sleep in experimental and control group subjects are assumed to be caused by the independent variable because everything is identical in the two conditions except for the independent variable. Measurements of the dependent variable for the two groups should be about the same, unless the independent variable has systematically influenced the dependent variable.

Sometimes researchers examine more than one independent variable at a time. Table 2.1 summarizes means (averages) on a final exam for a study comparing two teaching methods (rote memory and conceptual learning). Each subject also is classified as low or high in intelligence. Study this table before reading the next paragraph.

The study summarized in Table 2.1 concerns the effects of two independent variables (teaching method and intelligence) on one dependent variable (learning, defined as scores on the final exam). Each of the independent variables has two levels. The pattern of results in the table indicates (a) that students with high intelligence learned more than students with low intelligence; (b) that, overall, students learned more when taught by the rote memory method; (c) that bright students learned equally well, regardless of teaching technique; and (d) that students with low intelligence learned better using a rote memory method than using a conceptual method.

Studying two independent variables simultaneously provides information that could not be obtained by exploring one variable at a time. If we had studied only the independent variable of intelligence, we would have concluded that brighter students learn more. If we had studied only teaching methods, we would have concluded that rote memory methods lead to more learning. By using two independent variables, however, we were able to observe their joint effects on the dependent variable. Psychologists frequently study multiple independent variables to extract richer information.

TYPES OF STUDIES

Three basic types of research studies are conducted by psychologists: descriptive, correlational, and experimental. These studies may be conducted for exploratory, descriptive, relational, explanatory, or applied purposes.

Descriptive studies are conducted to summarize the characteristics of some person or group or to describe information contained in historical records. For example, a client with unusual symptoms may be carefully observed and described. The same could be done for groups of people, such as business or therapy groups, or for animals, such as troops of gorillas. The descriptions may serve to identify variables for exploratory purposes, to examine relationships between variables, to examine theory, or to uncover information for an applied study. Although descriptive studies may yield information useful for many purposes, their major function is to describe interesting phenomena.

Two major types of descriptive studies are case studies and archival research. **Case studies** are in-depth analyses of specific individuals or groups; and **archival research** is the analysis of records and artifacts. Archival researchers may examine newspapers or diaries to explain or to understand historical phenomena or to uncover relationships, such as the relationship between suicide rates and the deaths of popular athletes. Descriptive studies are described in detail in Chapter 10.

Correlational studies are conducted to examine relationships between naturally occurring variables. For example, psychologists may explore the relationship between parents' honesty and the honesty of their children. Other psychologists may correlate chemical properties of the brain with emotional states or suicide rates with population densities. Correlational studies can be used to explore relationships, to describe relationships within a particular population, to evaluate or to develop theories that postulate relationships, or to provide information relevant to applied questions. Their major purpose is to examine relationships. Correlational studies are discussed in detail in Chapter 11.

Experimental studies are conducted to systematically evaluate the effects of independent variables on dependent variables, such as the effect of light intensity on pupil size or the effect of repeated practice on learning. They generally are used to evaluate or to develop theories, and they may provide useful applied information. For example, an experimental study may be used to systematically evaluate how dial-reading accuracy is affected by the degree of detail provided. Should speedometers have numbers for every 5, 10, or 20 miles per hour? Results can be applied to the development of displays to be read by pilots, engineers, or bus drivers.

There are two major types of experiments: quasi-experiments and true experiments. **True experiments** have random assignment of subjects to conditions and manipulated independent variables. **Quasi-experiments** may have manipulated or measured independent variables, and subjects are not randomly assigned to conditions. Suppose we wanted to compare the effectiveness of two models of treating schizophrenia. If subjects are randomly assigned to therapy modes, the study is a true experiment; but if people select their own therapist, the study is a quasi-experiment. Types of experiments are described in detail in Chapters 12 and 13.

STEPS IN A RESEARCH STUDY

Students hear about classic studies and may develop the impression that researchers are a special class of people born with research skills and ideas. This is far from the truth. Researchers, like all people, frequently ask questions that flow from their own lives and develop theories that are consistent with their own experiences (Golden, 1976). They may become interested in abnormal psychology because of an affected friend or relative, or they may develop an interest in race relations because of a personal commitment to social justice.

Sources of Research Ideas

Psychologists' research ideas may come from many sources, including theories, common sense, personal observations, past research, serendipity, and the need to solve practical problems.

Theories are a common source of research ideas. For example, the theory of cognitive dissonance has inspired hundreds of studies, each examining some aspect of the theory (e.g., Croyle & Cooper, 1983). Other researchers may explore theories of how visual perceptions are formed or how propaganda influences beliefs.

Common sense includes a number of sayings that we find useful, such as "absence makes the heart grow fonder" and "out of sight, out of mind." As these examples illustrate, however, sometimes they lead to contradictory predictions. Researchers may decide to explore these "truisms" to uncover the limits of their accuracy. For example, "spare the rod, spoil the child" suggests that punishment is an effective way to handle disobedient children; but psychologists find evidence that positive reinforcement may be more effective than punishment for developing children's inner sense of right and wrong. Punishment also has some undesirable side effects, such as the suppression of all activity and increases in violence among children who have been punished (Newsom, Favell, & Rincover, 1983). Intuition is related to common sense, and researchers may design studies to test intuitive ideas. For example, a researcher may intuitively believe that people litter because they are rebellious toward authority; but research may demonstrate that most people litter when trash cans are not easily accessible.

Personal observations can lead to research questions. For example, teachers have noticed that some unruly children become more disruptive when punished. To these children, punishment acts as a reinforcer, perhaps by providing them needed attention. Researchers can explore this theory to see if it adequately explains the observations. Schieber (1988) made a personal observation. He noticed that older drivers have more trouble reading street signs than younger drivers, and he examined physical properties of the letters and numbers on street signs. His results suggest that we increase the width of lines composing these characters.

SELECTING A RESEARCH QUESTION: TWO CASE STUDIES

Are Women Prejudiced Against Women?

Philip Goldberg asked the question: Are women prejudiced against women? (1968). He presented women college students edited versions of six different published articles. Half the time each article was ascribed to a female author, and half the time each article was ascribed to a male author. Except for the author's name (Joan vs. John), the articles were identical. The answer to his question was yes; the students rated the articles higher in quality if they believed the articles were written by a man than they did if they believed the articles were written by a woman.

Why did Goldberg ask this question? He reports an ongoing interest in self-prejudice sparked in the 1950s when he noticed hair straightener and skin lightener products sold in Harlem and became aware that some Jewish people were flattered by being told that they "don't seem Jewish." He toyed with ways to study this phenomenon, but did not begin research in this area until after he became a faculty member at a women's college. There he was struck by the students' passivity, especially in contrast with equally intelligent male students at another campus. He decided that these bright, young women were prejudiced against themselves and their own gender. Thus sprung the research question: Are women prejudiced against women? Goldberg claims that the "hard" part was asking this question. The research, itself, followed its natural course (Goldberg, 1976).

How Do You Measure Romantic Love?

Zick Rubin (1970) decided to measure romantic love, separating it from the concept of "liking" and from other forms of love (such as parental love). He developed questionnaire items by reviewing the literature on romantic love, examining the ideas of student and faculty volunteers, and including his own views. He demonstrated that his romantic love test was related to perceptions of the probability of getting married, was higher for dating partners than for same-gender friends, and was related to "gazing" behavior between lovers (those who scored more in love had more mutual eye contact).

What led Rubin to his research question? Rubin was looking for a dissertation topic and "love was *there*, like Mount Everest, shimmering in the distance, of obvious importance to the human experience, and yet almost completely untouched by nonpoetic human hands" (1976, p. 508). Rubin, as a social psychologist, was interested in relationships between people and their social environment; and he concluded that romantic love is an important social link. Rubin also was inspired by some psychologists and sociologists who were interested in studying positive aspects of human interactions, rather than aggression and violence. In particular, he was inspired by his dissertation chairman at the University of Michigan, who had conducted research on friendship formation. Rubin also enjoyed songwriting, so he had personal interest in developing a better understanding of romantic love (Rubin, 1976).

Psychologists review relevant published results when exploring research questions. By analyzing previous research, they may find inconsistencies or areas that need further exploration. Most research reports end with a discussion of the limits of the findings and suggestions for further research. These discussions identify new areas for research. In addition, we place more confidence in results that are replicated with different samples. Researchers may decide to precisely duplicate a study, or they may adapt stimuli or conditions to explore the generality of previous findings.

Serendipity is finding things one isn't looking for, and sometimes researchers discover interesting research questions by chance. For example, Pavlov was studying

HINTS FOR SELECTING A RESEARCH AREA

Perhaps your teacher is requiring you to conduct a research project for this course. Here are some hints, in case you're having trouble coming up with a good idea. Your problem probably will become selecting one idea from many possibilities, rather than locating a single idea.

1. Pick a psychological theory that interests you. Your introductory psychology textbook may be a good source to remind you of a variety of psychological theories. Find a few experiments that have been done to test this theory. Perhaps you can replicate or modify one of them. Design your own study to test the accuracy of this theory or to demonstrate its applicability to some issue.
2. Think of some familiar phrase, such as "A stitch in time saves nine" or "Absence makes the heart grow fonder." Consider stereotypes. Do women actually talk more than men? Are children's cartoons really violent? Perhaps you could design a study to analyze the accuracy of one of these stereotypes.
3. Don't be afraid to test your own intuition. Perhaps you've always believed that attractive people are more popular than unattractive people or that teachers give higher grades to typed papers than to handwritten papers. You could design a study to test your intuitive conclusions.
4. Spend some time in a public place observing people. What do you see? How do you

explain it? Can you test your theory? For example, you might notice that people tend to face the door in elevators. Maybe you can develop and test a theory that explains this behavior.
5. Scan some journals and read a few articles that interest you. Perhaps you could replicate one of the studies described, or part of it. Do the articles end with suggestions for further research or a discussion of limitations that you could explore?
6. Pick an issue that is important to you. Are you interested in affirmative action, AIDS, study skills, or alcoholism? Do some reading to find out what is already known about this area, and design a study that replicates previous research or that makes use of procedures or materials that have already been developed.
7. Ask a practical question and design a study to answer it. For example, you might be interested in how students can learn to study better, and you might decide to conduct an exploratory study contrasting students with high grades and students with low grades.
8. Don't lose track of the purpose of this assignment. The goal of this assignment is for you to practice conducting a study. You are not expected to invent a new theory that applies to all human behaviors. Keep your study simple. You will discover that even simple studies involve a series of tough decisions.

---

digestive juices when he noticed anticipatory behaviors. (His dogs began salivating before they received food.) From this chance observation of "psychic secretions," he developed the concept of classical conditioning. Alert researchers may chance upon new ideas in many settings. Piaget's interest in cognitive development grew out of his experience testing items for early intelligence tests. He became intrigued with the processes underlying children's wrong answers, and many of his observations were made on his own children. Serendipity can provide useful ideas to people whose minds are open to unexpected discoveries.

Sometimes research ideas are based on issues or practical problems. Researchers may be interested in understanding the causes of alcoholism or in developing strategies to convince people to recycle trash. Psychologists have addressed many practical questions. Which treatment is the best way to help clients overcome phobias? What is the best color for emergency vehicles? How can psychological tests improve the accuracy of hiring, admissions, or classification decisions? (Who should be hired for a job? Who should be admitted to graduate school? Should this army recruit be assigned to the motor pool or the kitchen?) Applied researchers focus on uncovering answers to questions that require immediate answers.

The Literature Review

After a general research area has been identified, researchers conduct a **literature review**, an analysis of relevant published information, in order to uncover what is already known. Science can be thought of as a complex castle constructed of blocks. The accumulated literature serves as a foundation for further research, and each useful research study adds a block to a tower or a new wing to the castle. The entire body of knowledge is larger than any single study. Science develops when new research findings are integrated with prior research findings.

Your campus library probably has some reference tools, such as *Psychological Abstracts*, the *Social Science Citation Index*, and the computer-based *PsychLit*, that are useful for locating relevant references. There are hundreds of psychology journals, and psychologists may also consult journals in related fields, such as medicine, social work, education, and sociology. Reference tools such as *Resources in Education, Current Index to Journals in Education, Biological Abstracts,* and *Index Medicus* may be consulted.

The literature review serves a second function. It allows investigators to locate procedures and instruments found useful by other researchers. These techniques may be replicated exactly, or may be adapted; and some researchers may branch into research examining the quality of different research tools for approaching the problem of interest. Hundreds of research studies on particular psychological tests, such as the MMPI, are published each year, so that clinicians and researchers can better understand the meaningfulness of scores obtained with these instruments.

After the literature review is completed, the researcher knows what has been established and what research strategies and tools have been effective. Sometimes the completed literature review reveals interesting information about important variables and is published in a journal such as *Annual Review of Psychology, Psychological Bulletin,* or *Psychological Review*. Sometimes the results of many studies are statistically examined using meta-analysis. **Meta-analysis** is used to summarize the results of multiple studies of the same phenomenon. The summary may be simple (e.g., "80% of researchers find that distributed practice is more effective than massed practice") or may be based on complex statistical models that allow for combined estimates of the effects of independent variables.

Research Development

Researchers frequently state explicit research hypotheses based on theory, intuition, and/or the literature review. They may hypothesize that extinction will be slower if partial reinforcement is used instead of continuous reinforcement, that opinions on abortion are related to religious affiliation, or that abused children will be less trusting of adults than children who have not been abused. After stating hypotheses, researchers are ready to select an appropriate descriptive, correlational, or experimental design.

PUBLISHING A JOURNAL ARTICLE

Students may wonder whether researchers make money from publishing journal articles. The answer is no. In fact, sometimes journals charge authors for the number of pages in the article (page costs), for the set-up of extensive tables or figures, and for reprints (copies of articles that are sent to interested readers). Some journals also have a submission charge, to partially offset the cost of reviews. Journal editors usually send submitted manuscripts to several reviewers who are experts in the field. The article may be subjected to **blind review** (the reviewers are not told the author's name). Not every submitted manuscript is accepted. For example, in 1991, 90 percent of the articles submitted to *Psychological Review* and 87 percent of the articles submitted to *American Psychologist* were rejected ("Summary Report of Journal Operations, 1991," 1992).

Research psychologists are motivated by their desire to develop an understanding of the issues they investigate. Publication is the best way to reach a broad audience, to catch the interest of their peers, and to add to our knowledge of psychology. Neal Miller, winner of an American Psychological Association Outstanding Lifetime Contribution to Psychology award, expressed this well: "I feel particularly lucky that I love my work so much that I chose to continue it even after my salary has been retired.... One source of satisfaction is learning new things by study and by experience; another is solving challenging problems that are met in basic and applied research..." (1992, p. 848). Scientists like Miller conduct research and publish their studies because they enjoy it.

Procedures must be developed, ethical principles must be considered, and appropriate subjects must be recruited. Most research must be approved by an ethics committee before data can be collected. The ethics committee generally requires a formal research proposal that describes procedures and ethical safeguards.

Sometimes a pilot study precedes the actual study. A **pilot study** is a small-scale version of a project in which procedures and instrumentation are checked, much like a dress rehearsal of a play before the audience sees it. Results from the pilot study generally lead to revision and refinement of research procedures. Pilot studies are one type of exploratory research.

Data are collected. Data collectors generally are monitored to ensure conformity to the research proposal. Statistics are used to describe data and to evaluate research hypotheses. If results are meaningful, researchers may present the study at a convention and/or publish it in a journal or book. Written research reports are the most common route for sharing findings with professional colleagues. Researchers must be skilled writers to prepare reports that are published and read.

An Illustrative Example

Box 2.1 describes an experiment conducted by Robert Croyle and Joel Cooper. This is a true experiment because the researchers manipulated the independent variable and randomly assigned subjects to conditions. Familiar with the theory of cognitive dissonance and the accumulated literature on this theoretical construct, Croyle and Cooper (1983) hypothesized that physiological arousal should accompany a state of dissonance. Their study was designed to support or to falsify the theory by testing this hypothesis. They first conducted a pilot study to verify that their manipulation

---

Box 2.1

Physiological Arousal and Cognitive Dissonance

Cognitive dissonance theory (Festinger, 1957) specifies that people whose beliefs, attitudes, or behaviors are inconsistent will become uncomfortable and be motivated to reduce this discomfort. They may alter the belief, attitude, or behavior to reduce this inconsistency. For example, Festinger and Carlsmith (1959) had subjects participate in a boring experiment, then asked them to lie to a new subject, saying that the experiment was interesting. Subjects were paid either one or twenty dollars for this lie. All subjects would notice the inconsistency between their belief (the experiment is boring) and their behavior (telling another subject that the experiment is fun); but subjects paid twenty dollars could justify their lie ("I did it for the money") more easily than subjects who were paid a dollar. This implies that subjects paid only a dollar will experience more cognitive dissonance. When later asked about their feelings, subjects who were paid a dollar were more likely to report that the experiment was enjoyable than were those who had been paid twenty dollars. According to cognitive dissonance theory, this attitude change reduced their dissonance.

Many studies have been conducted on cognitive dissonance. Dissonance is manipulated by inducing subjects to do something that contradicts their true beliefs or attitudes. For example, subjects may be induced to write essays supporting opinions contrary to their own. Subjects with little justification for their inconsistency experience dissonance, and subjects with more justification for their inconsistency are expected to have little dissonance because they can justify their compliance to researcher requests. Basically, cognitive dissonance theory predicts dissonance will occur when subjects are induced into inconsistencies without receiving large amounts of external pressure or reward.

Croyle and Cooper (1983) decided to investigate Festinger's notion that discomfort is caused by dissonance. They hypothesized that subjects in a dissonance-inducing condition will demonstrate more physiological arousal than subjects in a non-dissonance-inducing condition. Based on previous research, Croyle and Cooper selected two measures of physiological arousal: heart rate and nonspecific electrodermal activity (skin conductance of electricity). They also conducted a pilot study to verify that their manipulation of cognitive dissonance was effective.

They used three conditions: subjects were induced to write a counterattitudinal essay under a high-choice condition, to write a counterattitudinal essay under a low-choice condition, or to write a consonant essay under a high-choice condition. Subjects in high-choice conditions were reminded that their participation was completely voluntary. They were told that they would be paid even if they chose not to write an essay; and they were asked to sign a permission slip allowing the researchers to release their essay to outsiders. Subjects in the low-choice condition were told to write an essay, without the extra instructions or consent procedures. The high-choice counterattitudinal group should experience dissonance because they wrote an essay that contradicted their own opinion with little external reward. The low-choice counterattitudinal group also wrote an essay that contradicted their opinion, but they could justify this because of experimenter pressure. The high-choice consonant group should not experience dissonance because their attitude and behavior were consistent.

creates cognitive dissonance; then they monitored heart rate and skin conductance among subjects who were randomly assigned to dissonance- or non-dissonance-inducing conditions.

All subjects in the pilot study were male undergraduates at Princeton University. Prior to being invited to the research laboratory, a group of potential subjects completed a survey that included a question about their attitude toward alcohol on campus. Thirty subjects who supported the availability of alcohol on campus were invited to the laboratory, were offered $2.50 for their participation, and were asked to write a set of "strong and forceful" (p. 785) arguments in support of or against banning alcohol on campus. Their arguments were supposedly being collected to submit to a committee that was considering banning alcohol on campus. Subjects were randomly assigned to one of the three conditions.

After writing the list, subjects filled out another survey, and this survey repeated the original question about their attitude toward alcohol on campus. The survey also contained a manipulation check, an item that asked subjects to report whether they felt free to decline writing a list. Data analyses confirmed that the manipulation was effective and that only the high-choice counterattitudinal subjects changed their attitude.

Twenty-nine more subjects were tested in the same way; but these subjects were told that the physiology division of the psychology department was examining the effects of various tasks on heart rate and skin electrical activity. Each subject was tested with heart and skin monitors in place and was first asked to solve a couple of filler tasks (solving some anagrams and remembering activities from the previous day). This allowed subjects to become comfortable with the recording equipment and study, and researchers obtained baseline heart and skin recordings. Each subject was randomly assigned to one of the three experimental conditions and was treated like one of the groups in the pilot study. Recordings made in the three-minute period following the experimental condition were compared, taking baseline readings into account, to assess physiological arousal caused by dissonance. Data analyses confirmed the effectiveness of the manipulation and verified that the high-choice counterattitudinal group exhibited more physiological arousal than the other groups.

Croyle and Cooper used two control groups, allowing them to conclude that cognitive dissonance caused the physiological arousal, not just coercion to write a list of arguments and not just the requirement that the list be counterattitudinal. They also found that pilot subjects in the dissonance condition changed their attitude, consistent with the findings of Festinger and Carlsmith (1959); but dissonance subjects in the second experiment did not change their attitude. Croyle and Cooper argued that subjects in the second experiment noticed their physiological arousal, but interpreted it as a response to the recording equipment, rather than the writing task; so they were not motivated to reduce the discomfort by changing their opinion. They believed that the discomfort would end when recording equipment was removed. Croyle and Cooper presented other research supporting this interpretation. They also discussed relationships between their findings and other theories, such as control theory and impression management theory, tying their results into the accumulated literature on cognitive dissonance and attitude change.

Croyle and Cooper conducted a manipulation check by asking subjects if they felt free to decline writing a list. This allowed them to verify that "high-choice" and "low-choice" conditions were accurately labeled. **Manipulation checks** involve questions or procedures that verify that subjects interpreted the conditions as researchers intended. For example, if the researcher manipulated degree of stress, subjects may be asked how stressful the experiment was. Subjects in high-stress conditions should report more stress than subjects in low-stress conditions. Subjects who report deviant stress levels (e.g., low stress in the high-stress condition) may be analyzed separately from subjects who responded appropriately to the manipulation.

Data analysis confirmed Croyle and Cooper's hypothesis and supported the theory of cognitive dissonance. In addition, they discussed how their results apply to alternative theories and how their interpretations of some aspects of the results are supported by other research findings. Their study is a good example of theory-based research. They used deductive reasoning to create their research hypothesis (physiological arousal will accompany dissonance), and they used inductive reasoning to tie their results to relevant theories and research findings in the accumulated literature.

Currency of Information

Psychologists frequently belong to local, state, regional, and national associations that hold annual conventions. The two major national organizations are the **American Psychological Association (APA)** and the **American Psychological Society (APS)**. Current studies and ideas are shared at conventions and may be available to the research community a year or more before they are published. Journal submissions are reviewed by editors who may take months to examine a proposed article. Frequently articles are tentatively accepted, contingent on suggested revisions; and accepted articles may not be published for months after they are accepted. For example, journals published by the American Psychological Association report a six- to nine-month lag before articles are published ("Summary Report of Journal Operations, 1991," 1992). The best ways to stay current are to attend conventions and to personally contact researchers who are prominent in the area of interest. Most researchers are proud to show visitors their laboratory and are willing to mail information on current research to accommodate reasonable requests. Your teacher or department chair probably is your best source of information on upcoming conventions.

CHAPTER SUMMARY

Scientists use inductive and deductive reasoning, and the research process involves alternating inductive and deductive conclusions. Researchers examine variables, and they reduce complex variables to levels that can be operationally defined. Frequently, psychologists examine the effects of independent variables on dependent variables. Independent variables can be manipulated or measured; and more than one independent variable may be examined simultaneously. Sometimes researchers compare scores collected in experimental and control groups. Control subjects may be given a placebo.

Three basic types of studies are descriptive, correlational, and experimental. Descriptive studies are conducted to describe interesting phenomena, correlational studies are conducted to examine relationships, and experimental studies are conducted to evaluate the effects of independent variables on dependent variables. Descriptive studies may involve case studies or archival research, and experimental studies may involve true experiments or quasi-experiments.

Researchers select research questions in a variety of ways; research ideas may come from theories, common sense, personal observations, past research, serendipity, or the need to understand issues or to solve practical problems. Once a general area has been identified, a literature review is conducted to uncover what is already known and to identify procedures that have been found useful. Literature reviews may be summarized and published; and the summaries may involve meta-analysis.

Researchers plan studies by forming research hypotheses, developing procedures, and considering ethical issues. Pilot studies may precede the actual research, and manipulation checks may be conducted to verify that procedures function well. After data are collected, they are analyzed. Meaningful results may be presented at a convention or published. Psychologists may attend national conventions (such as the APA or APS convention) or regional conventions to learn about current research findings.

Key Concepts

American Psychological Association (APA)
American Psychological Society (APS)
archival research
blind review
case study
control group
correlational study
deductive reasoning
dependent variable
descriptive study
experimental group
experimental study
independent variable
inductive reasoning
levels of a variable

literature review
manipulated variable
manipulation check
measured variable
meta-analysis
operational definition
pilot study
placebo
reductionism
research hypothesis
serendipity
quasi-experiment
true experiment
variable

Review Questions

1. Dr. Jenkins notices that there are more men than women in engineering classes, and she forms the theory that women are socialized to emphasize people and men are socialized to emphasize things. She prepares a test to measure relative interests in people and things, and she gives this test to a sample of university students. Her research hypotheses are that men will indicate greater interest in things and that women will indicate greater interest in people. How has Dr. Jenkins used deductive and inductive reasoning?

2. John decides that dogs are smarter than cats because his dog can fetch the newspaper, and his cat can't. You convince John that he needs a better operational definition of animal intelligence. Suggest some possible alternative operational definitions.

3. John decides to use memory as one aspect of his operational definition of animal intelligence, and he plans to do a study comparing the memories of dogs and

cats. What are the independent and dependent variables in his study? How many levels does the independent variable have? Is the independent variable manipulated or measured?

4. Marta plans to study the effect of caffeine on energy level. How could she do this as a descriptive study? How could she do this as a correlational study? How could she do this as an experiment with a manipulated independent variable? How could she do this as an experiment with a measured independent variable?

5. Ask a research question that you might like to investigate. How did you select this question? Did you have anything in common with Goldberg or Rubin?

6. Select a topic in psychology that you find interesting and use your library to locate three journal articles. You may need help from your teacher or reference librarian if you do not know how to use the research tools in your library.

7. Fran conducts a literature review and finds a meta-analysis of a group of research studies. Explain to Fran what a meta-analysis is.

8. You plan to do research on the effects of reading difficulty on children's understanding of written material, and you have prepared three booklets: one written in simple language, one written in moderately difficult language, and one written in very difficult language. You have developed six questions for each booklet and plan to ask children these questions after they read the material. What could you learn from a pilot study? How could you integrate a manipulation check into your study?

9. How could the above study be conducted as a true experiment? How could it be conducted as a quasi-experiment?

10. You read in the campus newspaper that Norman Simms had a paper accepted for the APA convention. What does this mean?

3

Research Ethics

Researchers have ethical obligations to their discipline, the public, and their research subjects. Ignorance is no excuse for unethical research. Researchers must know their ethical responsibilities and must design research that meets ethical guidelines. Each researcher is responsible for the ethics of the whole research team and cannot abdicate this responsibility to others.

AMERICAN PSYCHOLOGICAL ASSOCIATION ETHICAL GUIDELINES

The American Psychological Association (APA) has developed guidelines for ethical research (the most recent set was published in 1990), and most institutions have an **Institutional Review Board (IRB)** that must approve research plans before they are enacted. In addition, the APA has an Ethics Committee that provides educational materials to members and to the public and that investigates complaints about unethical research. The Committee publishes an annual report in the APA journal, *The American Psychologist*, and has presented illustrative cases in the *Casebook on Ethical Issues* (APA, 1987).

APA Ethical Principles stress the protection of fundamental human rights and a commitment to increasing our understanding of human behavior for the benefit of human welfare. Principles for the use of animal subjects also are provided.

Ethical decisions are based on subjective criteria, and decisions frequently balance costs to individual research participants and benefits to society. For example, it is important that we understand details about the transmission of AIDS so that health educators can provide accurate information to the public. In order to examine this topic, we may have to obtain details of individuals' sexual and drug habits that normally are protected from invasion of privacy. A research program that guarantees respect for subjects is essential before data can be collected. One rule of thumb to use when considering the ethics of a research project is to ask the question: "Would I be a subject in this study and would I let my family members participate?" If the answer is not an unqualified "yes," the proposed study is questionable.

KEY ETHICAL CONSIDERATIONS

There are seven key **ethical considerations** for research on human subjects: privacy, confidentiality, subjects' right to decline and withdraw participation, subjects' right to have protection from harm and removal of harmful consequences, deception, debriefing, and informed consent.

Privacy is the right of research participants to control the amount of information about themselves that will be revealed to researchers. Subjects may choose not to reveal aspects of their personal lives, values, or attitudes. They have the right to refuse to answer any questions and to refuse to participate in any aspect of the study that may reveal information they consider too private to share with others.

Confidentiality deals with who has access to research information provided by individual subjects. Subjects have the right to have their confidentiality protected. Generally no one, not even the researcher, is aware of which scores are associated with individual subjects. Data are stored with code numbers, rather than with identifying information, so that no one can attach an individual's name to a set of data. Research reports describe characteristics of subjects as a group (average age, for example), so that individual subjects cannot be identified by readers.

Sometimes data are collected over a period of time for a group of subjects. These studies require that subjects' scores be identifiable in some way, so that new data can be matched to earlier data on the same person. Safeguards are built into such studies, with specially protected procedures that link individuals to their scores.

Research participants must give prior permission if identifiable information is to be provided to anyone other than the experimenter. For example, if a researcher must report all incidents of child abuse to legal authorities or if a researcher may be ordered by a court to reveal data collected from prisoners, research participants must be warned and must be allowed to decline to participate. Confidentiality includes protection from informal revealing of information, too. Data collectors are prohibited from discussing individual subjects with friends or research colleagues.

Privacy and confidentiality are sometimes confused. Privacy concerns the content of the information; confidentiality concerns access to the information. Subjects have the right to both privacy and confidentiality.

There also is a distinction between confidential and anonymous data. Researchers are able to associate **confidential data** with individual subjects but cannot associate **anonymous data** with individual subjects. Anonymous data are collected without associating individuals to their responses. For example, a survey may be given to a large group of prisoners, with subjects asked not to put their names on forms. These data probably would be anonymous. Some of the data might be confidential, however, rather than anonymous. If the group contains only one American Indian woman and she responded to questions on gender and ethnicity, the researcher would be able to identify her data. Anonymous data protect subjects and researchers from outside demands for identifiable information. Research on sensitive topics, such as sexual habits, may yield more honest responses if subjects are assured their responses are anonymous.

Subjects have the right to decline to participate and the right to withdraw participation during the study. These rights were first highlighted by investigators of Nazi atrocities. The resulting Nurenburg Code banned involuntary research participation (Keith-Spiegel & Koocher, 1985). Subjects who elect to exercise their rights to decline or to withdraw cannot be penalized in any way. For example, professors who conduct research on their students must have their students' permission; and if participation is a graded component of a course, students who choose to decline or to withdraw must be provided alternative ways to earn their grade. This example also illustrates a dual relationship, a concept that developed out of clinical psychology. A therapist and a client should have one relationship: the therapist-client relationship. It is unethical for them to have other relationships, such as employer-employee, spousal, or sexual relationships. **Dual relationships** occur when people have two or more relationships with each other. Researchers should have one relationship with their subjects: the researcher-subject relationship. When researchers also are the subjects' employers, teachers, therapists, or friends, the research process is jeopardized because judgements about risk, informed consent, and objectivity are threatened. If circumstances require dual relationships, researchers must be extremely careful to observe ethical obligations.

Subjects' rights include protection from harm and the removal of harmful consequences. Subjects must be able to trust that their health, safety, and welfare are not threatened, and, if harm does occur, that the researcher will help them recover. For example, if researchers are investigating the effects of sleep deprivation on alertness, they must be sure that subjects do not become physically sick from lack of sleep, that subjects are not required to endanger themselves by driving themselves home after a night in the lab, and that appropriate medical attention is provided if subjects become ill.

Even simple questionnaires may involve some risk to subjects. For example, a questionnaire on sexual abuse history may make subjects uncomfortable by bringing back painful memories. Appropriate intervention and referral to mental health personnel may be required. Research involving risk of considerable harm is conducted only with subjects' awareness and permission. Sometimes such research is ethically reasonable if subjects are at greater risk if nothing is done, as in studies on the effectiveness of therapy for people who are considering suicide.

Deception is involved when subjects are given incorrect or misleading information. In general, psychologists do not deceive their subjects, but some research may require elements of deception. For example, subjects' reactions to an accident victim would be different if they were told in advance that the accident was simulated in order to examine people's reactions to emergencies.

Researchers may give subjects misleading directions, such as referring to a personality test as an opinion questionnaire or suggesting that a task is more difficult than it is, or they may mislead subjects about the nature of a study. For example, researchers examining the effect of group size on speed of decision making might inform subjects that the study concerned problem solving. The research might be undermined if subjects were told that group size was a major independent variable. This "white lie" probably would not affect people's willingness to participate. Ethical researchers and review boards must evaluate the relative costs and benefits of the

ALTERNATIVES TO DECEPTION

Psychologists who conduct experiments using deception argue that the deception is necessary because subjects will respond differently if they know the true purpose of the study. Some argue, however, that deception is always unethical and is never justified because it undermines the relationship between researcher and subjects and does not respect subjects' dignity and right to choose whether or not to participate (e.g., Baumrind, 1971, 1985).

Role playing has been suggested as an alternative to deception. **Role playing** involves full and honest informed consent procedures in which subjects are asked to respond as if something had happened. Subjects may be asked to respond as if they had just witnessed a car accident or as if they had just flunked an important test. Role playing "entails a more ethically dignified atmosphere" and works with the subjects' cooperation, rather than their suspiciousness, apprehensiveness, or docility (Miller, 1972, p. 625).

The Stanford prison study (Haney, Banks, & Zimbardo, 1973) used role playing. Stanford student volunteers were asked to simulate a prison, with some students designated as guards and others designated as prisoners. Critics argue that role playing experiments like this are not equivalent to studies involving deception. Basically, subjects are acting, rather than reacting to "real" events, so their behavior is not natural or spontaneous. For example, students in the Stanford study would have behaved differently if they were actually imprisoned or given jobs as guards. Some research supports this argument and suggests that role playing is not the solution to the ethical problems of deception studies (Adair, Dushenko, & Lindsay, 1985; Miller, 1972). In addition, Feild and Barnett (1978) demonstrated that college student subjects' role playing results are significantly different from results utilizing "randomly selected citizens" when simulating jury decisions. College students gave significantly lighter sentences. This suggests that role playing by college students may not generalize to role playing by other adults.

Another way to avoid deception is to tell subjects they will not be fully informed about the nature of the study until its completion (Holmes & Bennett, 1974). This might lead to suspicion, problem solving, and false or accurate conclusions about the nature of the study; and these reactions may undermine the purpose of the research.

Rubin (1973) suggested several alternative strategies. Some research can be done in public settings without subjects' awareness. For example, the effects of modeling can be examined by walking briskly past subjects on a city street, then measuring the subjects' change in walking speed. Modeling would have an effect if subjects increased their speed. Deception is not used; the subjects are not even aware they are being studied. Researchers also can examine the effects of naturally occurring variables, such as whether or not the home team wins an athletic contest or whether a boy or girl infant is born. Applied research offers opportunities for the examination of theoretical issues. For example, a consumer psychologist examining the effectiveness of grocery store displays may stock the merchandise on lower shelves, upper shelves, at the end of aisles, or in special eye-catching exhibits. Opportunities to study theoretical issues in human perceptual styles exist in such studies.

Investigators using these alternative research strategies generally do not obtain consent from research subjects and deliberately misrepresent the researchers' roles, so they may violate other ethical or legal principles (Silverman, 1975). For example, experiments in which researchers pretend to be store customers may violate trespass laws, and experiments in which researchers simulate accidents or injuries may violate harassment or disorderly conduct laws.

Another alternative is to inform subjects that they might be deceived. Gamson, Fireman, and Rytina (1982) suggest that researchers poll potential research subjects on the types of experiments they would be willing to join, including experiments involving deception. Only those volunteers who indicated a willingness to be deceived would be subjected to such studies. Critics argue that this technique might restrict the subject pool to an unusual collection of people, and research results may not hold true for people unwilling to volunteer to be deceived.

deception. Deception might be acceptable if the costs to the subjects are low, the potential benefits are high, and there is no better research strategy for investigating the phenomenon of interest. Debriefing is very important if deception has been used.

Debriefing involves summarizing the research to the subjects after data are collected. Debriefing educates the subjects about the project and assures them that their responses are important. Subjects should be told the purpose of the research, the expected results, and any reasonable information they desire. Some researchers volunteer to send copies of the completed research report to subjects who desire more information. Much research is relatively innocuous, and volunteers are not particularly interested in its fine details. Debriefing does not require that subjects be bored to death after participating; however, subjects who want to better understand the research and its implications have a right to expect reasonable explanations.

Holmes (1976a, 1976b) described two types of debriefing: dehoaxing and desensitizing. **Dehoaxing** involves informing subjects about experimental deception, to be sure that they understand the true nature of the study. **Desensitizing** involves making subjects comfortable with their own performance in the study, to be sure they do not have residual discomfort about themselves. For example, a researcher gives false feedback on test performance, arbitrarily telling half the subjects they did well and half the subjects they did poorly. This researcher would dehoax subjects during the debriefing. A researcher who conducts a study that reveals to subjects that they are more aggressive, prejudiced, or naive than they believed themselves to be should desensitize them during the debriefing. This can be accomplished by convincing subjects that unusual laboratory conditions elicited atypical behavior and that their behaviors were not aberrant, but were similar to other subjects' performance.

Full debriefing is not always desirable. For example, pointing out to subjects that they were selected because of traits that could be considered negative or that their performance was unusually weak would not serve a useful purpose. Keith-Spiegel and Koocher (1985) describe a student research volunteer who was told that he was selected because he had a feminine personality, causing considerable discomfort that was not alleviated by further discussion. The researcher should have been more careful in her choice of words and more sensitive to the student's response.

Obtaining informed consent generally is a crucial step in ethical research. **Informed consent** is obtained by providing subjects information about the research and allowing them to decide whether they are willing to participate. Subjects should participate in research *"voluntarily, knowingly,* and *intelligently"* (Keith-Spiegel & Koocher, 1985, p. 390). It is not necessary to give every detail of the study, but it is necessary to provide all information that might influence a subject's decision to participate. Subjects should be told what procedures will be followed, what risks and benefits are involved, what will be done to protect their privacy and confidentiality, what time commitment is required, and who is conducting the research. Subjects also are told that they may decline to participate and may withdraw at any time. If the research involves treatment for a disorder, subjects are informed about alternative treatments. The best way to decide if some detail should be included is to ask whether knowing this information might affect subjects' willingness to participate.

According to APA guidelines (1990), informed consent is required for all studies having more than **minimal risk**, i.e., the typical amount of risk that is involved in day-to-day living or "during routine physical or psychological exams" (Code of Federal Regulations, 1983, 46.102[g]). As part of the informed consent process, a clearly de-

---

DEBRIEFING: THE OBEDIENCE EXPERIMENTS

In the 1960s, Stanley Milgram (1963, 1964a, 1965a, 1965b) conducted a series of experiments that are well known to psychology students. Community volunteers were asked to serve in a learning experiment. In the first study, each volunteer was paired with a cohort of the researcher, and when they drew straws to decide who would be the teacher and who would be the learner, the real subject always became the teacher. The researcher instructed the teacher to punish incorrect answers by delivering a shock of increasing intensity to the learner, with thirty shock levels ranging from "slight shock" though "danger: severe shock," and, finally, "xxx." The learner, who was in an adjacent room, began complaining of the pain as the study progressed. He pounded the wall and begged the teacher to stop because of his heart condition. Eventually, the learner was silent and did not respond to the teacher's questions. Although the teachers became very uncomfortable, the researcher insisted that the study continue. To the amazement of Milgram and his professional colleagues, 65% of the subjects obeyed the researcher's instructions and delivered shocks through the "xxx" level.

Milgram's study required both dehoaxing and desensitizing. Dehoaxing was accomplished by assuring the volunteers that no shocks had been administered. The researcher's cohort entered the room for a "friendly reconciliation" (1964b, p. 849) so that subjects could see that no harm was done. The researcher explained the deception; the study really dealt with obedience to authority, rather than the effectiveness of punishment on learning.

Desensitizing subjects was crucial, especially those subjects who apparently gave lethal doses of punishment. "Obedient subjects were assured of the fact that their behavior was entirely normal and that their feelings of conflict or tension were shared by other participants.... In some instances, additional detailed and lengthy discussions of the experiments were also carried out with individual subjects" (1964b, p. 849). A five-page report of the study's results was sent to each subject a few months later, and it was designed to further assure subjects that their behavior was not aberrant. A year after the experiment, a psychiatrist interviewed forty subjects judged to be most at risk for lingering problems. Although he found that some of the subjects had earlier suffered from stress, he concluded that all had recovered (Milgram, 1964b).

Further research (Holmes, 1976a, 1976b; Ring, Wallston, & Corey, 1970) has demonstrated that proper dehoaxing and desensitizing can effectively eliminate misconceptions and discomfort among participants in deception experiments. Although Milgram was careful to dehoax and desensitize subjects, it is unlikely that current ethical review committees would allow anyone to replicate his procedures.

---

fined set of mutual expectations are developed, and the researcher must follow through on all commitments made to subjects.

Informed consent may be obtained in writing, with subjects receiving a copy of the consent form and instructions about how to contact the researcher. This is especially important for research that runs the risk of long-term harm to subjects. Sometimes both the subject and the researcher sign the consent form. Here is an example of a simple informed consent form used by a group of students in a Research Methods course. They found that most research subjects did not mind volunteering to provide data, as long as they understood that they were in control of their degree of participation.

Researchers collecting data from special populations must take precautions against potential exploitation or abuse. Such populations include children, people in

---

AIDS AWARENESS STUDY

The information that you provide on the following pages is to be used in a confidential manner for the sole purpose of the psychological study of student awareness of the causes of AIDS. Your responses are completely voluntary and only the researchers will have access to the information you provide. You may choose not to answer any questions that you prefer not to answer, and you may choose to terminate your participation in this study at any time. The questionnaire generally can be completed in under ten minutes. This project is conducted by students in a psychology research methods course under the supervision of Dr. Mary Allen, and it has been approved by the campus Human Subjects Institutional Research Board.

You are agreeing to participate in this study if you complete this form.

If you are interested in the outcome of this study, you may see a summary of the results posted on the door of DDH-D103. Results will be posted before the end of the quarter.

You may tear off and retain this sheet of paper in case you have any questions about the research.

Thank you for your participation.

Names of Researchers

---

institutions (such as prisons, hospitals, schools, and the military), and people undergoing stress (such as family members of a mentally ill client or people who have just survived an earthquake). Informed consent of a parent or conservator is required for all children and adult subjects incompetent to make an informed judgment.

What effect does informed consent have on research? Adair, Dushenko, and Lindsay (1985) reviewed the literature on this question and concluded that informed consent procedures can reduce the number of research participants, increase the number of questions that are not answered, alter subjects' responses because they are less naive and spontaneous, and create biased samples. For example, subjects who are explicitly told that they may withdraw from the study at any time respond less negatively to obnoxious stimuli (such as loud noises and crowding) than subjects who are not so informed, probably because they have a sense of control over the situation (Adair, Dushenko, & Lindsay, 1985).

INSTITUTIONAL REVIEW BOARDS

Any institution that receives financial support from the federal government must have an Institutional Review Board (IRB), and all research must be approved by the IRB before subjects are recruited and data are collected. The IRB proposal generally contains at least the following information: the purpose and anticipated benefits of the study, a description of how subjects will be recruited and treated, informed consent procedures, and a complete discussion of possible risks and benefits to subjects. IRB members are not always trained in psychology, so proposals must explain concepts in language that the intelligent layman will understand. Although this phase of the project may appear inconvenient, at best, the exercise of preparing the proposal and obtaining IRB approval better guarantees ethical research by all psychologists and sensitizes researchers to ethical requirements. Considering the potential for abuse of research subjects, this is a small price to pay.

ETHICAL DECISION-MAKING

Research goals and ethical standards can come into conflict. For example, a study requiring deception cannot provide all the information that might be needed for appropriate informed consent. The researcher and IRB must make subjective judgments that balance the need for quality research with the need for ethical restrictions. Even if an IRB review is not required, APA standards require researchers to seek the guidance of experienced, knowledgeable people when difficult ethical decisions must be made.

Imagine that you are on an IRB and are asked to evaluate the following study. A research team is interested in studying helping behavior toward people with disabilities, and they design a simple study to conduct at a shopping mall. They plan to randomly select people who are walking alone in the mall. Coming toward the subject, one researcher will drop three books on the floor and a confederate will record the person's behavior. Does the subject ignore the books, pick up one book, pick up two books, or pick up all three books? They plan to have two conditions: the books will be dropped by an ambulatory researcher or by the same researcher in a wheelchair.

This study has one independent variable (whether or not the researcher is in a wheelchair) and one dependent variable (how many books the subject picks up); and it takes less than one minute per subject. The only data to be recorded are the gender of the subject, the age group of the subject (adolescent or adult), and the number of books the subject picks up.

They do not plan to have informed consent or debriefing. They will, however, treat all subjects with respect and will not compromise confidentiality. They argue that the research is ethical because it involves minimal risk to subjects (other than perhaps a bit of guilt if they choose to ignore the researcher), that it takes place in a public area where people are aware that others can observe their behavior, and that the research answers an important question about helpfulness toward people in wheelchairs. If you were on the IRB, would you approve this project? If you would not approve the project, what alternative procedures would you suggest?

RESEARCH ON ANIMALS

Psychologists sometimes do research with animal subjects. They do this to study variables that could not be ethically studied among human subjects (such as the effect of alcohol on prenatal development) or because they are interested in animal behavior. Animals also are convenient research subjects because their living conditions can be carefully controlled, and standard genetic strains have been selectively bred. In addition, many animals have a gestation period (time from conception to birth) and lifespan that are far shorter than those of humans, so multiple generations can be studied in a short period of time.

Much of modern medicine would not exist without ongoing research on animals, including tests of drugs and surgical strategies. Research on animals has allowed psychologists to understand the physiological and psychological effects of stress (e.g., Selye, 1976) and to develop principles of learning (e.g., Thorndike, 1911). Miller (1985) noted that animal research has allowed psychologists to develop therapies for humans with a variety of problems, including bedwetting, phobias, neuromuscular disorders, chronic pain, anxiety, Parkinson's disease, and depression, and to better understand drug addiction and treatment, the effects of premature birth and prenatal drug exposure, and the effects of aging on memory. In addition, behavioral research on animals has led to more humane methods for dealing with animals that damage crops or livestock and more effective ways to protect endangered species.

Ethical standards require that animals not be subjected to undue or excessive pain. Ethical review boards that specialize in animal research, **Institutional Animal Care and Use Committees**, carefully examine proposed studies to evaluate their conformity to ethical principles.

The American Psychological Association (1990) has developed guidelines for the ethical use of animals in research. Many of the principles are the same for human and animal research. For example, researchers are responsible for the ethical, humane, and legal treatment of all research subjects and are responsible for the behavior of all research colleagues involved in their project. Special training and supervision must be provided all animal caretakers and data collectors to ensure that animals are appropriately fed and maintained. Procedures that cause discomfort to animals are carefully reviewed to verify that they are necessary and justified by research goals and that appropriate anesthesia, medication, and care are provided to prevent unwarranted pain. Sometimes research animals are terminated at the end of a study. This must be done "rapidly and painlessly" (APA, 1990, p. 395).

OTHER ETHICAL CONSIDERATIONS

In addition to ethical treatment of subjects, psychologists have other ethical obligations to their peers and to the public. They must select reasonable research strategies that are likely to uncover the truth; and they must carefully conduct their data collection and data analyses. They must honestly report results, even those that are inconsistent with their hypotheses; and they must not deliberately withhold information that might support an alternative explanation. They must be honest in their dealings with granting agencies and research associates. They must give credit to those who have contributed to the project. Anyone who has made substantial contributions to the scholarly importance of the finished study should be acknowledged as a co-author or in a footnote. Psychologists also have an obligation to the community to see that the media do not misrepresent their findings, that providers of psychological services are accurately interpreting and applying results, and that community leaders are well informed on how research results relate to public policy.

CASEBOOK ON ETHICAL PRINCIPLES OF PSYCHOLOGISTS

The *Casebook on Ethical Principles of Psychologists* (American Psychological Association, 1987) presents specific cases reviewed by the APA Ethics Committee, with details changed to protect the confidentiality of those involved. Anyone may bring an ethics charge against an APA member, and members are required to cooperate with the investigation. The Committee may find the accused psychologist not guilty or may reprimand, censure, or file formal charges leading to dropping the person from APA membership. **Reprimands** are given for minor offenses that did not hurt another person, **censures** are given for offenses that hurt another person, and **formal charges** are given for offenses serious enough to warrant expulsion from the Association. Plea bargaining also occurs, with voluntary resignation from the APA for a specified period of time. Most of the cases in the Casebook involve ethical violations by therapists and teachers, but some involve violations by researchers.

Case P.2 dealt with a psychologist who was accused of arbitrarily firing a graduate student employee of a research lab that he directed. Although the Committee found the psychologist not guilty of this act, they did find him guilty of refusing to cooperate with their investigation. The psychologist agreed to resign from the APA for two years, and he has been subsequently readmitted.

Case 1.b.2 involved a psychologist who was doing stress research among hospital employees. The researcher allowed the hospital director to observe some of the data collection because the psychologist and hospital director were long-term friends and the director was curious about the procedures. The Ethics Committee censured the psychologist for allowing the director into the laboratory.

Case 1.e.2 concerned accusations by graduate students that a senior faculty member gave a research colloquium that was prejudiced against women students. The psychologist concluded that, in his experience, men conducted more rigorous, significant theses than women because of their biological superiority; and he refused to discuss alternative explanations of this perception. The Ethics Committee reprimanded the psychologist for his actions.

Case 2.d.2 involved a social psychologist studying voodoo in a Black Haitian community. The director of a local community health center complained that the researcher and her graduate assistants were culturally insensitive and demeaning. The Ethics Committee found that the psychologist inadequately trained her student assistants in cultural sensitivity. They sent an educational letter to the psychologist accepting her offer to write a letter of apology to the director and suggesting she give more attention to the political aspects of conducting research.

CHAPTER SUMMARY

Researchers have ethical obligations to their discipline, the public, and their research subjects; they cannot abdicate this responsibility to others. Key ethical considerations for research on human subjects are privacy, confidentiality, subjects' right to decline and withdraw participation, subjects' right to protection from harm and removal of harmful consequences, deception, debriefing, and informed consent. Data can be anonymous or confidential. Debriefing can involve dehoaxing and desensitizing subjects. Informed consent is required for all studies having more than minimal risk. Dual relationships between researchers and subjects should be avoided.

Institutional Review Boards evaluate the ethics of research on humans, and Institutional Animal Care and Use Committees evaluate the ethics of animal studies.

Case 5.d.1 concerned complaints from a parent that a school psychologist had interviewed sixth-grade children about sexuality without parental permission. The psychologist was evaluating the sex education program, had received oral permission from each child, and had asked the children to consult with their parents before the interview. The Ethics Committee censured the psychologist for not obtaining explicit parental permission and recommended that she take a university ethics course.

Case 5.d.2 concerned a psychologist at a nursing home for the elderly. He instituted a training program to increase self-management skills among the residents, and punished those who did not do well by withdrawing privileges, such as television watching. He planned to publish the results if the program proved effective. A staff member complained to the Ethics Committee. The Committee censured the psychologist for failing to respect the best interests of each resident and for failing to obtain IRB approval and informed consent.

Case 7.e.1 involved a clinical psychologist who was accused of ethical violations for adding a research survey to the intake battery of the church-affiliated clinic that employed her. She added the survey without permission because she feared the church authorities would refuse her request to ask clients about childcare, birth control, and abortion. The

Ethics Committee reprimanded the psychologist for not obtaining permission.

Case 7.e.2 dealt with a school psychologist who worked with culturally deprived, low self-esteem students. In an effort to increase their self-esteem, she coached 25 children to improve their IQ scores by providing them with the test's answers. A colleague complained to the Ethics Committee. The Committee reprimanded the psychologist for making the IQ test invalid for these children and for a possible breach of test security.

Case 7.f.1 was brought by a graduate student who worked under a faculty member's grant. The graduate student collected data, ran computer data analyses, and conducted a literature review, but was only given footnote credit in the published articles. The Ethics Committee found the faculty member not guilty of ethical violations because the student did not make substantial contributions to the scholarly nature of the research.

Case 7.g.2 concerned charges of plagiarism. Conducting a literature review, a psychologist discovered extensive verbatim plagiarism of sections of two of her students' dissertations in articles published by a faculty colleague. The Ethics Committee decided to file formal charges, and the plagiarist was dropped from the APA.

Some alternatives to deception have been suggested, such as role playing, but none completely eliminate problems. The APA Ethics Committee has published a casebook that illustrates ethical violations among APA-member researchers.

Key Concepts

anonymous data
Casebook on Ethical Principles of Psychologists
censure
confidential data
confidentiality
debriefing

deception
dehoaxing
desensitizing
dual relationship
ethical considerations
formal charge
informed consent

Institutional Animal Care and Use
    Committee
Institutional Review Board (IRB)
minimal risk
privacy

reprimand
right to decline and withdraw
right to protection from harm and the
    removal of harmful consequences
role playing

Review Questions

1. Wilson plans to tell subjects that he is working for a marketing firm and is investigating people's reactions to three new flavors of yogurt. He will ask each subject to take one tablespoon of yogurt from each of three containers, taste it, and rate it. The yogurt in Container A is sweet and pleasant, the yogurt in Container B has a neutral flavor, and the yogurt in Container C is bitter and unpleasant. Wilson will tell the subjects that it is important that they be fair in their judgements, so they must eat the same amount of all three flavors; then he will have them rate the yogurts while he is out of the room. Wilson really is studying honesty. By carefully measuring the weights of the three yogurt containers, he will be able to uncover which subjects dishonestly claimed to eat the same amount of all three flavors. He will record data using identification numbers, and he will report statistical results for all subjects combined. His hypothesis is that dishonest people will rate the bitter flavor more favorably than honest people. After data are collected, he will tell subjects the true purpose of the study. You are on the IRB panel. Evaluate Wilson's conformity to the seven key ethical considerations in research with human subjects. Would you approve his study? Explain your answers.

2. Tracy was examining endurance among college students by asking them to run on a treadmill "as long as they possibly could." A pregnant subject faints while on the treadmill. What should Tracy do?

3. Shannon plans to collect data on her sexual history questionnaire by interviewing her friends. Her teacher tells her that this would involve dual relationships. What possible problems could Shannon have because of these dual relationships?

4. Would Wilson (question 1) have to dehoax or desensitize subjects? Explain your answers.

5. Write a sample informed consent form for Tracy's study (question 2). Make up necessary details that are not provided above.

6. A biology major tells you that psychologists should not do research with animals, because they torture animals and learn nothing from them. How would you respond to this statement?

7. You find out that there is a psychologist on campus who is doing unethical research, and that this psychologist is a member of the American Psychological Association. You discuss your concerns with the psychologist, but are not satisfied with the responses. You are considering reporting the psychologist to the APA. Whom would you contact? What are the possible outcomes of their investigation?

Presenting Research: APA Style

Most psychological research is published using APA style, which is defined by the *Publication Manual of the American Psychological Association*. APA style describes good technical writing and requires specific formats for some aspects of the paper, such as reference citations. The latest (fourth) edition was published in 1994 and contains more than 350 pages of instructions and illustrations. A complete description of APA style cannot be provided here, but we will be able to cover some important points. The *Publication Manual* was not created for casual reading. It is a technical manual that is consulted when needed. The information in this chapter should help you learn when to look something up in the *Publication Manual* and how to find it.

ORGANIZATION OF THE MANUSCRIPT

APA-style manuscripts contain the following sections, in order: title page, abstract, introduction, method, results, discussion, references, appendices, author note, footnotes, tables, and figures. (Some of these sections, such as appendices and footnotes, are not included in every manuscript.)

The **title page** identifies the topic, authors, and authors' affiliations. For example, Beth Marie Yamato and David Icardo at UCLA and Wendy Madison Scrams at Michigan State University did a study on how the development of moral reasoning in children is affected by parental style. Dr. Yamato was the primary author of the paper, with Dr. Icardo as second author and Dr. Scrams as third author. (The order of the authors indicates their relative contributions to the project.) An appropriate title page for this paper is shown in Figure 4.1.

The title summarizes the topic of the paper in about ten to twelve words and identifies the major variables. The authors are identified by first name and middle initial, and their academic department is given only if it is not psychology. The short

---

FIGURE 4.1 SAMPLE TITLE PAGE

```
                                                    The Effect 1


          Running head: PARENTAL STYLE AND MORAL DEVELOPMENT




                  The Effect of Parental Style on the
               Development of Children's Moral Reasoning


                  Beth M. Yamato and David Icardo
                  University of California, Los Angeles
                          Wendy M. Scrams
                       Michigan State University
```

---

title in the upper right corner appears on every page of the submitted manuscript with a page number, and the running head (centered at the top of the title page) should be a maximum of fifty characters and will appear at the top of the journal page if the article is published. Like the rest of the manuscript, the title page is double-spaced.

The **abstract** has an abbreviated introduction, method, results, and discussion that summarize the article. Journal readers scan abstracts to decide which articles to read. Research article abstracts should be about 100 to 150 words, and abstracts for review articles should be about 75 to 100 words. The abstract should describe the study's topic, research participants, procedures, results, and implications. It is written last, after the rest of the paper is completed.

The **introduction** describes the research problem and reviews relevant literature. It generally ends with explicit statements of the hypotheses and their rationale. Citations of others' work or ideas are made in APA style. For example, if several studies found that distributed practice produced better learning than massed practice, the introduction may have a sentence like this: `Research demonstrates that distributed practice is more effective than massed practice (Jones, 1988, 1991; Smitt & Thompson, 1987; Wong, 1991).` As an alternative, the sentence could read: `Jones (1988, 1991), Smitt and Thompson (1987), and Wong (1991) found that distributed practice is more effective than massed practice.` Notice that the studies are listed in alphabetical order by the first author, the publication year is given for each article, only last names of authors are given, and ampersands are used within parentheses, but not within the body of sentences. Jones published two articles on the topic, one in 1988 and one in 1991. Material that is directly quoted is placed in quotation marks and is cited by author, date, and page number, such as `"Distributed practice was 50% more efficient than massed practice"` `(Jones, 1988, p. 127).`

Students who write their first introduction to a research paper tend to organize it by reference, serially describing a set of studies. Researchers, though, organize their introductions by topic, integrating all research relevant to several related themes. For example, researchers reporting a study of the effects of gender and social class on musical talent would devote sections of the introduction to reviews of what constitutes musical talent, known gender differences in musical talent, and known social class differences in musical talent. If a theoretical model, such as social learning theory, is to be applied, the researchers would include a summary of the theoretical perspective and how it relates to gender, social class, and musical talent. Finally, based on these reviews, specific hypotheses would be developed.

The **method** section summarizes the sample and procedures in sufficient detail that the reader can understand how the data were collected and how the study could be replicated. This section generally is organized into three major parts, in order: participants, apparatus (or materials), and procedure. The **participants** section describes the research participants: their number, how they were selected, their demographic characteristics (gender, age, ethnicity, and other identifying features, such as class level for student subjects or occupation for adult subjects), and how they were assigned to experimental conditions. The **apparatus** section describes specialized equipment or data collection materials. Detailed information on frequently used materials, such as the Wechsler Adult Intelligence Scale (WAIS) or a standard blood pressure cuff, are not provided. The **procedure** section describes specifically how data were collected, including instructions to the subjects. Details about conditions and information on ethical procedures, such as informed consent and debriefing, also are provided. Sufficient detail must be provided so that the reader could precisely replicate the study.

The **results** section presents the data analyses. Tables and figures may be used to present complicated findings. Each hypothesis is specifically analyzed. Tests that are statistically significant are reported in detail. For example, a paragraph in the results section may state: `The` $\underline{t}$ `test comparing men to women on musical ability was significant,` $\underline{t}(50) = 1.84,$ $\underline{p} < .05$ `Men averaged 12.73 (`$\underline{SD} = 2.14$`), and women averaged 14.68 (`$\underline{SD} = 1.61$`).` Equivalently, the section could read: `Men (`$\underline{M} = 12.73,$ $\underline{SD} = 2.14$`) were significantly different from women (`$\underline{M} = 14.68,$ $\underline{SD} = 1.61$`) in musical ability,` $\underline{t}(50) = 1.84,$ $\underline{p} < .05.$ This may seem like a foreign language to you. Basically, each of these phrasings indicates that a test was used to compare men to women on musical ability. The test was statistically significant; i.e., the test led to the conclusion that men and women have significantly different means. The means are the average scores for each of the two groups, and the standard deviations (**SDs**) are measures of dispersion (how much the members of each group differed among themselves).

Notice that both phrasings identified the type of test that was used (a *t* test), the independent variable (gender), the dependent variable (musical ability), details of the statistical test (a *t* test with 50 degrees of freedom, a value of 1.84, and a significance probability less than .05), and relevant descriptive statistics (means and standard deviations). The .05 indicates that the observed gender difference would be expected less than 5% of the time if men and women were identical in average musical talent. Because this outcome is unlikely, we conclude that women and men have significantly different means. Notice that all statistical symbols are underlined in the manuscript, which is a message to the journal's typesetter to set these symbols in italics. Symbols, such as **M** for mean and **SD** for standard deviation, are used within parentheses, but the words are spelled out in the body of a sentence.

Fewer details are provided for results that are not statistically significant, but even for these results the test that is conducted, the significance level, and the independent and dependent variables are identified. For example, if the above test had not been significant (i.e., if we concluded that men and women are not significantly different in musical ability), the phrasing could be: `The t test comparing women to men on musical ability was not significant at the .05 level.` Statistics commonly used in psychological research are reviewed in Chapter 5.

The **discussion** section evaluates and interprets results. The researcher integrates, elaborates, and speculates in this section. Each hypothesis is discussed, results are integrated into the theory and literature review, and speculations about implications and suggestions about possible subsequent studies are developed. Beginners tend to simply repeat the results section, rather than to fully discuss the results and integrate them into the rest of the paper.

The **references** section lists detailed information on every source cited in the paper, so that readers can locate the original. References are ordered alphabetically by the last name of their primary author. APA style dictates the format for different types of sources. For example, a journal article written by Janet Q. Gorman, Frances Sara Campbell, and Vernon Hill would be cited like this:

> `Gorman, J. Q., Campbell, F. S., & Hill, V. (1992).`
> `The effect of parasites on human memory. Cognitive Re-`
> `view, 42(6), 14-23.`

Notice the capitalization of just the first word of the article's title and the fact that only the authors' initials and last names are given. This article can be found in Issue 6 of Volume 42 of the journal *Cognitive Review* on pages 14 to 23. Generally, each volume corresponds to one year. The issue number is provided only if each issue begins on page 1. Some journals use continuous page numbers within volumes. For example, if issue 1 contained pages 1 through 197, issue 2 would begin on page 198. Providing the issue number is not necessary for such journals because page numbers are sufficient for readers to locate the article.

Here is an example of a book reference:

> `Hartley, J. G., & Black, M. (1991). The history of`
> `psychology (4th ed.). Phoenix, AZ: Jacobson.`

This book was published in 1991 by the Jacobson Publishing Company in Phoenix, Arizona and is in its fourth edition (three earlier versions of this book were published previously).

Sometimes an editor creates a book by compiling sections written by other authors. To cite one section in such a book, the format is like this:

```
Beal, J. D. (1990). Measurement of androgyny. In W.
Hunter (Ed.), Current research in androgyny (pp. 118-
137). New York: Webber.
```

The reader would locate the book edited by Hunter in order to find the chapter written by Beal.

APA style dictates formats for other types of references, such as newspaper and magazine articles, conference presentations, and translated books. Because all APA-style publications use the same format for references, readers can easily use the information provided to locate original sources.

Appendices present complicated materials that would distract from the body of the paper. They are rarely used in journal articles, but would be appropriate for presentation of a new psychological test, details of a long script or set of procedures used in data collection, a new computer program, or a complicated mathematical proof.

The **author note** adds additional information, such as the author's department and acknowledgment of grant or other support for the research. You can write to the researcher to request copies of the article or to ask questions.

Footnotes provide materials that supplement information in the body of the paper. Like Appendices, they are rarely used in journal articles.

Tables and **figures** are used sparingly and are very effective ways to communicate complicated information. They are given at the end of the submitted manuscript, but are placed near the relevant section when the paper is published. Simple examples of tabular and graphic presentations of the t test results given above and one other t test comparing men to women on vocabulary size are presented in Figure 4.2. For illustrative purposes, the second t test was significant at the .01 level. This distinction will be explained in Chapter 5. Notice that the entire table is double-spaced, that a descriptive title is provided, and that labels are given to all columns. Also notice that the formats for table and figure titles are different. Each table and figure is given on a separate manuscript page at the end of the article, and figure captions are typed on a separate page that precedes the figure.

GENERAL WRITING STYLE

The paper should have an overall organization that facilitates readers' comprehension, with a smooth flow of ideas. Good technical writers carefully select each word to be precise and understandable. Beginners sometimes forget that the goal is not to impress readers with the size of their vocabulary or the cleverness of their expressions. (Concise, elegant expressions are appropriate; cute expressions are not appropriate.) Transition words (e.g., therefore, in addition, however) are used to provide continuity.

The *Publication Manual* requires "an economy of expression: Say only what needs to be said" (1994, p. 26). Wordiness is to be avoided. For practice, see if you can reduce

FIGURE 4.2 SAMPLE TABLE AND FIGURE

Short Title 25

Table 1
Means and Standard Deviations for Men and Women on Two Tests

| | Gender | | | |
| | Men | | Women | |
Variable	M	SD	M	SD
Musical ability	12.73*	2.14	14.68	1.61
Vocabulary size	14.13**	1.06	9.18	2.10

*p < .05. **p < .01.

Short Title 26

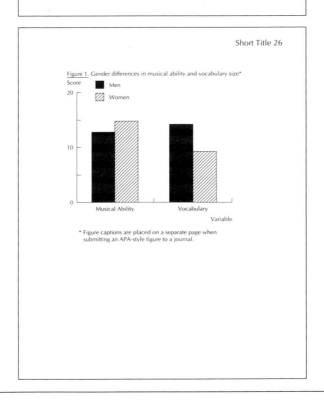

Figure 1. Gender differences in musical ability and vocabulary size*

* Figure captions are placed on a separate page when submitting an APA-style figure to a journal.

the wordiness of this sentence: `The reason that the girls were older was based on the fact that because buses absolutely required girls under 13 to have a mother or father ride with them, girls who were twelve years old or younger, who did not have a mother or father willing to ride with and accompany them, were unable to attend the summer camp.` Perhaps your sentence is closer to this: `Girls were older because bus regulations required that a parent ride with girls under 13, so fewer younger girls attended camp.`

Researchers sometimes refer to their own opinions or actions in their writings. Earlier publication manuals required the impersonal third-person voice, such as `The researcher asked each subject to answer five questions`, rather than the first-person voice: `I asked each subject to answer five questions`. Present APA style recommends the first-person voice to specify unambiguously the subject of such sentences. Writers should do this sparingly; the first-person voice should not dominate the article (Polyson, Levinson, & Miller, 1982). The singular form ("I"), rather than the plural form ("We"), is used for single-authored articles.

Beginners frequently misuse certain words or include expressions that are too informal or ambiguous for technical writing. *Feel* is not equivalent to *think* or *believe*. To feel something is to sense it, such as to feel cold or to feel a hard surface. *Effect* and *affect* are frequently confused. Both words can be used as nouns and verbs. An effect is an outcome or result; to effect is to bring about something. An affect is an emotional state; to affect is to influence. Nonhumans cannot perform human functions; for example, a study cannot think or make decisions. *While* and *since* refer to time and should not be substituted for *although* or *because*. *Between* and *among* refer to groups of two and to groups of three or more, respectively. *Hopefully* means "full of hope" or "in a hopeful manner" and should not be confused with "I hope" or "It is hoped." Some people also have trouble with pronouns. *It's* is a contraction for *it is*; and *its* is a possessive pronoun that indicates ownership. *They're* is a contraction of *they are*; *their* is the possessive form of *they*. Here are examples illustrating these concepts:

Wrong: `The researcher feels that smaller doses should be used.`
Correct: `I believe that smaller doses should be used.`

Wrong: `The parent was effected by the child's behavior.`
Correct: `The parent was affected by the child's behavior.`

Wrong: `The committee affected a plan.`
Correct: `The committee effected a plan.`

Wrong: `The affect of the noise was hearing loss.`
Correct: `The effect of the noise was hearing loss.`

Wrong: `Frustrated participants had an angry effect.`
Correct: `Frustrated participants had an angry affect.`

Wrong: `Johnson's (1992) results concluded that ...`
Correct: `Johnson (1992) concluded that ...`

Wrong: `While I agree with their perspective, I feel that ...`
Correct: `Although I agree with their perspective, I believe that ...`

Wrong: `The man refused since he disliked the questions.`
Correct: `The man refused because he disliked the questions.`

Wrong: `Among the two choices, I prefer the round one.`
Correct: `Between the two choices, I prefer the round one.`

Wrong: `Participants had to decide between the three alternatives.`
Correct: `Participants had to decide among the three alternatives.`

Wrong: `Hopefully, participants will recover from the shock.`
Correct: `I hope participants will recover from the shock.`

Wrong: `Its the answer to it's own question.`
Correct: `It's the answer to its own question.`

Wrong: `Their taking they're tests in the other room.`
Correct: `They're taking their tests in the other room.`

Technical writing generally uses the **active voice**: The subject of the sentence acts, rather than passively receives the verb's action. For example, `Rossell (1990) concluded that haste makes waste` is preferred over `The theory that haste makes waste was concluded by Rossell (1990)`.

Singular subjects require singular verbs and pronouns; plural subjects require plural verbs and pronouns. A frequent problem among beginners is the word *data*, which is a plural word. `Data were analyzed` is correct. `Data was analyzed` is wrong. Another common problem involves *each* and *their*. `Each girl closed her eyes` is correct. `Each girl closed their eyes` is wrong. Some words have plurals that may be new to you: the plural of analysis is analyses, the plural of criterion is criteria, the plural of hypothesis is hypotheses, and the plural of stimulus is stimuli.

Parallel ideas are expressed in parallel language. For example, `Results indicate that late risers prefer louder music, more colorful clothes, and dated younger than early risers` is wrong because the three phrases presented after "prefer" are not parallel. (If this is hard for you to see, leave out some words to see if the sentence works: `Results indicate that late risers prefer dated younger.`) A correct version of this sentence is: `Results indicate that late risers begin dating at a younger age and prefer louder music and more colorful clothes than early risers.` Similarly, `The participants liked fishing, boating, and to watch birds` involves nonparallel language and could be replaced by `The participants liked fishing, boating, and bird watching` or by `The participants liked to fish, to boat, and to watch birds`.

The present tense is used to define terms and to discuss current ideas, such as `Most psychologists view positive reinforcement as a major factor in learning.` The past tense is used to describe something that occurred at a definite time in the past, such as previous research findings. The present perfect tense is used to describe something that began in the past and continues into the present or that did not occur at a definite time in the past. For example, `Jones (1991) found support for Anderson's theory` (the past tense) and `Researchers have tried to discover a chemical basis for schizophrenia` (the present perfect tense). These tenses generally are used in the introduction.

The method and results sections generally are written in the past tense (e.g., `Participants were given five minutes to complete the test. Scores significantly improved.`), and the discussion of results in the discussion section generally is written in the present tense (e.g., `Results indicate that training improves performance.`). Of course, other tenses are sometimes appropriate. For example, the subjunctive is used to describe unlikely events, such as `If an alien were in his body, more people would notice the antennae.`

APA style prohibits the use of sexist or ethnically biased language that is discriminatory, offensive, or demeaning toward gender or ethnic groups. In addition, writers should be sensitive to groups varying in other ways, such as in religion, religiosity, or sexual orientation. Sometimes biases occur when the authors assume their group is the norm and other groups are deficient rather than different. Another common error is to assume that all members of a group are alike. For example, Levine (1982) points out differences among the elderly that must be taken into account. In addition, appropriate designations of groups change over time. For example, Negroes became blacks, black Americans, Afro-Americans, and African-Americans over a few decades; appropriate references to this group and others may evolve further.

The APA *Publication Manual* provides several pages of examples of sexist language. It includes use of the generic male (e.g., "Each participant covered *his* left eye" or "*Men* need to understand their environment") and assumptions about gender roles ("Each kindergarten teacher asked *her* students to be quiet" or "The children suffered from *maternal* neglect") when both genders are being discussed. These sentences could be corrected as follows: "Participants covered their left eyes," "People need to understand their environment," "The kindergarten teachers asked their students to be quiet," and "The children suffered from parental neglect." Sometimes plural phrasing is inappropriate or awkward, and an occasional "his or her" or "her and his" is used, such as "Each participant wrote his or her list on a notecard."

The APA Committee on Lesbian and Gay Concerns (1991) provided guidance for avoiding **heterosexist language** (language that is biased in favor of a heterosexual orientation or that assumes that all people are heterosexual), and their suggestions have been integrated into the *Publication Manual*. One must understand the history of their concerns to appreciate their sensitivity to some language, and this history is less well known than the history of racism or sexism in our culture. The Association of Lesbian and Gay Psychologists was established in 1973 and lobbied hard to remove "homosexuality" from the list of clinical diagnoses, to create an official APA policy statement that affirms the competence and civil rights of lesbians and gay men, and to develop affirmative psychotherapy models for gay persons (Morin & Rothblum, 1991).

The guidelines to avoid heterosexist language suggest a number of changes in reference to sexuality. The phrase *sexual orientation* is preferred to the phrase *sexual preference* because *orientation* does not imply that the gender of sexual interest is "chosen." Words like *lesbianism, homosexuality,* and *bisexuality* are avoided because of their historical association with pathology. ("Homosexuality" was removed from the

RESEARCH ON POLITICALLY SENSITIVE TOPICS

Sensitivity to cultural pluralism sometimes creates conflicts for researchers. It is no longer "politically correct" to refer to African-American citizens as Negroes, women as girls, or gay people as homosexuals. Researchers who wish to examine cultural differences may be accused of having an "ism" (racism, sexism, ageism, heterosexism), especially if they uncover results unflattering to minority groups. Sandra Scarr, who has conducted research on race and genetics, reports that researchers who examine racial and ethnic issues are "in danger of ostracism and worse from one's socially well-intentioned colleagues. The messenger with the bad news seems to be blamed for having invented the message" (1988, p. 56).

Although empirically verified weaknesses may be incorrectly used to justify exploitation or oppression, remediation programs will not be established and funded until we understand what needs must be met and their etiology. Understanding differences also should reduce misunderstandings between groups. For example, personal space requirements (the distance around the body that is maintained between people) vary across cultures; people unaware of these differences may misinterpret the behaviors of those from another culture. In addition, if we don't look for differences, we don't uncover similarities; thus, we allow inaccurate stereotypes to persist. Rather than ignore possible differences, perhaps researchers should routinely look for them and report both significant and nonsignificant results (Eagly, 1987).

Fearing criticism, researchers may abandon lines of research that could have politically unpopular results. For example, Baumeister (1988) suggests that we should stop studying sex differences because "politically, the study of sex differences may do more harm than good. By seeking, reporting, and discussing sex differences, psychologists lend scientific prestige to the distinction between men and women" and this "endorses a way of looking at the world in which men and women are fun-

damentally different" (p. 1094). This line of reasoning could be applied to other group differences. IRBs may be so sensitive to this perspective that they refuse to approve research studies that follow stated ethical guidelines, but that examine politically sensitive issues, such as affirmative action and reverse discrimination (Ceci, Peters, & Plotkin, 1985). Concerns about politically sensitive research may lead to censorship.

Scarr (1988) enumerates a number of research programs with results that were misused by others, such as the application of aversive conditioning to political prisoners and the application of sleep research to brainwashing. She concludes that researchers have the obligation to consider possible misuses of their results and to take a proactive stand explaining their conclusions in a public forum. Their explanations need not be consistent with politically correct ideology, but science "must operate with free inquiry, free discussion, and the competition of ideas" (p. 58).

A number of publications in the *American Psychologist* (the major publication of the American Psychological Association) have suggested ways to reduce biased research (e.g., Denmark, Russo, Frieze, & Sechzer, 1988; Herek, Kimmel, Amaro, & Melton, 1991; Zuckerman, 1990). Bias may affect every stage of a research study, from its first formulation to the final explanation of results. Here are some examples of bias in research:

1. Researchers who compare other groups to their own group and assume their group is "normal" are bound to find other groups "abnormal." IQ tests may have cultural biases that work against some minority cultures, and definitions of healthy behaviors and ways to handle stress and conflict may vary across cultures. Groups may be different, but this does not imply that one group is deficient compared to the other.

2. Literature reviews may lead to biased conclusions, especially if results are based on samples restricted to one group. For example,

research on male subjects shows that aggressive stimuli are sexually stimulating, but other studies have shown that this is not true for female subjects (Denmark et al. 1988). Much research leaves minority groups "invisible." For example, lesbian, gay male, and bisexual research participants may not be identified or separately analyzed in studies in which they may respond differently from subjects with a heterosexual orientation, such as studies concerning marital relationships. Members of other minority groups may not be identified or separately analyzed. Studies may involve biased samples for comparison purposes. For example, gender and ethnic comparisons among employees of a major corporation might compare people who also vary in income, educational level, and social class. Differences may reflect these other factors, rather than gender or ethnicity. Clinical research frequently is conducted among clinical samples, but minority group members may seek therapy for different types of problems that are not handled within their subculture or that are the effects of discrimination from the rest of society; and conceptions of normal and abnormal behavior may vary across cultures.

3. Biological explanations that do not take possible cultural differences into account may not be justified, and researchers should not assume genetic or cultural uniformity within groups. For example, Latino or Asian-American subjects may include recent immigrants, fifth-generation American citizens with few ties to their ethnic roots, and people with backgrounds from a variety of cultural traditions. An Indian farmer in Bolivia and a Cuban business owner may both be classified as Latino, but the Bolivian may have genetic roots in Asia and the Cuban may have genetic roots in Europe. Similarly, there is enormous genetic and cultural variation among people classified as African- or European-American.

4. Definitions of group membership may be inaccurate. For example, ethnic backgrounds may be mixed in American samples of minority groups. The whole concept of race is questionable among American samples because its definition assumes isolated inbreeding groups, a situation probably never true in our society (Zuckerman, 1990). The researcher's assumptions about group membership may be in error. People who attend Alcoholics Anonymous meetings may not be alcoholic; people at gay bars may not be gay; people who claim to be in a group may not belong to it.

5. Small differences may be exaggerated, leading to discussions of trivial, but statistically significant differences. This is especially common in studies with large sample sizes, as will be seen in Chapter 5. In addition, group differences cannot be applied to individuals. For example, the average man scores higher than the average woman on tests of mathematical reasoning, but some women score higher than most men and some men score lower than most women. Group differences cannot be used to justify discrimination against individuals, such as barring women from engineering programs.

6. Alternative interpretations may be ignored. For example, women use more tag questions than men. (Tag questions are short questions at the end of declarative sentences, as in *It's hot today, isn't it?*) This could be interpreted as an indicator of the lack of self-confidence in women or as an indicator that women make more attempts to involve others in mutual conversation (Hyde, 1991).

Psychologists must avoid biased research, and there are many possible pitfalls. Openly discussing research issues with members of other groups is an excellent way to highlight biased assumptions. A willingness to discuss group differences in an open forum should lead to increased mutual understanding and awareness. Researchers who examine socially important issues without bias are following APA ethical guidelines that promote research for the benefit of human welfare.

list of mental disorders in 1973, and "ego-dystonic homosexuality" was removed in 1987.) Preferable are the phrases *lesbian sexual orientation, gay male sexual orientation,* and *bisexual orientation.* The phrase *lesbian and gay male* is preferable to *homosexual* because it avoids the language previously associated with pathology and makes clear that both women and men are being described. *Gay* may be used as an adjective and *gay persons* may be used as a collective noun for lesbians and gay men when the context clarifies that both groups are being discussed.

The Committee also points out that many language habits suggest heterosexism. For example, classifying people as single or married omits cohabiting relationships. People with heterosexual orientations frequently assume that all sexual activity is heterosexual and could result in pregnancy, and surveys and papers use language such as *sexual intercourse* that implies heterosexual sex, rather than *sexual activity* which includes a wider range of behaviors. Language that suggests deviance should not be used, such as comparing lesbians to "normal women" or comparing gay and bisexual persons to "the general public."

Contributors to the psychological literature must be sensitive to biased language and must work to eliminate it. Changing writing habits may require extra effort, but is an important aspect of doing psychological research.

EXAMPLES OF APA STYLE

The *APA Publication Manual* has too many rules to summarize all of them here. If you have access to a *Publication Manual,* try to find the appropriate section and to correct the errors in the following sentences. Remember, the trick is to learn when to use the *Publication Manual* and how to use it. Key words in the manual's index are provided in parentheses after each example. In addition to the technical problems, most of these sentences are awkwardly phrased and require rephrasing.

1. `The 1st set contained 17 trials and the second set contained thirty-three trials and the 3rd set contained four trials.` (Numbers)

2. `There are 3 major theories relevant to this hypothesis: 1) the spinal-reflex theory; 2) the cortical theory; and 3) the thalamic-reflex theory.` (Seriation)

3. `Johnson & Jones (1932) did a study and it was about biofeedback and it said on page 37 that 'the "weakest link" between smoking and breathing is the mind'.` (Quotations)

4. `Some research has already concluded that token economies work for controlling temper tantrums in five year old children and children who are 6 years old: Rothbert's 1991 study published in the Western Psychologist, Jane Smith and Vincent Pepper's 1984 study conducted in Chicago, and Watson, Waldo, and Hale's 1981 study and also their 1985 study.` (Hyphenation, Reference citations in text)

5. `The first path was 4 centimeters wide and the second path was fifteen percent wider than the first path and the`

third path was fifteen percent wider than the second path and the fourth path was fifteen percent wider than the third path and the fifth path was fifteen percent wider than the fourth path. (Numbers, Metric units)

6. We did an F test for homogeneity of variance and it was significant at the .005 level and it had four and fifteen degrees of freedom and its value was 19.540002 and the young subjects had a standard deviation of 3.8723225 and the old subjects had a standard deviation of 17.117242. (Statistical copy)

7. Each participant was given one parachute (except for the control subjects) and then were asked to jump out of the plane. (Verbs)

8. Randomly-assigned participants were subjected to either high intensity or low-intensity lighting to see who would have a higher-chance of misreading the labels on the low-calorie soft drinks. (Hyphenation)

9. On Day 6 of condition two each participant received an injection of adrenalin. (Capitalization, Numbers)

10. Participants were given the CBT (California Baseline Test). CBT IQ's were provided to the participant's parents, teachers and counselors. (Abbreviations, Comma in series)

11. Each participant was asked to throw his hat into the circle. (Sexist language)

12. Smith (1992) has found that adrenalin injections increase activity levels in rats. (Verb tense)

Here are correct rephrasings of the above sentences. Many other phrasings also would be accurate. Check with your teacher if you have questions about the answers you developed.

1. The first set contained 17 trials, the second set contained 33 trials, and the third set contained 4 trials.

2. There are three major theories relevant to this hypothesis (a) the spinal-reflex theory, (b) the cortical theory, and (c) the thalamic-reflex theory.

3. Johnson and Jones (1932) concluded that "the 'weakest link' between smoking and breathing is the mind" (p. 37).

4. Rothbert (1991), Smith and Pepper (1984), and Watson, Waldo, and Hale (1981, 1985) concluded that token economies can be used to control temper tantrums in five- and six-year-old children.

5. The first path was 4 cm wide, and each of the next four paths was 15% wider than the preceding path.

6. The test for homogeneity of variance was significant, $F(4, 15) = 19.54$, $p < .005$. Young subjects had a standard deviation of 3.87, and old subjects had a standard deviation of 17.12.

7. Experimental participants were given parachutes, and all participants were asked to jump out of the plane.

8. Randomly assigned participants were subjected to either high-intensity or low-intensity lighting and were asked to read the labels on the low-calorie soft drinks.

9. On Day 6 of Condition 2 each participant received an injection of adrenalin.

10. Participants were given the California Baseline Test (CBT). CBT IQs were provided to their parents, teachers, and counselors.

11. Participants were asked to throw their hats into the circle.

12. Smith (1992) found that adrenalin injections increase activity levels in rats.

SAMPLE MANUSCRIPT

Figure 4.3 shows a sample manuscript prepared in APA style. Manuscripts that are to be submitted to journals for possible publication would be prepared in this way. Figure 4.3 also contains some reminders of style rules previously discussed in this chapter. (The study and references are not authentic, so pay more attention to the style than to the content.)

FIGURE 4.3 SAMPLE RESEARCH PAPER

Double-space entire paper. Number each page.

Note use of capital and lowercase letters.

Parental Style 1

Running head: THE EFFECT OF PARENTAL STYLE

The Effect of Parental Style on the Development of Children's Moral Reasoning

Joan P. Sample
Morro State University

Parental Style 2

Abstract is on a
separate page.
No paragraph indent.

Summarize whole
paper.

Abstract

Research indicates considerable variability in the development
of moral reasoning. According to modeling theory, children are
likely to imitate their parents. Children of parents with
consultative styles should have more developed moral reasoning
than children of parents with dictatorial styles. Twenty-five
one-child, two-parent families were classified by parental style,
and the children's responses to a Kohlberg dilemma were
categorized by developmental level. The children had a mean
age of 10.56 years, and they represented three ethnic groups.
Twelve of the children were girls; and thirteen were boys.
Consistent with the hypothesis, children with consultative
parents exhibited significantly higher levels of moral reasoning.
The relatively high proportion of consultative parents and
postconventional children suggests the need for increasingly
sophisticated public service campaigns.

Begin a new page.

Parental Style 3

Repeat the title.

Review relevant
literature.

The Effect of Parental Style on the Development of
Children's Moral Reasoning

Kohlberg (1969) classified moral reasoning into three levels,
with two stages at each level, and developed a technique for
classifying people's level by their responses to dilemmas. For
example, a woman has a fatal illness that can only be helped by
one medication; and the pharmacist who developed and
markets the drug is charging an enormous rate for it. The
woman and her husband do not have enough money to buy the
medicine. Her husband fails in attempts to borrow the money,
and the pharmacist refuses to sell him the drug on credit; so he
decides to steal the medicine.

Subjects are asked if the husband's decision was reasonable,
and they are asked to explain their answer. The lowest level,
preconventional morality, is indicated by responses that stress
external authority or hedonism. A child at this level may reason
that the husband should not steal because he would have to go
to jail or that he should steal to make himself feel better.
Conventional morality stresses rules and what others will think,
rather than punishment or hedonism. A child at this level may
conclude that the husband should steal the drug to avoid being
labelled a coward or that the husband should not steal the drug
because others would think him criminal. The last level,
sometimes achieved in adolescence, is one of postconventional
morality, and it is marked by the application of a personal code
of ethics. A postconventional child might conclude that the
husband should steal because a woman's life is worth more than
money or that the husband should not steal because his

Parental Style 4

Use et al. for
second and subsequent
citations of sources
with at least three
authors.

choosing to steal violates the contract among citizens to
conform to legally agreed upon rules.

Children vary considerably in the rate at which they progress
through the stages (Johnson, 1982), and many never go beyond
the conventional level (Hower, Garcia, & Fielding, 1983).
Johnson (1982) found that only 52% of American adults are
beyond stage 4, and Hower et al. (1983) found that only 38% of
American teenagers are beyond stage 4.

Introduce theory.

According to social learning theory, many aspects of
behavior are learned by imitating models (Watson, 1976).
Many aspects of cognitive and attitudinal development are
learned through the imitation of role models (Watkins, Ralley,
and McDonald, 1978; Zarf, 1991); and parents are the primary
models for pre-pubescent children (Watson, 1976).

Two parental models describe global characteristics of
parenting (Bodmer, 1983): a dictatorial and a consultative
model. Dictatorial parents "expect obedience without question

Give page number for
quoted materials.

or debate" (p. 121); and consultative parents expect obedience,
but they explain to their children why rules exist and negotiate
with their children on rules that are based on flexible guidelines.

Considerable evidence suggests that children of consultative
parents are more likely to obey rules that have been achieved
through discussion and consensus, even when parents are not
present (Bodmer & Alison, 1984). This suggests that such
children have internalized a higher level of moral reasoning.
They have learned a higher level through observing adult
models that explain moral reasoning and through participating
in this process. This study examines the hypothesis that

State research
hypotheses.

Parental Style 5

Do not go to a new
page for method
section.

children with consultative parents exhibit higher levels of moral
reasoning than children with dictatorial parents.

Describe participants.

Method

Participants

Twenty-eight one-child, two-parent families were identified
with the cooperation of two local elementary schools; and each
family was individually contacted by a member of the research
team with an invitation to participate in the project. All families
lived within a five-mile radius of the university. All but three
families agreed to participate. Six families had step-fathers and
one family had a step-mother; and all step-parents had been in
the home at least seven years. The children ranged from 10
years, 3 months to 10 years, 11 months, with a mean of 10.56

Underline statistical
terms.

years ($\underline{SD}$ = .12). Twelve of the children were girls, and thirteen
were boys. Fourteen of the families were African-American,
eight were Latino, and three were European-American. All
children were monolingual in English.

Notice that headings
at the same level are
in the same format.

Procedure

Two members of the research team spent six hours in each
home observing parent-child interactions. They arranged their
visits so that they observed at least one meal and at least one
period when the child participated in housekeeping chores.

Describe procedures.

Observers applied Bodmer's eight criteria (1983) and reached
agreement on parenting style through discussion. Eight sets of
parents were categorized as dictatorial, and seventeen sets of
parents were classified as consultative.

Each child was tested individually to determine moral
development level. The interviews were videotaped, and two

Parental Style 6

scorers reached agreement through discussion of each child's
responses. The dilemma described above was presented,
following Kohlberg's procedure (1969).

Results

Summarize findings.

Observed developmental levels ranged from stage 3 through
stage 6, as shown in Figure 1. A $\chi2$ test comparing the levels of
children raised by consultative and dictatorial parents could not
be conducted because of small expected frequencies, so stages
were grouped into two levels (conventional and
postconventional) and a Fisher's exact test was conducted.
Results were significant, p < .00005. The percentage of children
at the two developmental levels is provided in Table 1.

Test research
hypothesis.

Discussion

Discuss research
hypothesis.

The hypothesis that the level of moral development exhibited
by children is affected by parental style was supported.
Children with parents who model moral thinking and who
involve children in discussion of moral issues are significantly
more likely to exhibit postconventional moral reasoning than
children whose parents dictate moral rules without discussion or
participation by the children.

The proportion of ten-year-olds in our sample who exhibited
postconventional reasoning was much larger than found by
Kohlberg (1969) and others (e.g., Howard & Fielding, 1983;
Johnson, 1982); and the proportion of consultative parents in
our sample also exceeded earlier studies (e.g., Bodmer, 1982;

Relate findings to
the literature.

Parental Style 7

Bodmer & Alison, 1984). Two explanations are possible.
Previous research indicates a trend across time, with increasing
reliance on consultative parenting styles between 1982 and
1991 (see review by Jantzen, 1992), so our results are consistent
with this trend. Alternatively, it is possible that families in a
university community are more likely to adopt consultative
models. For example, Bodmer and Allison (1984) found that
parents who adopt a consultative model have higher
educational attainments than parents who adopt a dictatorial
style. The high proportion of postconventional children in our
sample appears to be an artifact of the high proportion of
consultative parents, consistent with a causal relationship
between parenting style and child's moral reasoning.

Discuss implications.

If trends noted by Jantzen (1992) continue, school and social
service personnel who design prevention programs for children
must recognize that increasing numbers of children are
reasoning at high levels, even among ten-year-olds. The
sophistication of the reasoning in public service campaigns for
children (such as the "just say no to drugs" campaign) should
target a more sophisticated audience. Further research on the
moral development of children, their actual behavior, and the
routes to influence attitude and behavioral changes is needed.

Suggest new research
ideas.

Arrange in alphabetical order by authors' last names.

Parental Style 8

References

Bodmer, G. (1983). Two models of parenting behavior. Child Development Journal, 46(3), 118-131.

Bodmer, G., & Alison, A. J. (1984). Parenting for the future. New York: Harcourt.

Hower, R. T., Garcia, J., & Fielding, D. (1983). Kohlberg's stages of moral development. In T. G. Riley (Ed.), Developmental trends (pp. 145-196). New York: Bethany.

Jantzen, U. (1992, July). Trends in parenting styles. Current News, pp. 67-72.

Johnson, F. (1982, August). Reexamining the development of moral reasoning. Paper presented at the meeting of the Child Development Association, San Francisco, CA.

Kohlberg, L. (1969). Stages and sequence: The cognitive-developmental approach to socialization. In D. A. Goslin (Ed.), Handbook of socialization theory and research (2nd ed. pp. 293-325). Chicago: Rand-McNally.

Watkins, J., Ralley, H. B., & McDonald, R. (1978). Imitation of parental violence. Human Aggression, 32, 145-157.

Watson, J. C. (1976). Learning altruism by imitation. Altruism Journal, 3, 417-431.

Zarf, W. C. (1991). The role of imitation in child development. New York: Westinghouse.

Journal article

Book

Chapter in an edited book

Magazine article

Conference presentation

Second edition of a book

Parental Style 9

Author Note

Author's address

Correspondence concerning this article should be sent to Joan P. Sample, Department of Psychology, Morro State University, Morro, California 91174.

Underline title.

Notice arrangement
of headings.

Notice horizontal
lines above and
below the table.

Table 1
Percentage of Children at Each Developmental Level

	Moral development level	
Parenting style	Conventional	Postconventional
Consultative	12	88
Dictatorial	100	0

Figure caption is
on a separate page.

Notice lowercase
letters and period.

Figure Caption
Figure 1. The number of children at each developmental level.

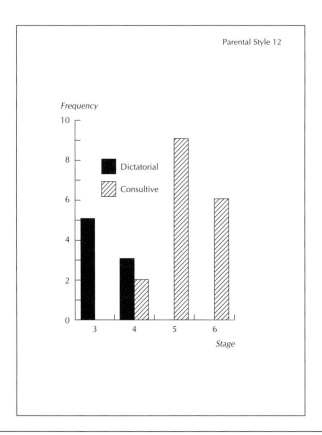

PLAGIARISM

Plagiarism is a concept that appears simple but becomes tricky in practice. **Plagiarism** is the presentation of another's words or ideas as if they were your own, without crediting the source. Plagiarism is unethical and illegal; it can result in serious professional and legal consequences.

The American Modern Language Association (Gibaldi & Achert, 1988) has developed a detailed set of criteria for identifying plagiarism. Plagiarism includes presenting verbatim passages, paraphrased passages, or rephrased ideas without citing their source. Problems with plagiarism occur in published research (Riordin & Marlin, 1987), magazines and newspapers (Easterbrook, 1991), and classrooms (Hale, 1987).

Take the preceding paragraph as an example of a section in an original source. The following two sentences are plagiarism: *Plagiarism includes presenting verbatim passages, paraphrased passages, or rephrased ideas without citing their source. Plagiarism includes presenting verbatim materials, paraphrased materials, or rephrased concepts without citing their source.* In the first sentence, a verbatim passage is given without citation and without quotation marks; in the second sentence, a paraphrased passage is given without citation.

Paraphrasing that maintains the grammatical structure of the original source is plagiarism, such as substituting "materials" for "passages" in the above paragraph, even when the source is cited. You must change the grammatical structure of cited materials to avoid plagiarism. Although common knowledge may be stated without a source (e.g., Freud developed psychoanalysis), interpretations of common knowledge do require citations (e.g., someone's analysis of psychoanalysis).

One important aspect of plagiarism is that the definition does not specify intentionality. Unintentional plagiarism is still plagiarism. Students who write papers by taking notes and then combining their notes into an original composition plagiarize if they inadvertently "borrow" language from the source or lose track of which aspects of their notes are in their own language and which aspects have been lifted verbatim or paraphrased too closely. To avoid plagiarism on your final paper, be careful when you take notes. Use quotation marks and record page numbers for quotations, and avoid borrowing phrases and grammatical structures.

APA style requires citation of all sources of information for a paper and special treatment of materials that are quoted verbatim. Beginning writers often overquote sources, perhaps indicating fear of plagiarism or lack of confidence about their ability to accurately summarize another's ideas. Direct quotes are used sparingly in good technical writing. Paraphrasing is relatively easy to avoid if writers think through the ideas to be cited and rephrase them without repeatedly checking the source. To create your own phrasing, imagine summarizing someone's ideas to one of your friends. Remember that ideas are organized by concepts, rather than by source, so papers are unlikely to contain many direct quotes.

CHAPTER SUMMARY

Psychological research generally is published using APA style, which is based on the *Publication Manual of the American Psychological Association.* APA-style manuscripts contain the following sections, in order: title page, abstract, introduction, method, results, discussion, references, appendices, author note, footnotes, tables, and figures. APA style dictates the content and organization of each section.

The manuscript should have a smooth flow of ideas with precise, concise language. It should be in the active voice, with appropriate use of parallel sentence structure, subject-verb and subject-pronoun agreement, tense, and nonbiased language. A number of suggestions have been made for avoiding bias when planning and interpreting research. Plagiarism involves inappropriate use of quotations, paraphrased language, and presenting another's ideas without citation. Plagiarism is unethical and illegal.

Key Concepts

abstract	author note
active voice	discussion
APA style	figure
apparatus	footnote
appendix	heterosexist language

introduction

method

participants

plagiarism

procedure

Publication Manual of the American

Psychological Association

references

results

table

title page

Review Questions

1. Create an APA-style title page for the following research project: Daryl Stanley Freeman, Psychology Department at Connecticut State Teacher's College, was the first author, and Maria Benjamin and Shane W. McNaughton of the Criminology Department at the University of Hawaii were the second and third authors, respectively. Their study examined the effects of expert witness testimony on parental custody decisions by comparing custody decisions made on the basis of reports filed by social workers, psychologists, and psychiatrists. (They found that judges most often made decisions consistent with psychologists' recommendations.)

2. You conduct a literature review on gender differences in phobias and discover that three studies found that men were more needle phobic than women, but one study found that women were more needle phobic than men. The three consistent studies were written by Hazel Norman and Stan Singleton (published in 1991), Hazel Norman and Stan Singleton (published in 1992), and Terry Bates (published in 1990). The other study was written by T. L. Thorton (published in 1987). Write an appropriate sentence or two for the introduction of your paper.

3. Here is the participants section in Cynthia's research report: "Participants were 108 alcoholics, mostly women. All were volunteers solicited at an Alcoholics Anonymous meeting, and they agreed to respond to the survey in order to allow me to examine their opinions." Is this complete? What additional information should have been provided?

4. Dawn conducted a *t* test and found that athletes had larger lung capacities than nonathletes. The *t* test had 50 degrees of freedom, a value of 2.17985, and a significance level of .05. Athletes had an average lung capacity of 8.61, with a standard deviation of 2.32; and nonathletes had an average lung capacity of 6.78, with a standard deviation of 1.53. Write an appropriate results statement for Dawn's findings.

5. Write APA-style references for the following sources:

   a. A journal article written by Mickey M. Rodent and Donald D. Bird. The article's title was "Tune in to Toons," and it was published in 1989 on pages 3 through 17 in Volume 35, Issue 4 of the journal called *Animated Psychology*.

   b. A book written by Steven Caruthers called *Research Careers in Psychology*. The book's third edition was published in 1992 by Jenson Publishers, a company based in Carleton, Virginia.

   c. A chapter in a book. The book was edited by Martha Ramey and was entitled *Psychological Studies on Enchantment*. It was published in 1991 by Howard Press in London. The chapter was written by Ellen Tyler and Laird M. Watkins, and its title is "The Theory of Romantic Enchantment." The chapter is on pages 415 to 475.

6. Rephrase the following sentences.
   a. The data collection was stopped and terminated after five minutes of elapsed time had gone by.
   b. The researchers conclude that the present study's results indicate that more than three weeks of healing time are required.
   c. The participants felt that racism was unfair.
   d. Tears indicated that the participants were effected by the movie.
   e. The study decided to test participants separately.
   f. Since the two raters generally agreed, their scores were averaged.
   g. When forced to choose between cats, dogs, and birds, participants most often selected dogs.
   h. Participants looked at the line and estimated it's length.
   i. The line lengths were estimated by subjects.
   j. Participants included 15 doctors, 14 teachers, and 10 in careers as lawyers.

7. Here are some sentences from sections of a paper. Correct any errors in tense.
   a. (Introduction) Smith (1957) had first described regulation theory.
   b. (Method) Participants are 109 volunteer undergraduates.
   c. (Results) The test comparing employers to employees is significant.
   d. (Discussion) Data analyses showed that training improved performance.

8. Identify possible biases in these sentences.
   a. Participants were 82 men and 89 girls.
   b. Minority children grow up in violent neighborhoods.
   c. The professors asked their wives to prepare the menu.
   d. Bisexuals were compared to normal subjects.
   e. Each participant was asked to describe his favorite teacher.
   f. Sherry reported a lesbian sexual preference.

9. What biases may be involved in the following examples?
   a. A psychologist assumes that differences between Asian-American and European-American subjects must be genetic.
   b. A researcher operationally defines influence as obtaining behavioral changes by directly ordering someone to change.
   c. A researcher finds that minority participants scored relatively poorly on a test of verbal reasoning and does not offer an explanation of these results.
   d. A researcher concludes that results found for European-American women must be true for all women.
   e. A researcher fails to mention that 90% of the participants were male.
   f. A clinical researcher concludes that gay men are unhealthy because his gay clients are seeking therapy.

    g. A researcher assumes that all Asian-Americans are gifted in mathematics.

    h. A researcher assumes that all people in American airports are American citizens.

    i. A researcher gives an IQ test to recent immigrants.

10. Clark read the following sentence in a book written by Miller: "Dosages under 10 mg had only marginal effects on hallucinatory images." Are the following sentences in Clark's paper plagiarism?

    a. Miller (1982) concludes that dosages under 10 mg had only marginal effects on hallucinatory visions.

    b. Visual hallucinations are not greatly affected by dosages that are less than 10 mg (Miller, 1982).

    c. Dosages under 10 mg had only marginal effects on hallucinatory images.

    d. "Dosages under 10 mg had only marginal effects on hallucinatory images" (Miller, 1982, p. 107).

5

Statistics

Many students have a statistics phobia. They are convinced that statistics are too hard to understand. As we will see in this chapter, however, statistics are understandable, logical, and essential.

Most of this chapter will be a review if you have already studied statistics, but it will be new to you if you have never studied the logic of statistical analysis. This chapter is not a substitute for a statistics course. Instead, it introduces the basic logic and vocabulary of statistical analysis that researchers must understand. Mastering this chapter will not make you a statistician, but it will help you understand how statisticians think, and it will familiarize you with some commonly used procedures.

Don't expect to read this chapter like a novel. Read it slowly, mastering each concept before you go on. Once you get an overview of statistical thinking, you'll be better prepared to design and to interpret research.

BASIC VOCABULARY

Descriptive and Inferential Statistics

Researchers use statistics to describe their findings and to tentatively decide whether their findings are caused by chance or by real phenomena. These two functions are served by descriptive and inferential statistics.

Descriptive statistics summarize aspects of samples. For example, descriptive statistics are used to summarize the average age of subjects and their gender and ethnic composition.

An investigator may be interested in all babies born to cocaine-using mothers. It would be impossible to study the entire population, so a group of such babies is examined. The **population** is the entire group of interest (all babies born to cocaine-using mothers); a **sample** is a subset of the population (the group of babies actually studied). Researchers generally are interested in reaching conclusions about populations, but they must study samples. **Inferential statistics** are used to make generalizations from samples to populations.

Researchers use descriptive statistics to describe sample characteristics; they use inferential statistics to generalize from samples to populations. If the goal is simply to describe what was found, descriptive statistics are used. If the goal is to make generalizations about populations, inferential statistics are used.

Qualitative and Quantitative Variables

Psychologists deal with two types of variables: qualitative variables and quantitative variables. Qualitative variables are also known as categorical variables. Variables are **qualitative** (**categorical**) when subjects are classified into groups. For example, gender is a categorical variable; subjects are classified into two groups (male and female). Variables are **quantitative** when subjects are given scores along a continuum. IQ, weight, and GPA are quantitative variables.

Distributions of Variables

There are two basic types of distributions: frequency distributions and probability distributions. A **frequency** is a count, how many times each value occurred in the sample. A score of 72 has a frequency of 12 if 12 subjects earned 72 points. A **probability** is the chance of observing a specific value by randomly selecting observations from the population. If the probability of observing an American with red hair is .02, and we observe Americans selected at random, we expect to observe red-haired people 2 percent of the time. **Random selection** means that each person in the population is just as likely to be observed. If we were to select our sample at a meeting of Asian-Americans, the probability of observing a red-haired person would be different because our selection would not have been chosen at random from the *entire* American population.

A **frequency distribution** gives the frequency for each value of a variable in the sample. Say the ages in our sample range from 12 to 25. The frequency distribution for ages could be summarized in a table or in a figure, as illustrated in Table 5.1 and Figure 5.1. Both the table and figure show that the sample included one 25-year-old, three 24-year-olds, and so on.

A **probability distribution** gives the probability for each value of a variable in the population. Probability distributions, like frequency distributions, can be displayed in tables or figures. Say we roll a fair die; each of the six possible outcomes has the same probability, ⅙. This probability distribution is presented in Table 5.2 and Figure 5.2.

There are two major differences between frequency and probability distributions. Frequency distributions are based on sample data and contain frequencies. Probability distributions are based on populations and contain probabilities. Researchers use inferential statistics to estimate aspects of population (probability) distributions from sample (frequency) distributions.

FREQUENCY DISTRIBUTION OF AGES IN THE SAMPLE **TABLE** 5.1

Age	Frequency
25	1
24	3
23	5
22	7
21	4
20	2
19	5
18	7
17	6
16	8
15	6
14	4
13	2
12	1

FREQUENCY DISTRIBUTION OF AGES IN THE SAMPLE **FIGURE** 5.1

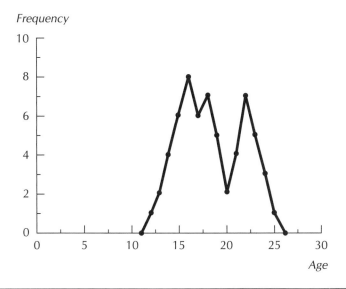

TABLE 5.2 PROBABILITY DISTRIBUTION FOR A FAIR DIE

Outcome	Probability
1	⅙
2	⅙
3	⅙
4	⅙
5	⅙
6	⅙

FIGURE 5.2 PROBABILITY DISTRIBUTION FOR A FAIR DIE

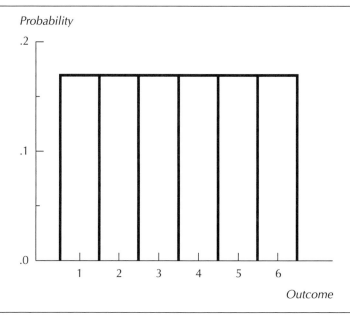

The Normal Distribution

The most well-known probability distribution is the normal distribution. All normal distributions have the same general shape, as shown in Figure 5.3a, but they vary in other ways, such as their average score and width. Notice that most of the scores are near the middle, fewer people obtain extreme scores, and extreme scores at both ends of the distribution are equally likely. The area under a probability distribution is the probability of observing the indicated range of scores, and the total area under the distribution is 1.0. The shaded area in Figure 5.3b is the probability of observing a score between 18 and 20.

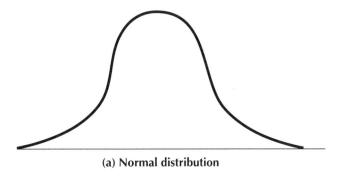

(a) Normal distribution

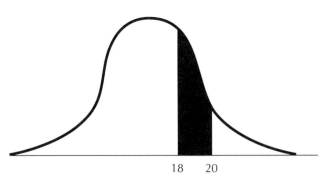

(b) Probability of observing a score between 18 and 20

Normal distributions are important in psychological research for three reasons. First, many variables of psychological interest are normally distributed. For example, IQ scores have a normal distribution. Most people have average intelligence. Extremely low or high IQs are less probable and are found about equally often. Second, most statistical procedures used by psychologists are based on the assumption that variables are normally distributed. Third, statisticians have demonstrated that many of the statistics based on the assumption of normality can be used when sample sizes are large, even if variables are not normally distributed.

DESCRIPTIVE STATISTICS

Descriptive statistics generally summarize two major properties of distributions: central tendency and variability. In addition, descriptive statistics summarize relationships between variables.

Central Tendency

Central tendency is the location of the score distribution. Are scores near −500, 75, or 10,000? Three statistics are used to summarize central tendency: the mode, mean, and median. The **mode** is the most frequently occurring score. The modal age for the distribution in Table 5.1 is 16 because more subjects were 16 than any other age. The **mean** is the arithmetic average. (Add up all the scores and divide by the number of scores to calculate the mean.) The mean age for the data in Table 5.1 is 18.44 (1125 divided by 61). The **median** is the score in the middle of the distribution; half the scores are below it and half the scores are above it. The median age in Table 5.1 is 18 because half the scores are below 18 and half are above 18.

Why do we need three different statistics to describe central tendency? Each is "best" under different circumstances. The mode is the only central tendency indicator that can be used for categorical data. We can state which category occurred most often, but we cannot calculate a mean or median for categorical data. (For example, we could not report that the mean or median ethnicity is 2.43.) The mode also is the easiest to calculate; it can be found simply by examining the distribution. Unfortunately, the mode is not very stable from sample to sample, some distributions have multiple modes, and the mode is not conducive to mathematical manipulation, making it less valuable. The median generally is considered the best summary of central tendency for skewed distributions. **Skewed distributions** have most of the scores piled up at one end and other scores trailing off at the other end, as illustrated in Figure 5.4. For such distributions the median is near the bulk of the scores, and the mean is pulled out by extreme scores. This is easy to see in a simple example with only three scores: 4, 5, and 6. The mean and median are 5. If the highest score were 600, instead of 6, the median would still be 5, but the mean would be 203 (609 divided by 3). The mean is pulled out toward the skew.

Of the three statistics, the mean is used most frequently as an indicator of central tendency. It generally is the most stable of the three statistics, it gives equal weight to each score, and its formula is easy to understand and manipulate.

Variability

Variability is how much scores differ from each other. Are all scores identical (zero variability) or do scores vary a great deal? Three statistics are commonly used to describe variability: the range, variance, and standard deviation. The **range** measures the width of the obtained distribution. For example, the ages in Table 5.1 range from 12 to 25, so their range is 13 (25 − 12 = 13). The range, like the mode, is relatively unstable. Adding one extreme score greatly affects its value. (What would happen to the range of ages if the sample included one 50-year-old?)

The **variance** is the average squared deviation from the mean. This may seem like a strange statistic, but its underlying logic is straightforward. If scores differ from each other, they differ from their mean; so variation of scores from their mean summarizes variability. For each person, we first calculate a deviation score (how much the person deviates from the mean). Deviations from the mean are squared so their sum is not zero. (The sum of deviations from the mean always is zero.) The squared deviations are averaged, so that variances calculated on samples with different sizes can have similar variances if they have similar amounts of variability. The variance is close

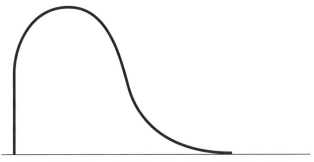

(a) Positively skewed distribution (skewed to the right)

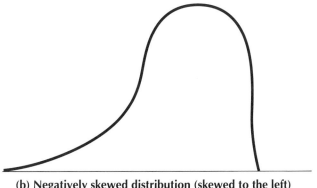

(b) Negatively skewed distribution (skewed to the left)

to zero when variability is low (because deviations from the mean are small), and it increases as scores differ more from each other.

The variance of ages in Table 5.1 is 11.22 squared years. Variances are expressed in squared units, not a particularly pleasant situation. An easy solution to this problem is to take the variance's square root, which is the standard deviation. The **standard deviation** is the square root of the variance. Because it is expressed in original, nonsquared units, the standard deviation is the most frequently used descriptive statistic to summarize variability. The standard deviation of ages in Table 5.1 is 3.35. Scores have a standard deviation of zero if they are all identical, and the standard deviation increases as scores differ more from each other.

If the variable is normally distributed, about 68 percent of scores are within one standard deviation of the mean, about 95 percent are within two standard deviations of the mean, and about 99 percent are within three standard deviations of the mean. For example, scores on the Wechsler IQ tests have a mean of 100 and a standard deviation of 15. About 68 percent of the population have IQs between 85 and 115; about 95 percent score between 70 and 130; and almost everyone is between 55 and 145.

Central tendency and variability are the two characteristics most frequently summarized by descriptive statistics. Usually the mean and standard deviation are reported. As seen in Chapter 3, APA style uses $\underline{M}$ for mean and $\underline{SD}$ for standard deviation within tables and within parentheses. If this sentence did not make sense to you before, it should be understandable now: "The mean age was 18.44 years ($\underline{SD}$ = 3.35)."

Relationships Between Variables

Relationships between variables are most frequently summarized using the Pearson product-moment correlation coefficient. Although other correlation coefficients exist, the Pearson product-moment correlation is assumed when people speak of "the correlation." A few concepts must be developed before this statistic can be defined.

A **scatterplot** is a picture of the distribution of two variables. Figures 5.5a, b, c, d, e, and f are scatterplots of the variables X and Y. X is on the horizontal axis, and Y is on the vertical axis. Each dot in a scatterplot represents one person's pair of scores. For example, the person represented by the leftmost symbol in Figure 5.5a has a score of 3 on X and a score of 0 on Y. The distribution of points in the scatterplot illustrates the relationship between the two variables.

Relationships can be positive or negative. Variables have a **positive relationship** if people who score higher on one variable tend to score higher on the other. Variables have a **negative relationship** if people who score higher on one variable tend to score lower on the other. Figures 5.5a and c demonstrate positive relationships, and Figures 5.5b and d demonstrate negative relationships. Height and weight have a positive relationship; taller people tend to weigh more. Caloric intake and weight loss have a negative relationship; the more you eat, the less you lose.

Relationships can be linear or nonlinear. Variables have a **linear relationship** if points in the scatterplot cluster around a straight line; they have a **nonlinear relationship** if points in the scatterplot do not cluster around a straight line. The first four figures demonstrate linear relationships; Figure 5.5e demonstrates a nonlinear relationship. Anxiety level and performance on a typing test have a nonlinear relationship like that illustrated in Figure 5.5e. Anxiety level would be X and test performance would be Y in the scatterplot. People with moderate anxiety perform better than people with low or high anxiety because low-anxiety people aren't motivated to work quickly, and high anxiety interferes with performance.

Relationships vary in strength. Some relationships are very strong, so one variable can be used to predict the other accurately; but some relationships are weak, so predictions cannot be made with confidence. Plots that are confined to a tight pattern demonstrate **strong relationships**, and plots that are not confined to a tight pattern demonstrate **weak relationships**. Figures 5.5a and b demonstrate very strong linear relationships; Figures 5.5c and d demonstrate weaker linear relationships; and Figure 5.5e demonstrates a strong nonlinear relationship. The relationship in Figure 5.5c is stronger than the relationship in Figure 5.5d because the pattern is tighter.

Two variables may not be related at all. Figure 5.5f demonstrates no relationship between X and Y. For example, there probably is no relationship between income and number of close friends. Wealthy, middle-class, and poor people may have few or many close friends.

The Pearson correlation can be defined using the above concepts. The **Pearson product-moment correlation coefficient** is a number between −1 and +1 that

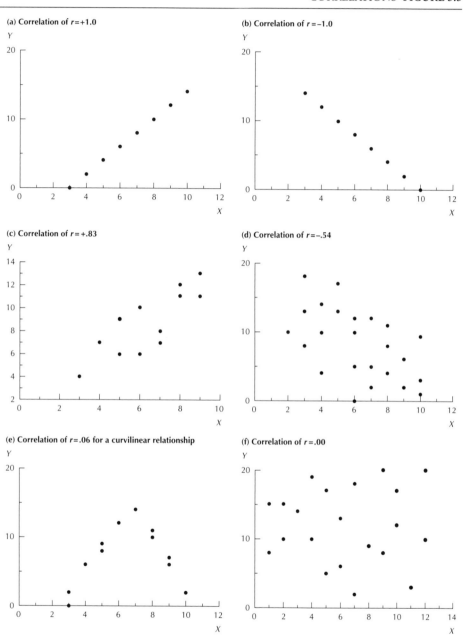

(a) Correlation of $r=+1.0$

(b) Correlation of $r=-1.0$

(c) Correlation of $r=+.83$

(d) Correlation of $r=-.54$

(e) Correlation of $r=.06$ for a curvilinear relationship

(f) Correlation of $r=.00$

summarizes the direction and strength of the linear relationship between two variables. The sign of the correlation indicates the direction of the linear relationship. Positive correlations indicate positive relationships; negative correlations indicate negative relationships. The size of the correlation indicates the strength of the linear relationship. Correlations close to zero indicate weak linear relationships; correlations close to 1.0 indicate strong linear relationships. A correlation of −.50 is as strong as a correlation of +.50, but the direction of the relationship is reversed. The symbol for a correlation coefficient calculated in a sample is r. The strongest linear relationship ($r = +1$ or $r = -1$) is found when all points in the scatterplot are on a line. The wider the spread of scores from the line, the closer the correlation is to zero.

Reexamine Figures 5.5a, b, c, d, and f. Correlations for these data are +1.0, −1.0, +.83, −.54, and .00, respectively. Notice that positive relationships have positive correlations, negative relationships have negative correlations, and the size of the correlation summarizes the strength of the linear relationship. Beginners sometimes forget the word *linear* in the definition. Pearson correlations summarize the direction and strength of the *linear* relationship between two variables. Strong nonlinear relationships, such as the one in Figure 5.5e, have small Pearson correlations because they do not have a linear pattern. The Pearson correlation for these data is only .06. Other correlation coefficients that describe the strength of nonlinear relationships exist.

Typical APA-style statements involving correlations are: "The correlation between height and weight was positive ($r = .81$)" and "The correlation between the two opinions was −.17."

INFERENTIAL STATISTICS

Hypothesis Testing

Inferential statistics are used to make inferences from samples to populations. They are used to test research hypotheses. For example, a researcher evaluating a new teaching technique hypothesizes that students taught in a new way will do better on a final exam than students taught in the old way. The statistician turns this into a pair of statistical hypotheses: either the students taught with the new method score the same as students taught with the old method (the null hypothesis) or they perform better (the alternative hypothesis). Based on the data analysis, the statistician will reject the null hypothesis (tentatively concluding that the new technique is better) or will not reject the null hypothesis (tentatively concluding that the new technique is not better). If the null hypothesis is rejected, the results are significant; if the null hypothesis is not rejected, the results are not significant.

Let's look more closely at the concepts illustrated in this example. First, the process: This is called hypothesis testing. **Hypothesis testing** involves tentatively deciding between two hypotheses: the null hypothesis and the alternative hypothesis. The **null hypothesis** states that variables are not related (independent variables did not cause changes in dependent variables, the correlation is zero, and so on), and the **alternative hypothesis** states that variables are related (independent variables did cause changes in dependent variables, the correlation is *not* zero, and so on). Together, the two hypotheses describe the only two conceivable outcomes for the study. Researchers usually predict that variables are related. They hypothesize that experimental and control groups will be different or that variables will be correlated. The research hypothesis is the basis for the alternative hypothesis.

HYPOTHESIS TESTING OUTCOMES **TABLE 5.3**

		Reality	
		H_0 is true	H_A is true
Tentative conclusion	H_0 is true (don't reject H_0)	Correct	Wrong Type II error β
	H_A is true (reject H_0)	Wrong Type I error α	Correct Power $1-\beta$

Statisticians are conservative; they start by assuming the null hypothesis is true, that variables are not related. The null hypothesis is rejected only if evidence clearly indicates that this assumption is unwarranted. This is much like our legal system: The accused is presumed innocent until proven guilty. The statistician assumes that the null hypothesis is true unless there is very good evidence against this assumption. After examining the data, the null hypothesis is rejected or is not rejected. If the null hypothesis is rejected, we have concluded that variables are significantly related; the results are **statistically significant**. If the null hypothesis is not rejected, we have concluded that the variables are not significantly related; the results are **not significant**. Researchers generally want significant results; they want to conclude that results support their research hypotheses. The requirement of statistical significance protects the discipline from overzealous researchers who might mistakenly conclude that their research hypotheses are accurate.

Calculating the statistics for hypothesis testing sometimes involves tedious arithmetic, but most researchers use computers for data analysis. The formulas will not be covered here. What is more important now is the logic of statistical analysis.

There are two ways to be right and two ways to be wrong when doing hypothesis testing. Table 5.3 depicts the four possible outcomes. In reality, either the null hypothesis (H_0, pronounced "H"-naught) or the alternative hypothesis (H_A, pronounced "H"-"A") is true; and, based on the statistical analysis, we tentatively conclude that H_0 or H_A is true. (We tentatively conclude that H_A is true if we reject H_0 and that H_0 is true if we don't reject it.) Two of the four possible outcomes are correct: concluding H_0 when H_0 is true and concluding H_A when H_A is true. These are good outcomes because we have made accurate conclusions. The two wrong decisions also are illustrated in the figure: rejecting H_0 when H_0 is true (a **Type I error**) and not rejecting H_0 when H_A is true (a **Type II error**). The probabilities associated with these two types of errors are symbolized as α (alpha) and β (beta). **Alpha** is the probability of a Type I error and is the probability of rejecting H_0 when H_0 is true. **Beta** is the probability of a Type II error and is the probability of not rejecting H_0 when H_A is true.

The goal of research is to reach the correct conclusion, so investigators want to design research with low alpha and low beta. Alpha is kept arbitrarily low by convention.

FIGURE 5.6 EVALUATION OF A NEW TEACHING METHOD

Reality

	$\mu_{New} = \mu_{Old}$	$\mu_{New} > \mu_{Old}$
Tentative conclusion $\mu_{New} = \mu_{Old}$	*Correctly* conclude that the new method is *not* better.	*Incorrectly* conclude that the new method is *not* better. (Type II Error)
$\mu_{New} > \mu_{Old}$	*Incorrectly* conclude that the new method is better. (Type I Error)	*Correctly* conclude that the new method is better.

H_O: The two means are the same. $\mu_{New} = \mu_{Old}$
H_A: The mean for students taught by the new method is higher than the mean for students taught by the old teaching method. $\mu_{New} > \mu_{Old}$

Generally alphas above .05 are not acceptable. Beta generally is considered by dealing with power. The **power** of a statistical test is the probability of rejecting H_0 when H_A is true; power is $1-\beta$. When H_A is true, we either reject or don't reject H_0. If the probability of not rejecting H_0 is β, the probability of rejecting H_0 is $1-\beta$, which is the power. (For example, if β is .10, $1-\beta$ is .90. If there is a 10 percent chance of making the wrong conclusion when H_A is true, there is a 90 percent chance of making the correct conclusion when H_A is true.) Researchers who design studies with low alpha and high power are likely to reach correct conclusions and avoid both types of error.

These concepts seem difficult when first encountered, but mastering them is important for understanding the logic of hypothesis testing and research design. Let's return to the original example: testing the effectiveness of a new teaching method. Details are presented in Figure 5.6.

The null hypothesis states that the two teaching methods are equally effective. This has been translated into statistical terms: $\mu_{New} = \mu_{Old}$. μ **(mu) is the symbol for the population mean.** (μ should not be confused with M, the sample mean.) μ_{New} is the population mean for students taught by the new method, and μ_{Old} is the population mean for students taught by the old method. The alternative hypothesis has been translated into statistical symbols, too: $\mu_{New} > \mu_{Old}$ is another way to say that the mean for the new method is higher than the mean for the old method.

Researchers use an inferential statistic to infer conclusions about the population means (μ_{New} and μ_{Old}) by examining the sample means (M_{New} and M_{Old}). Figure 5.6 illustrates the two ways to be right and the two ways to be wrong. We are likely to uncover the truth if we have low α and high power. Low alpha makes it unlikely that we commit a Type I error (concluding that the new technique is better when it is *not* better), and high power makes it unlikely that we commit a Type II error (concluding that the new technique is *not* better when it is better). Alpha is kept low by the arbitrary .05 convention. Power is kept high by careful research design. This will be described in Chapter 7.

A *t* test usually is conducted to compare two means. There is a set of *t* distributions just as there is a set of normal distributions. All *t* distributions have the same general shape, but they vary in width. The degrees of freedom (*df*) for this test indicate which of the *t* distributions to use. To find the degrees of freedom, we take the total number of people in the two groups and subtract 2. If there were 30 students in each group, the *t* test has 58 degrees of freedom. The calculation yields a value for the *t* statistic, and this value is compared to the *t* distribution with the appropriate degrees of freedom. If the calculated *t* value is sufficiently large, the null hypothesis is rejected, the test is significant, and we conclude the new teaching method is significantly better than the old teaching method. If the calculated *t* value is not sufficiently large, the null hypothesis is not rejected, the test is not significant, and we conclude the new teaching method is not significantly better.

Significance Probabilities

You may remember from Chapter 4 that results of tests like the *t* test are reported like this: "The new teaching method was significantly more effective than the old teaching method, $t(58) = 2.56$, $p < .01$." Most of this should make sense to you: the *t* test was conducted with 58 degrees of freedom (60 subjects minus 2), and it had a value of 2.56. The .01 is the significance probability for this result. The **significance probability** is the lowest alpha that could be used to reject the null hypothesis. The statement that $p < .01$ tells the reader that the results could have been rejected with an alpha of .01 or more (including the customary .05), but could not have been rejected using an alpha of .005, .001, or smaller.

The significance probability communicates how extreme the findings were; smaller significance probabilities correspond to more extreme results. Although computers can give us exact significance probabilities (such as .03872), we traditionally report them as values that have a series of zeroes followed by 1 or 5, such as .05, .01, .005, and .001. An actual significance probability of .0027 would be reported as $p < .005$, and an actual probability of .0091 would be reported as $p < .01$. Significance probabilities reflect the strength of the independent variable's influence on the dependent variable, plus other factors, such as sample size; so significance probabilities from different studies cannot be compared to decide which study had more "significant" results.

One- and Two-Tailed Tests

The teaching method example involves a one-tailed test and a directional alternative hypothesis. **Directional alternative hypotheses** state the expected direction of the results. **Nondirectional alternative hypotheses** do not state the expected direction of the results. The alternative hypothesis for the teaching method example is directional; it states that μ_{New} is greater than μ_{Old}. Had it been nondirectional, the alternative hypothesis would have stated that μ_{New} is not equal to μ_{Old}; i.e., the new teaching method leads to an amount of learning that is different from the old method, and the new method may be superior or inferior to the old method.

Directional hypotheses generally are tested with one-tailed tests, and nondirectional hypotheses generally are tested with two-tailed tests. One- and two-tailed tests differ in the set of obtained values of the statistic that lead to rejecting the null hypothesis. For both tests we first calculate the necessary statistic in our sample, such as the value of t for a t test. The statistic that must be calculated in order to conduct a test is called the **test statistic**. **One-tailed tests** reject H_0 only for large values of the test statistic (**upper-tailed tests**) or only for small values of the test statistic (**lower-tailed tests**). (We could use a lower-tailed test to test the hypothesis that the experimental group scored lower than the control group.) **Two-tailed tests** reject H_0 for both large and small values of the test statistic. This affects the significance probability.

As shown in Figure 5.7, the significance probability (the shaded area) is twice as large for two-tailed tests as for one-tailed tests when the test statistic is the same value. This picture illustrates the population distribution for the test statistic. This distribution is called a sampling distribution to distinguish it from other population distributions. **Sampling distributions** give probabilities associated with a statistic calculated on all possible samples of the same size. A t test is conducted by examining the test statistic within the appropriate t sampling distribution. The sampling distribution for the teaching methods example is the t distribution with 58 degrees of freedom.

One-tailed tests are called one-tailed because the area in one tail of the sampling distribution beyond the observed value of the test statistic is the significance probability. The significance probability is the area above the test statistic for upper-tailed tests (Figure 5.7a) and the area below the test statistic for lower-tailed tests (Figure 5.7b). We need to include both areas for two-tailed tests, as shown in Figure 5.7c, so these tests have doubled significance probabilities. This means that two-tailed tests must have more extreme values of the test statistic to reject the null hypothesis. To be significant at the .05 level, the observed value of the test statistic must be in the top 5 percent of the sampling distribution for upper-tailed tests, but must be in the top 2.5 percent (or the bottom 2.5 percent) of the sampling distribution for two-tailed tests. For example, in order to reject the null hypothesis with an alpha of .05, the t statistic with 2 degrees of freedom requires a test statistic to be larger than 2.920 for upper-tailed tests, smaller than −2.920 for lower-tailed tests, and larger than 4.303 (or smaller than −4.303) for two-tailed tests. An observed t of 3.04 or −3.04 would be statistically significant for one-tailed tests but would not be significant for two-tailed tests.

Why are the shaded areas significance probabilities? These are probability distributions, and areas under probability distributions are probabilities. The shaded areas are the probabilities of obtaining the observed value of the test statistic or more extreme values of the test statistic if the null hypothesis is true. A significance probability of .05 means that the obtained value of the test statistic is among the most extreme 5 percent of possible results. A significance probability of .01 means that the obtained value of the test statistic is among the most extreme 1 percent of possible results. When obtained outcomes are that unlikely, we reject the null hypothesis and conclude that results are significant at $p < .05$ or $p < .01$, respectively. Something really did happen. (Of course, we recognize that our conclusion may be a Type I error.)

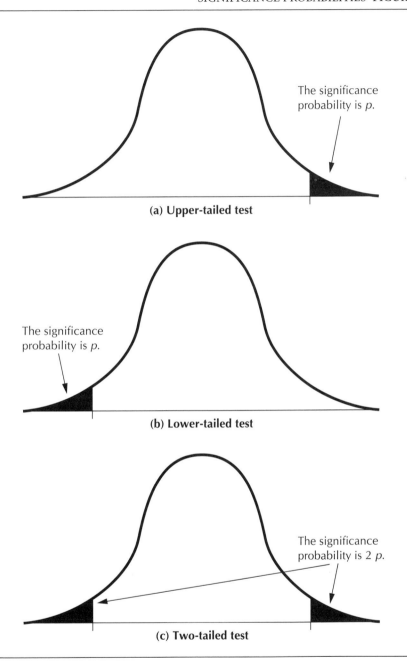

The significance probability is *p*.

(a) Upper-tailed test

The significance probability is *p*.

(b) Lower-tailed test

The significance probability is 2 *p*.

(c) Two-tailed test

All hypothesis testing works the same way. First, the researcher states the null and alternative hypotheses. The alternative hypothesis may be directional or nondirectional. The obtained value of the test statistic (such as a *t* statistic) is calculated in the

TABLE 5.4 STEPS IN HYPOTHESIS TESTING

Step	Teaching method example
1. State the null and alternative hypotheses.	1. H_0: The two means are the same. $\mu_{New} = \mu_{Old}$. H_A: The mean for students taught by the new method is higher than the mean for the old teaching method. $\mu_{New} > \mu_{Old}$.
2. Collect the data.	2. For 30 students taught with the new method: $M = 87.27$, $SD = 8.84$. For 30 students taught with the old method: $M = 78.07$, $SD = 10.91$.
3. Choose the appropriate test statistic and sampling distribution.	3. t, with 58 degrees of freedom
4. Calculate the test statistic in the sample.	4. $t = 3.589$
5. Find the significance probability.	5. $p < .001$
6. Make a decision.	6. Reject H_0 because $p < .05$
7. Reach a tentative conclusion.	7. The new method is significantly better than the old method, $p < .001$

sample. Then the test statistic is evaluated using the relevant sampling distribution. The significance probability for the test is found by examining one or both tails of the sampling distribution: one tail for one-tailed tests and two tails for two-tailed tests. If the significance probability is .05 or less, the results are statistically significant and the null hypothesis is rejected. If the significance probability is greater than .05, the results are not significant and the null hypothesis is not rejected. Table 5.4 illustrates the steps for the teaching method study. The arithmetic to calculate the descriptive statistics (mean and standard deviation) and the inferential statistic (the t statistic) was done using a computer. If this paragraph and Table 5.4 make sense to you, you have a good understanding of the logic of hypothesis testing.

Significant Results

The word *significant* has two meanings that should not be confused: statistical significance and meaningful significance. **Statistical significance** occurs when the null hypothesis is rejected; the results are statistically significant. Such results may not have meaningful significance, however. Results have **meaningful significance** if they are important or useful. For example, a researcher may find a statistically significant difference between girls and boys on a test of verbal reasoning. Girls average 56.54, and boys average 56.53. Such a small difference probably lacks meaningful significance, but it could be statistically significant if the study had high power. This is why researchers are encouraged to summarize results with an estimate of effect size.

Effect size indicates how strongly the independent variable influences the dependent variable, or the strength of the relationship between the variables. You may have learned that researchers interpret r^2, rather than r, when dealing with correlation coefficients because r^2 is a better indicator of effect size. You also may have learned about other statistics that summarize effect size, such as η^2 (eta squared) or ω (omega).

These effect size indicators estimate the proportion of variance in the dependent variable accounted for by the independent variable. For example, if η^2 is .60, the independent variable accounts for 60 percent of the observed variability of the dependent variable; and the other 40 percent of observed variability is not explained by the independent variable. Results with larger effect sizes are more likely to have meaningful significance than results with smaller effect sizes. Effect sizes will be discussed more fully in Chapter 7.

COMMONLY USED INFERENTIAL STATISTICS

Hypothesis testing can be used to evaluate a variety of hypotheses, and many inferential statistics are available. Some of the more frequently used tests will be summarized here.

Hypotheses deal with differences and with relationships. Researchers could hypothesize that two groups have different means or variances or that there is a relationship between two variables. The null hypothesis always states there is no difference or no relationship; the alternative hypothesis states there is a difference or a relationship. Alternative hypotheses can be directional or nondirectional. Directional hypotheses state the direction of the difference or relationship, i.e., Group 1 has a higher mean than Group 2 or there is a positive relationship between Variable X and Variable Y. Nondirectional hypotheses do not specify the direction of the difference or relationship: i.e., Group 1 and Group 2 have different means, or there is a relationship between Variable X and Variable Y.

Differences in Means

Hypotheses frequently concern means. **t tests** are used to compare two means, as illustrated earlier in this chapter. There are two basic t tests to compare two means, and the choice is determined by the nature of the independent variable. The independent variable can be between-group or within-subject. Variables are **between-group** when each subject is at only one level; variables are **within-subject** when each subject is at every level. For example, if we compare girls to boys, gender is a between-group variable with two levels (male and female), and each subject is classified into one of these two levels. On the other hand, if we are examining the effectiveness of a new type of therapy, each subject's mental health can be measured before and after therapy. The independent variable is time, and it has two levels (before therapy and after therapy). Each subject is measured at *both* levels. Time is a within-subject variable in this example.

Matching is a second way to create a within-subject variable. Each subject is matched to other subjects, and within each matched group, each level of the independent variable is experienced by one subject. In effect, we pretend that the same subject is measured at each level of the independent variable. Matching frequently involves littermates or twins, but may involve matching unrelated subjects. For example, if Group 1 includes a twelve-year-old African-American girl with parents who are college-educated, we could match her to an equivalent girl in Group 2 and pretend that the same girl is measured twice.

Between-group and within-subject *t* tests are calculated using different formulas, but they are interpreted in the same way. If the significance probability is .05 or less, the two means are significantly different. These tests generally are referred to as the **independent groups *t* test** (for between-group independent variables) and the **dependent sampling *t* test** (for within-subject independent variables). Both tests are used to compare two means. The degrees of freedom for independent groups *t* tests is the total number of subjects minus 2, and the degrees of freedom for dependent sampling *t* tests is the number of subjects (or matched pairs of subjects) minus 1. For example, a study involving 8 pairs of matched twins would have a *t* test with 7 degrees of freedom.

All statistical techniques rely on a set of assumptions. The *t* tests are based on the assumption that the dependent variable is normally distributed (or the sample size is large enough for the Central Limit Theorem to hold). Most students have learned a special case of the **Central Limit Theorem**: The sampling distribution of the mean becomes increasingly normal as the number of subjects in the sample increases. This theorem can be used to demonstrate that many sampling distributions, such as the *t* distribution, become more like the normal distribution as the sample size increases— even when the original distribution of the dependent variable is not normal. The independent groups *t* test also requires the assumption that the groups have identical variances (the **homogeneity of variance assumption**).

Analysis of variance is a set of techniques for examining means. Analysis of variance is used to analyze the effect of one or more independent variables. An analysis of variance is defined by the number of independent variables and their nature and number of levels. A **k-way analysis of variance** examines the effects of *k* independent variables on the dependent variable. A one-way analysis of variance examines the effect of one independent variable, a two-way analysis of variance examines the effects of two independent variables, and so on. We also can identify the number of independent variables and their levels when we describe the analysis of variance. For example, a 3 × 4 analysis of variance is a two-way analysis of variance. The first independent variable has three levels, and the second independent variable has four levels. A 2 × 2 × 2 analysis of variance has three independent variables, and each has two levels.

Analyses of variance require assumptions. Among them are the assumptions that the dependent variable is normally distributed and that the variance of each group is the same. As with the *t* test, the normality assumption can be violated for large sample sizes.

The type of analysis of variance is determined by the nature of the independent variables. The simplest analysis of variance is a one-way analysis of variance. The **one-way analysis of variance** is used when there is one between-group independent variable with at least three levels. (Although a one-way analysis of variance can be applied if there are two levels, an independent groups *t* test generally is used for this case. The two tests are directly related and always result in the same conclusion.) This design is called a **one-way repeated measures analysis of variance** if the independent variable is within-subject. The designs with more than one independent variable are **factorial** if all the independent variables are between-group, **repeated measures** if all the independent variables are within-subject, or **mixed** if both between-group and within-subject variables are involved.

Here are five studies. Identify the dependent variable, the independent variable(s), the number of levels of each independent variable, the nature of each independent variable (between-group or within-subject), and the appropriate test for each study. The answers are below, so don't read on until you have developed your answers.

1. A researcher examines the effects of gender and social class (lower, middle, upper) on IQ scores.

2. A researcher examines typing speed before a typing class begins, halfway through the class, and after the class is over.

3. A researcher asks each subject to rate the quality of six cookies. The six cookies vary in batter (sugar, peanut butter, or oatmeal batter) and in filler (raisins or chocolate chips). Each subject rates one of each type of cookie.

4. A researcher compares politically conservative to politically liberal students on their attitudes toward abortion.

5. A researcher examines the effect of gender and practice (one week, two weeks, three weeks, and four weeks) on swimming speed among a set of students in a swimming class. Each student's speed is measured four times.

Ready for the answers? Experiment 1's dependent variable is IQ score, and it has two independent variables: gender (two levels, between-group) and social class (three levels, between-group). Data should be analyzed using a two-way factorial analysis of variance. You also could call this a 2×3 factorial analysis of variance.

Experiment 2's dependent variable is typing speed, and there is one independent variable: time. Time has three levels and is within-subject. Data should be analyzed using a one-way repeated measures analysis of variance.

Experiment 3's dependent variable is cookie quality, and there are two independent variables: batter (three levels, within-subject) and filler (two levels, within-subject). Both independent variables are within-subject because each subject is measured at every level. Data should be analyzed using a two-way repeated measures analysis of variance, which we also could call a 3×2 repeated measures analysis of variance.

Experiment 4's dependent variable is attitude toward abortion, and there is one independent variable: political orientation (two levels, between-group). Data should be analyzed using an independent groups *t* test because the independent variable has two levels.

Experiment 5's dependent variable is swimming speed, and there are two independent variables: gender (two levels, between-group) and practice (four levels, within-subject). Data should be analyzed using a two-way mixed design analysis of variance, which we also could call a 2×4 mixed design analysis of variance.

Two types of hypotheses are examined using analysis of variance: those involving main effects and those involving interactions. A significant **main effect** for an independent variable is found if means for the levels of the independent variable are significantly different. For example, Experiment 2 would have a significant main effect for time if the three means are significantly different. **Interactions** occur if the effect of one independent variable depends upon the level of one or more other independent variables. For example, look at the data for Experiment 3 in Table 5.5. The mean for each condition is provided. First, the main effects: There is a significant main effect for batter if the 11, 19, and 12 are significantly different; and there is a significant main effect for filler if the 7 and 21 are significantly different. In order to examine interactions, we ask if the effect of filler depends on the batter (or we ask if the effect of

TABLE 5.5 MEAN RESULTS FOR COOKIE-TASTING EXPERIMENT

| Filler | BATTER | | | |
	Sugar	Peanut butter	Oatmeal	Average
Raisin	5	5	11	7
Choc. chip	17	33	13	21
Average	11	19	12	

batter depends on the filler). It appears that there is a significant interaction; raisins are most preferred in oatmeal cookies, and chocolate chips are most preferred in peanut butter cookies. The effect of filler does depend on the type of batter, so there is an interaction. The interpretation of main effects and interactions will be explained more fully in Chapter 13.

A two-way analysis of variance involves three statistical tests: one for the main effect of the first independent variable, one for the main effect of the second independent variable, and one for the interaction between the two independent variables. Complicated analyses of variance involve more tests. For example, a three-way analysis of variance examining the effects of independent variables A, B, and C would involve seven tests: the main effect of A, the main effect of B, the main effect of C, the AB interaction, the AC interaction, the BC interaction, and the ABC interaction. How many tests would occur in a four-way analysis of variance examining the effects of variables A, B, C, and D? There would be four tests for main effects (A, B, C, and D), six tests for two-way interactions (AB, AC, AD, BC, BD, and CD), four tests for three-way interactions (ABC, ABD, ACD, BCD), and one test for a four-way interaction ($ABCD$), or fifteen tests in all. Multi-way interactions may be difficult to understand and to explain, so beginners should restrict themselves to simple one-way or two-way designs. Nevertheless, a thorough understanding of complicated psychological phenomena may require more complicated research designs.

Differences in Variances

Hypotheses also can concern variances. For example, the homogeneity of variance assumption required by the independent groups t test is that the two groups have identical variances; this can be tested using the F sampling distribution and the **F test for homogeneity of variance**. **Statistical Package for the Social Sciences** (**SPSS**) is a commonly used computer program that conducts statistical analyses. SPSS automatically conducts the F test for homogeneity of variance whenever an independent groups t test is calculated. If the F test is significant, the homogeneity of variance assumption is rejected, and an alternative t test that does not require this assumption can be used. A number of other tests on variances exist, but the F test is the one you will most likely see as a beginning researcher. The F test requires the assumption that the dependent variable is normally distributed.

The F distribution involves the ratio of two variances, and the degrees of freedom specify the degrees of freedom for each of the variances. The larger variance goes in the numerator, so the F ratio always should be at least 1.0. If the group with the larger sample variance has n_1 subjects, and the group with the smaller sample variance has n_2

subjects, the F test for homogeneity of variance has $(n_1 - 1, n_2 - 1)$ degrees of freedom. For example, if the first group had 12 subjects, and the second group had 11 subjects, the F test would have (11, 10) degrees of freedom. A significant test could be reported like this: "Girls ($SD = 26.88$) and boys ($SD = 10.50$) had significantly different variances, $F(11, 10) = 6.55, p < .01$."

Relationships Between Quantitative Variables

The most frequent test for a relationship between quantitative variables involves the Pearson correlation coefficient. The null hypothesis states that the population correlation coefficient is zero; the alternative hypothesis states that the population correlation coefficient is positive or negative (directional hypotheses) or nonzero (a nondirectional hypothesis). Significant results lead to the rejection of the null hypothesis and the conclusion that the population correlation is significantly greater than zero, less than zero, or different from zero, respectively. Sometimes researchers simply conclude that the correlation between the two variables is significant. A typical APA-style results statement is the following: "There was a significant correlation between height and weight, $r(N = 25) = .56, p < .01$." The sample correlation coefficient of .56, based on a sample of 25 cases, was significantly different from zero, with a significance probability that was less than .01. The observed correlation was in the extreme 1 percent of the sampling distribution if the population correlation was zero, so the null hypothesis is rejected.

Relationships Between Categorical Variables

Pearson correlations are appropriate for most quantitative variables, but sometimes researchers are interested in relationships between categorical variables. The **chi square test for independence** is used to test for relationships between categorical variables.

Two variables are **statistically independent** if knowing the value of one provides no information about the other. For example, eye color and whether or not one is a genius are statistically independent. Knowing that someone has brown eyes does not provide information about his or her intelligence, and knowing that someone is a genius does not provide information about his or her eye color. By contrast, gender and being more than six feet tall are statistically dependent; they're related. Women are less likely than men to be more than six feet tall, so knowing a person's gender provides some information about probable height, and knowing that a person is more than six feet tall provides some information about probable gender.

The chi square test for independence tests the null hypothesis that two variables are statistically independent. The alternative hypothesis states that the two variables are related. This test is done to analyze categorical variables that are displayed in a contingency table. A **contingency table** gives the frequencies of the joint occurrence of two (or more) variables. For example, Table 5.6 is a contingency table for age and attitude toward cartoons. Out of a sample of 30 old people and 30 young people, 25 young people and 10 old people expressed favorable attitudes toward cartoons. The chi square test for independence on these data was significant at the .001 level. The APA-style summary could be written like this: "There was a significant relationship between age and attitude toward cartoons, $\chi^2(1, N = 60) = 15.43, p < .001$; 83% of the young respondents, and only 33% of the old respondents had favorable attitudes toward cartoons." This com-

---

TABLE 5.6 CONTINGENCY TABLE

| | | Attitude toward cartoons | |
		Favorable	Unfavorable
	Young	25	5
Age			
	Old	10	20

---

municates that the chi square test statistic (χ^2) with one degree of freedom, based on a sample of 60 cases, had a value of 15.43; and this result was significant because the significance probability was less than .001. As the example illustrates, the pattern of the relationship frequently can be described by reporting percentages.

The chi square sampling distribution, like the t distribution, is a set of distributions that have about the same shape, but that vary with the degrees of freedom. If the contingency table has r rows and c columns, the chi square test for independence has $(r-1)(c-1)$ degrees of freedom. For example, if the contingency table has 4 rows and 5 columns, the test has 12 ($3 \times 4 = 12$) degrees of freedom.

Assumptions for the chi square test for independence include the assumption that categories are mutually exclusive and exhaustive and that the expected frequencies are reasonably large. Categories are **mutually exclusive** when subjects are classified into only one level, and they are **exhaustive** if all subjects can be classified. For example, the age categories 1–5, 5–9, and 10–15 are not mutually exclusive because five-year-olds could be placed in two age groups, and these categories would not be exhaustive for subjects who were not between the ages of 1 and 15.

The chi square test compares observed and expected frequencies, where **expected frequencies** are what we expect to observe if the variables are statistically independent. (Expected frequencies are calculated as the product of the row total and the column total, divided by the total number of observations. For example, the expected frequency for the upper left cell in Table 5.6 is (30)(35)/60 = 17.50. There are 30 people in the Young row, 35 people in the Favorable column, and 60 people in the whole study.) The expected frequencies should be at least 5 for tests with 1 degree of freedom, and should be at least 1 (with at least 80 percent of them 5 or more) for tests with more than one degree of freedom. Sometimes categories have to be collapsed in order to increase expected frequencies. For example, the age categories 1–5 and 6–10 may have to be combined into one group (ages 1–10) to increase expected frequencies. Many computer programs (including SPSS) warn the researcher if expected cell frequencies are too small.

Parametric and Nonparametric Procedures

Analyses of variance, t tests, F tests for homogeneity of variance, and tests on Pearson correlations are parametric procedures. Their null and alternative hypotheses deal with parameters (means, variances, and correlations). The chi square test for independence is a nonparametric test; its hypotheses deal with relationships between variables. **Parametric tests** examine hypotheses about specific parameters; **nonparametric tests** do not examine hypotheses about specific parameters. There are nonparametric procedures that are similar to the t test, analysis of variance, and Pearson correlation; and these nonparametric procedures require weaker assumptions about the data. For example, the Mann-Whitney test is the nonparametric counterpart of the independent groups t test, and the Spearman rank-order correlation coefficient is a nonparametric counterpart of the Pearson correlation coefficient; and they only require that data can be rank-ordered. Nonparametric tests are less powerful than parametric tests, however, so they are used only when the assumptions for the parametric tests are violated. The appropriate choice of statistical procedure requires an understanding of the properties of the measured variables. This will be covered in the next chapter.

SUPPORTING AND FALSIFYING THEORIES AND RESEARCH HYPOTHESES

Imagine we are conducting an experiment to test the theory of positive reinforcement, and we form the research hypothesis that children who are positively reinforced for reading will spend more time reading than children who are not positively reinforced for reading. To test this hypothesis, we randomly assign a group of forty children to one of two conditions. Children in the reinforcement condition are offered a dollar for each hour of reading in the coming week, and children in the control group are not offered a reward for reading. All subjects are asked to keep a log of their activities; and the log includes a daily total of the amount of time spent in a number of activities, such as reading, writing, watching television, and playing with friends.

If we were interested only in the forty children examined in our study, we would simply compare the descriptive statistics. If the reinforced children spent more time reading than the control children, we would conclude that the two groups were different. However, we are interested in generalizing to the entire population of children who are rewarded for reading and the entire population of children who are not rewarded for reading. We must use an inferential statistic (the t test) to generalize from the two samples to the two populations they represent.

Even if the two sample means are different, it may be that they are not significantly different. The observed difference may be the result of random factors operating within the study. If we were to replicate our study with a second group of forty children, we would not expect to get identical means for the two groups because there is fluctuation from sample to sample. We must use an inferential statistic to examine the possibility that the observed mean difference was within the range of differences attributable to chance. If the observed mean difference is so large that it is unlikely to be due to chance, we reject the assumption that the two populations have the same mean and tentatively conclude that the observed difference is caused by our experimental manipulation.

How does rejecting or not rejecting the null hypothesis relate to our research hypothesis and conclusion? Not rejecting the null hypothesis is not the same as accepting it, and rejecting the null hypothesis is not the same as accepting the alternative hypothesis. Rejecting the null hypothesis means that our results are unlikely if the null hypothesis is true; but if we use the customary alpha of .05, we recognize that there is a 5 percent chance of making a Type I error (rejecting the null hypothesis when the two populations actually have the same mean). There is nothing magical about .05. Early researchers could have established .01, .03, or .10 as the customary level. We use a small alpha level like .05 to make Type I errors unlikely. In this chapter we have used phrases such as "conclude that the null hypothesis is true" or "conclude that the alternative hypothesis is true" because the logic of hypothesis testing is easier to understand when we discuss the accuracy of these conclusions. To be more precise, though, we should have used language such as "fail to reject the null hypothesis" and "reject the null hypothesis," respectively. The distinction is subtle when we discuss actual studies. Rejecting the null hypothesis normally leads to the conclusion that groups are different, and failure to reject the null hypothesis normally leads to the conclusion that groups are not different.

We began this section with a research hypothesis: Children who are rewarded for reading will read more than children who are not rewarded for reading. We translated this hypothesis into the alternative hypothesis: the mean for rewarded children is higher than the mean for control-group children; and we contrasted this with the null hypothesis that the groups have the same mean. Failure to reject the null hypothesis (nonsignificant results) tentatively falsifies the research hypothesis, but it is possible that the research hypothesis is accurate and we have committed a Type II error. This is more likely when the test has low power. We expected a difference, but we did not observe a statistically significant difference. Significant results (results that lead us to reject the null hypothesis) do not prove that our hypothesis is true, but they do indicate that our theory has survived one round of empirical analysis. Even when results are significant, there is a chance that a Type I error has been made; and even if a population difference does exist, it is possible that alternative theories explain it more accurately. For example, it is possible that the significant mean difference was caused by parents of reinforced children giving them more encouragement to read.

Beginning researchers sometimes want to conclude more than "results suggest that the theory is true." They want to conclude that "results prove that the theory is true." The latter conclusion involves the fallacy of affirming the consequences. If we place a burning match in contact with a piece of dry paper, the paper will burn. If we observe a piece of burning paper, however, we cannot conclude that a burning match ignited it. The paper may have been ignited by a cigarette lighter, flame thrower, or forest fire. Concluding the cause (a burning match) from the effect (burning paper) is a logical fallacy, the **fallacy of affirming the consequences**. If we carefully design our study and control for other possible causal variables, we can place more confidence in the accuracy of our conclusions. If we observe the burning paper in a room that contains no cigarette lighters, flame throwers, or forest fires, these alternative causes can be ruled out. Also notice that if the paper is not burning, we can conclude a match did not light it. We can falsify the hypothesis that a match ignited the paper if the paper is not on fire, but we cannot prove that a match ignited a piece of paper if the burning paper is our only evidence.

The burning paper example must have one added dimension to apply to research. What if the observed paper isn't burning, but its corners are singed? It is possible that a match had lit it, but the fire went out, or that the paper was singed before the experiment began. We can make only tentative conclusions. Researchers who rely on statistical analysis are not able to unambiguously confirm or falsify hypotheses because they reach conclusions based on probabilities. Investigators conduct research by examining samples; there always is some chance that a particular sample is unusual—that relationships in the population are not found in the sample or that relationships in the sample are not found in the population. The sample may include only people with aberrant responses to experimental manipulations. Psychologists conduct thousands of studies, so the improbable is likely to be observed occasionally.

How do we uncover the truth? Regardless of the outcome of the study, it is possible that a Type I or Type II error was made or that the causal link specified by the theory was incorrect. This is why the scientific method relies on replication and consensual validation, and this is why researchers conducting replications sometimes fail to reach the same conclusions. Good experimental design rests on designing studies that are likely to result in unambiguous findings. Much of the rest of this book describes the process of designing a research study.

CHAPTER SUMMARY

Descriptive statistics are used to summarize aspects of samples, and inferential statistics are used to generalize from samples to populations. Researchers work with qualitative (categorical) and quantitative variables. Variables have frequency distributions in samples and probability distributions in populations. The most well-known probability distribution is the normal distribution.

Descriptive statistics are used to summarize central tendency (mode, mean, and median), variability (range, variance, and standard deviation), and relationships (the Pearson product-moment correlation coefficient). Relationships are illustrated in scatterplots, and they vary in direction (positive or negative) and strength. Relationships can be linear or nonlinear.

Hypothesis testing involves deciding between null and alternative hypotheses. Significant results are obtained when the null hypothesis is rejected. Researchers try to avoid Type I errors (rejecting a true null hypothesis) by using a small alpha and to avoid Type II errors (not rejecting the null hypothesis when the alternative hypothesis is true) by designing studies with high power. Generally, significance probabilities must be .05 or less to have significant results. Alternative hypotheses can be directional or nondirectional, and tests can be one-tailed or two-tailed. All hypothesis testing is done in the same way. The null and alternative hypotheses are stated, the test statistic is calculated in the sample, the significance probability is determined by examining the appropriate sampling distribution, the null hypothesis is rejected or is not rejected, and tentative conclusions are made. Researchers must distinguish between statistical and meaningful significance when they interpret results, and they may calculate an estimate of effect size.

Hypotheses concern differences and relationships. Differences among means can be examined with *t* tests and analysis of variance. The independent variables can be between-group or within-subject, and the type of test to be conducted depends on the type and number of independent variables and their number of levels. *t* tests and analyses of variance require the assumption that the dependent variable is normally distributed, but this can be waived by applying the Central Limit Theorem if the sample size is large. Analyses of variance can be factorial, repeated measures, or mixed; and their tests concern main effects and interactions. The *F* test for homogeneity of variance can be used to examine the homogeneity of variance assumption, and tests can be conducted to see if correlation coefficients or relationships are significant. Hypotheses concerning parameters are examined with parametric tests, and other hypotheses are examined with nonparametric tests. Parametric procedures generally have more power and involve stronger assumptions about the data.

Statistical analysis leads to rejecting or not rejecting the null hypothesis, and results can be tentatively used to falsify or to support a theory. Supporting a theory does not prove its truth, but well-designed research allows us to place more trust in our conclusions.

Key Concepts

alpha

alternative hypothesis (H_A)

analysis of variance

beta

between-group variable

categorical variable

Central Limit Theorem

central tendency

chi square test for independence

contingency table

dependent sampling *t* test

descriptive statistic

directional alternative hypothesis

effect size

exhaustive categories

expected frequencies

F test for homogeneity of variance

factorial analysis of variance

fallacy of affirming the consequences

frequency

frequency distribution

homogeneity of variance assumption

hypothesis testing

independent groups *t* test

inferential statistic

interaction

k-way analysis of variance

linear relationship

lower-tailed test

main effect

matched subjects

mean

meaningful significance

median

mixed design analysis of variance

mode

mu (μ)

mutually exclusive categories

negative relationship

nondirectional alternative hypothesis

nonlinear relationship

nonparametric test

null hypothesis (H_0)

one-tailed test

one-way analysis of variance

one-way repeated measures analysis of variance

parametric test

Pearson product-moment correlation coefficient

population

positive relationship

power

probability

probability distribution

qualitative variable

quantitative variable

random selection

range

repeated measures analysis of variance

sample

sampling distribution

scatterplot

significance probability

skewed distribution

SPSS

standard deviation

statistical independence

statistical significance
strong relationship
t test
test statistic
two-tailed test
Type I error

Type II error
upper-tailed test
variability
variance
weak relationship
within-subject variable

Review Questions

1. David reports that the average age of his subjects is 18.42 (*SD* = 4.37) and that there is a significant gender difference in the heights of his subjects. What descriptive statistics did he use? What inferential statistic did he use?

2. Are the following categorical or quantitative variables?
Age, Gender, Income, Eye Color, Shoe Size, SAT-Verbal Score

3. Denise wants to examine a random sample of adults in her community. She calls every hundredth name in the phone book to obtain her sample. Is this a random sample?

4. Here is the frequency distribution of scores on Joey's assertiveness test.

X	f
17	3
16	2
15	4
14	8
13	10
12	16

Does it appear that assertiveness scores are normally distributed? Why or why not?

5. What would be the best descriptive statistic for the central tendency of each of the following distributions?
    a. The distribution of incomes for a cross-section of American citizens
    b. The distribution of dog breeds at an American Kennel Club show
    c. The distribution of heights among four-year-old children

6. You know that ambition scores on the Cross Ambitiousness Test have a normal distribution with a mean of 50 and a standard deviation of 5. Approximately what score range includes the middle 95 percent of people taking this test?

7. Would you expect the following relationships to be positive and linear, negative and linear, or nonlinear? Draw their likely scatterplot.
    a. The relationship between income and years of education
    b. The relationship between aggressiveness and popularity among children
    c. The relationship between income and satisfaction with life

8. A researcher is studying the effectiveness of a new sleeping pill. Half the research subjects are given the sleeping pill, and half the subjects are given a placebo (an inert substance that should not affect sleeping). Each subject reports the average number of hours slept after taking the pill. What would be the null and alternative hypotheses for this study? Should the alternative hypothesis be directional or

nondirectional? Why? What test statistic and sampling distribution would be used to analyze the data if there were 40 subjects in each group? What would be the Type I error for this analysis? What would be the Type II error for this analysis?

9. Significance probabilities are based on calculating values of test statistics and examining areas under sampling distributions. Define significance probability, test statistic, and sampling distribution. Explain how to find the significance probability for upper-tailed, lower-tailed, and two-tailed tests.

10. Jean conducted a research project and obtained significant results. Her teacher, though, concluded that Jean's results were trivial. How could results be both significant and trivial?

11. Independent groups *t* tests, dependent sampling *t* tests, one-way analysis of variance, and one-way repeated measures analysis of variance are used to analyze the effect of one independent variable on a dependent variable. How do you decide which one to use?

12. Identify the dependent variable, independent variable(s), the number of levels of each independent variable, the nature of each independent variable (between-group or within-subject), and the appropriate test for each of the following studies.

a. Ten sets of identical twins are studied to examine the effect of experience on motor development. Within each set, one child is given special training and exercises, and the other child is offered no special experiences. The age at which each child walks ten steps without assistance is recorded.

b. A researcher studies the effects of political party and gender on attitudes toward the Supreme Court by administering an attitude questionnaire to 800 subjects.

c. In order to examine the effect of gender and age on attention span, 50 girls and 50 boys are each measured four times (at ages 3, 5, 7, and 9).

13. Life satisfaction scores averaged 40 for married women, 50 for single women, 60 for married men, and 30 for single men. These data are based on four equally-sized groups of subjects. Do there appear to be any main effects or interactions in these results? Why?

14. Emilio uses SPSS to do an independent groups *t* test comparing 23 women to 14 men, and the program automatically does an *F* test. Why is the *F* test calculated? How is it interpreted? If the women had a standard deviation of 19 and the men had a standard deviation of 27, what would be the degrees of freedom for this *F* test? What would be the degrees of freedom for the *t* test?

15. Should the following relationships be examined using a test on the Pearson correlation or a chi square test for independence? Why?

a. The relationship between ethnicity and eye color

b. The relationship between age and the number of minutes of television viewing per day

16. You conduct a chi square test for independence using a computer program and the computer flags a problem with inadequately sized expected frequencies. What is the problem? How can it be addressed?

17. You can analyze your data using a parametric or a nonparametric test. Which would you use? Why?

18. Gloria finds a significant gender difference in activity level, as measured by the number of square feet of a room each child enters in a one-hour period. She finds that boys cover significantly larger areas than girls. She concludes that her study proves a genetic basis for activity level. Comment on her conclusion.

6

Measurement

Variables in psychological research are described by operational definitions, and researchers use a variety of measurement techniques. For example, descriptive studies may involve measuring creativity or depression level. Correlational studies may be used to examine relationships among measurements of anxiety, self-confidence, and test performance. Researchers conducting experimental studies manipulate independent variables, then measure dependent variables. Most research studies require measurements.

Measurement is assigning numbers to objects in a systematic way to reflect properties of those objects. For example, intelligence is measured by administering IQ tests, and weight is measured with a scale. Even categorical variables can be measured. If men are coded "1" and women are coded "2," gender is measured because numbers have been assigned in a systematic way to reflect this property. Although numbers have been assigned, arithmetic on these numbers would be unreasonable. It would not make sense to report that the average gender is 1.36. We must understand the properties of measurements in order to decide how they can be used.

PROPERTIES OF MEASUREMENT

The four major properties of measurement are distinctiveness, ordinality, equal unit size, and absolute zero. Measurements have **distinctiveness** if objects that are different receive different scores. For example, two people should be assigned different numbers if weight is being measured and they have different weights. Measurements have **ordinality** if the ordering of the numbers reflects the ordering of the trait. Someone

PROPERTIES OF THE LEVELS OF MEASUREMENT   TABLE 6.1

Property of measurement	LEVEL OF MEASUREMENT			
	Nominal	Ordinal	Interval	Ratio
Distinctiveness	Yes	Yes	Yes	Yes
Ordinality	No	Yes	Yes	Yes
Equal unit size	No	No	Yes	Yes
Absolute zero	No	No	No	Yes

who is 145 pounds weighs more than someone who is 140 pounds; 145 is larger than 140, and the person with a score of 145 has more weight than the person with a score of 140. Not all measurements have this property. For example, if we measure gender by assigning men a score of 1 and women a score of 2, the ordering of the numbers does not indicate the ordering of the trait. Women do not have more gender than men.

Measurements have an **equal unit size** if a difference of 1 means the same amount everywhere on the scale. For example, the difference between two people who weigh 186 pounds and 185 pounds is the same amount of weight as the difference between two people who weigh 156 pounds and 155 pounds. The unit (one pound) is the same size for all possible weights. Not all measurements have this property. For example, consider positions in a race (first-place, second-place, third-place, and so on). Numbers have been assigned in a systematic way to measure speed. The speed difference between the first- and second-place runners may be small, and the speed difference between the sixth- and seventh-place runners may be large. The measurement units are not necessarily equal in size.

Measurements have an **absolute zero** if assigning a score of zero indicates an absence of the trait being measured. Suppose the temperature in Fargo was 0 degrees Fahrenheit on December 29. The score of zero is not an absolute zero because it does not mean an absence of temperature. If we were to measure the number of people in each room in the Psychology Building, however, a score of zero would be absolute; it would mean there were no people in that room.

LEVELS OF MEASUREMENT

There are four levels of measurement, and each level has different properties. Researchers establish the **level of measurement** for their data to decide which statistical analyses are appropriate. The four levels of measurement, in order of increasing sophistication, are nominal, ordinal, interval, and ratio. Their properties are summarized in Table 6.1.

Data measured at the **nominal level of measurement (nominal data)** have distinctiveness but lack the other properties of measurement. Nominal variables are categorical variables with numbers assigned to categories. We could measure ethnicity by giving a 1 to African-Americans, a 2 to Asian-Americans, a 3 to European-Americans,

---

Box 6.1

Attitude Toward Martians Scale

Would you respond positively or negatively to the following events? Mark + if
you would respond positively and – if you would respond negatively.

_____	1.	Martians are documented in the universe.
_____	2.	Martians are documented in our solar system.
_____	3.	Martians land on Earth.
_____	4.	Martians move into your state.
_____	5.	Martians move into your county.
_____	6.	Martians move into your city.
_____	7.	Martians move into your neighborhood.
_____	8.	Martians live next door to you.
_____	9.	A Martian becomes friends with a member of your family.
_____	10.	A Martian dates a member of your family.
_____	11.	A Martian marries a member of your family.
_____	12.	A Martian and a member of your family have children.

and so on. These scores are on the nominal level of measurement. They have distinctiveness (people in different ethnic groups receive different scores), but they do not have ordinality, an equal unit size, or an absolute zero. We can form frequency distributions, calculate the mode, and use chi square tests to analyze relationships between nominal variables, but we cannot analyze them by doing arithmetic on the scores. We would not report that the mean ethnicity was 3.41 ($SD = .26$), do a t test comparing men's and women's ethnicity scores, or calculate a Pearson correlation between ethnicity and height.

Data measured at the **ordinal level of measurement (ordinal data)** have distinctiveness and ordinality, but lack an equal unit size and absolute zero. Rank-ordered data, such as positions in a race, levels of political participation, or social attitudes, are measured on an ordinal level. Box 6.1 provides an example of a social distance scale that measures attitudes toward Martians. Your score on this scale is the number of negative responses. **Social distance scales**, like this example, measure how large a social distance you want to maintain from a group. High scores indicate negative attitudes toward Martians (large social distances are desired); low scores indicate positive attitudes toward Martians (smaller social distances are acceptable). Data are on the ordinal level of measurement. Scores have distinctiveness because people with different attitudes get different scores, and they have ordinality because higher numbers indicate more negative attitudes toward Martians. The unit size, though, is not constant. The difference between Martians in the universe and Martians in the solar system may be small compared to the difference between having Martians as friends and having Martians as dates, or between dating a Martian and marrying one.

Ordinal data indicate which subjects are higher on the trait being measured, but do not allow comparisons that require equal units or an absolute zero. Ordinal data cannot be subtracted meaningfully. For example, we cannot say that the attitude difference between people with scores of 7 and 9 on the attitude toward Martians scale is the same as the difference between people with scores of 0 and 2. We can use the median or mode to indicate central tendency. Means are less meaningful because the unit size fluctuates arbitrarily, and variances and standard deviations are not meaningful because they require the calculation of deviation scores. (Deviation scores involve subtraction, so require equal unit sizes.) We also cannot form reasonable ratios. We cannot say that someone with a score of 8 is twice as prejudiced against Martians as someone with a score of 4. Generally, ordinal data are converted to rank orders, and these rank orders are analyzed. For example, the **Spearman rank-order correlation coefficient** is the Pearson correlation calculated on ranked data. Subjects' scores are converted to ranks (1 = lowest, 2 = second lowest, and so on); then these ranks are correlated. The Spearman correlation coefficient summarizes the direction and strength of the linear relationship between rank-ordered data for two variables.

Data measured at the **interval level of measurement (interval data)** have distinctiveness, ordinality, and an equal unit size, but lack an absolute zero. Temperature in degrees Fahrenheit is measured on the interval level. Temperatures have distinctiveness (days with different temperatures receive different scores), ordinality (hotter days receive higher scores), and an equal unit size (one degree of temperature always represents the same amount of heat), but a score of zero is not absolute. Days that are zero degrees do not have an absence of temperature. Scores on many ability tests are at the interval level of measurement.

Interval data can be meaningfully added and subtracted, so common descriptive and inferential statistics can be used, including the mean, standard deviation, Pearson correlation, and t test. However, meaningful ratios cannot be formed because interval data lack an absolute zero. A day that is 80 degrees is not twice as hot as a day that is 40 degrees, and a child with an IQ of 100 is not twice as intelligent as a child with an IQ of 50.

Data measured on the **ratio level of measurement (ratio data)** have distinctiveness, ordinality, an equal unit size, and an absolute zero. Typical ratio variables are counts and physical measurements. For example, body weight (in pounds and ounces) is measured at the ratio level. Such measurements have distinctiveness (people who weigh different amounts receive different scores), ordinality (people who are heavier receive larger scores), an equal unit size (a pound or ounce of weight is the same amount of weight for all people), and an absolute zero (as we record scores closer and closer to zero, we are observing people who are closer and closer to weightless). Ratio data can be manipulated using any arithmetic operation, and ratios are meaningful. A child who weighs 50 pounds is twice as heavy as a child who weighs 25 pounds. As with interval data, common statistical procedures (such as means and standard deviations) result in meaningful numbers.

Researchers should establish the level of measurement of their data in order to select appropriate statistical procedures. Frequency distributions and modes are reasonable for all variables; medians and statistics requiring rank orders are reasonable for variables that are at least at the ordinal level; means, standard deviations, Pearson correlations, and most parametric tests (such as t tests and analysis of variance) are reasonable for data that are at least at the interval level; and ratios of scores are appropriate only for ratio data. Many parametric procedures also require additional assumptions, such as normally distributed variables, so level of measurement is not the only determinant of statistic choice.

Most of the standard parametric procedures are quite robust. A **robust statistic** is reasonably accurate when assumptions are violated. It is not uncommon for psychologists to use parametric procedures for data that are on the ordinal level or that are not normally distributed. The degree of risk in choosing an inappropriate procedure depends on how severely the assumptions are broken. It probably is safe to use parametric procedures to analyze ordinal data with roughly equal unit sizes, but this is not reasonable for nominal data.

RELIABILITY AND VALIDITY

All measurements should have two qualities: reliability and validity. Measurements are **reliable** if individuals' scores are stable. Reliable scores are precise, but unreliable scores do not precisely indicate test-takers' characteristics. Measurements are **valid** if scores are meaningful. Reliability and validity are separate concepts, and data that are reliable are not necessarily valid. For example, we could use a ruler to measure height, but claim to be measuring intelligence. The scores are reliable because people receive about the same score each time they are measured, but height scores are not valid measures of intelligence. Valid measures of stable characteristics must be reliable to be valid. An unstable score could not validly measure a constant trait. Researchers should examine the reliability and validity of their measurements. Research conducted with unreliable and/or invalid measurements could lead to inaccurate conclusions.

Reliability

Reliability can be examined in three ways (Allen & Yen, 1979). **Test-retest reliability** is established by measuring a group of people twice using the same procedure, then correlating the two scores. High correlations suggest that scores are stable (reliable); and low correlations suggest that scores are unstable (unreliable). **Parallel (or alternate) forms reliability** is established by correlating scores gathered with two versions of the measurement procedure. For example, two versions of an anxiety test may be developed. Subjects are given both tests, and the two scores are correlated. If the two forms correlate highly, the tests appear reliable; if they have a low correlation, the tests appear unreliable. **Internal consistency reliability** is established by correlating parts of the test with each other. For example, **split-half reliability** is based on giving each subject two scores, each based on half the test, then correlating the two scores. **Coefficient alpha** also is used to estimate a test's internal consistency reliability, and is based on correlating each item with every other item on the test. Longer tests are more reliable than shorter tests, so split-half reliability estimates and coefficient alpha are adjusted to estimate the reliability of the whole test, rather than a half-test or item. Internal consistency reliability estimates range from 0 to 1.0. High coefficients indicate high internal consistency, and low coefficients indicate low internal consistency.

High reliability coefficients are obtained when scores being correlated have strong linear relationships, and there should be strong linear relationships if tests are reliable. Most test developers establish more than one type of reliability for their tests because the three types of reliability examine different aspects of reliability: stability across time (test-retest reliability), stability across different versions of the measurement procedure (parallel or alternate forms reliability), and stability within the measurement procedure (internal consistency reliability).

Validity

Valid measurements are meaningful. Validity can be examined in three ways (Allen & Yen, 1979). Researchers examine content validity, criterion-related validity, and construct validity.

Content validity is based on evaluation of the measurement procedure by experts. The experts make a qualitative judgment that the procedure appears to be valid or invalid. Global judgments examine the **face validity** of the test: Does the test measure, on the face of it, the intended characteristic? **Sampling validity** involves a more structured qualitative assessment, based on carefully defining details that the test must cover. For example, a test that is designed to measure the ability to add two-digit numbers would have face validity if it contained items such as 35 + 17 = ? and 59 + 36 = ?. Imagine you are a student in a course and the instructor announces that Tuesday's exam will cover Chapters 1 through 5. You could assess the exam's sampling validity by verifying that the questions cover the major concepts in these five chapters. You would question its sampling validity if all the questions were on Chapter 1, if the test emphasized only trivial points made in Chapters 1 through 5, or if questions on Chapter 6 were included.

Criterion-related validity is used when the measurement procedure yields scores that are used to predict a specific criterion. The correlation between the measurements and scores on the criterion assesses **criterion-related validity**. For example, scores on the attitudes toward Martians scale should correlate with actual observations of people's willingness to associate with Martians. If these two variables correlate highly, the test has good criterion-related validity. If they have a low correlation, the test has weak criterion-related validity. Similarly, an assertiveness test should correlate with measurements of assertive behaviors, and an employment screening test should correlate with success on the job.

Construct validity involves empirically assessing how well a test measures the theoretical construct it was designed to reflect; this is done by conducting studies that examine hypotheses concerning scores. Construct validity studies are part of an ongoing process. Researchers define the theoretical construct the test measures, and predictions are based on this theoretical construct. For example, developers of a new intelligence test make predictions based on their theory of intelligence. They may hypothesize that their test will correlate positively with other intelligence tests and with school grades and that older children will perform better than younger children. Each prediction is examined through empirical research. If results are consistent with predictions, the test appears to have construct validity. If results are inconsistent with predictions, there is something wrong with the study, the test, or the theory, and researchers must ascertain what happened. This process leads to accumulated knowledge about the scores' meaningfulness. Construct validity studies can be used to test hypotheses about experts' judgments and criterion-related validity, so construct validity encompasses the entire concept of validity.

Psychometrics

Psychometrics is the study of properties of psychological tests. Reliability and validity are psychometric concepts that are examined through empirical research. Many tests frequently used in psychological research and professional practice have been examined in thousands of psychometric studies. Researchers must reevaluate the psychometric properties of their tests periodically because test items and scoring criteria may become obsolete or invalid. A summary of research on the psychometric properties of the Beck Depression Inventory is provided here. This illustrates one of many ongoing research programs on the psychometric properties of psychological tests.

TYPES OF MEASUREMENT

Psychologists measure variables in a number of ways. They measure physical characteristics, they make behavioral observations, and they administer tests and surveys.

Physical Characteristics

Physical characteristics, such as birthweight, illumination level, and room size, can be measured objectively. Most of us have had medical exams, so we are accustomed to blood pressure cuffs, eye charts, and thermometers. Psychologists also have used other physical measures. A frequently used physiological indicator of emotional arousal is the **galvanic skin response (GSR)**, a decrease in electrical resistance in the skin that indicates autonomic nervous system arousal. The GSR, combined with blood pressure, heart rate, and breathing rate, is used in **polygraphs** (lie detectors). **Electromyograph (EMG)** recordings indicate muscle contractions. EMG recordings have been used to analyze the effect of relaxation therapy on tension headaches and are used by physical therapists to help in the rehabilitation of damaged muscle groups. An **electroencephalogram (EEG)** measures electrical activity in the brain by obtaining readings from electrodes attached to the scalp. EEGs have been used to study sleeping patterns and brain localization of thought processes.

Physiological measures of sexual arousal have been developed. Instruments measure increased pressure in genital areas due to increased blood flow. Such devices have been used to study sexual arousal in response to various stimuli (such as photographs or movies) and to treat sex offenders with behavioral techniques that discourage arousal to inappropriate targets.

We must consider the reliability and validity of physical measurements. A pattern on a polygraph recording may be unreliably evoked by a stimulus; it may occasionally occur spontaneously. This pattern, if reliable, may indicate guilt for a crime, or it may indicate some other emotional response to the stimulus. The person who responds emotionally to mention of Aunt Milly's stolen diamonds may have stolen the diamonds or may be aroused by memories of other associations to the gems. The psychometric properties of our physical recordings are important if we are to plan and to interpret research.

PSYCHOMETRIC PROPERTIES OF THE BECK DEPRESSION INVENTORY

The Beck Depression Inventory was originally developed in 1961 and was revised in 1971. It is one of the most widely used instruments for the assessment of depression in clinical practice and research, and foreign-language versions also are in use. The test generally is self-administered (test-takers rate themselves) and involves ratings of the intensity of twenty-one symptoms of depression (such as guilt feelings, irritability, crying, and loss of appetite). A short (thirteen-item) version of the test also is available. See Beck, Steer, and Garbin (1988) for a summary of twenty-five years of research on the psychometric properties of the Beck Depression Inventory.

Each of the three types of reliability has been examined. Test-retest reliability studies of clinical populations are complicated by subjects' involvement in therapy. Scores among therapy clients should decrease over time, rather than remain stable; this has been found true. Test-retest reliability coefficients among psychiatric patients in a number of studies range from .48 to .86, and the corresponding range in nonpsychiatric subjects is from .60 to .83. Periods between test administrations ranged from a few hours to a few weeks, so comparison of the studies is difficult. Results, as would be expected, suggest more stability in nonclinical populations.

Psychological tests can be classified as state or trait measurements. A **state** is temporary, but a **trait** is relatively constant. Tests of mood generally measure states; tests of ability and many aspects of personality are generally interpreted as measuring traits. The Beck Depression Inventory measures a state. We are less concerned about the long-term stability of tests of states than tests of traits, so the internal consistency and parallel forms reliability of the Beck Depression Inventory are more important than its test-retest reliability. Beck et al. (1988) summarize 25 internal consistency reliability studies based on a variety of samples. Reliability coefficients ranged from .73 to .95, with an average in the .80s for both psychiatric and nonpsychiatric samples and for both the long and short forms

of the test. Overall, this is good for a clinical instrument. (Established ability tests generally have reliabilities in the .90s, but personality tests generally have reliabilities in the .80s or less.)

Parallel forms reliability information is obtained by examining correlations between different versions of the test. Various studies have found correlations between the long and short forms of the Beck Depression Inventory that range from .89 to .97. Beck et al. (1988) report a correlation of .94 between the original and revised Inventory.

Validity analyses are based on a number of different types of studies. Content validity analyses comparing Inventory items to the definitions of depression in the *Diagnostic and Statistical Manual of Mental Disorders* (DSM-III, 1980), the American Psychiatric Association's official criteria for diagnostic categories, uncovered the omission of some symptoms of depression, but Beck and his colleagues deliberately omitted these symptoms because they are found less frequently in depressed clients than those included in the Inventory. Including less-frequent symptoms would make diagnoses of false positives (nondepressed people incorrectly labelled depressed) more common, an error they wanted to avoid.

Criterion-related validity studies relate Inventory scores to other measures of depression. Analyses of thirty-five studies using other measures of depression, such as clinical ratings and other depression test scores, revealed correlations that generally averaged in the .70s, with correlations a bit higher among clinical than among nonclinical samples. Such results are typical for widely used personality tests.

A number of different types of construct validity studies have been conducted. Repeated research finds that psychiatric populations score higher than nonpsychiatric populations, as would be expected. Other studies have established correlations between Inventory scores and suicidal behaviors, maladjustment ratings, depressive thoughts, loneliness, stress, anxiety, and biological indicators of depression. Overall, the pattern of results is consistent with predictions.

Behavioral Observations

Psychologists may measure characteristics by carefully observing and recording behaviors. These may be naturally occurring behaviors, such as acts of sharing among children at a nursery school, or may be behaviors in response to a stimulus, such as people's reactions to feigned seizures in public buildings. Behaviors of interest to experimental psychologists include errors in mazes and bar pressing by rats and other animals. Developmental psychologists working with nonspeaking infants rely on behavioral measures, such as reaching or gazing, to examine children's cognitive development.

Behavioral observations are recorded by an observer, who may be at the scene or who may work from videotapes. Observers may be hidden from view, so that subjects are not aware they are being observed. This involves some ethical problems, notably issues of informed consent and privacy. Observers may be identified, such as researchers who visit homes to record family interactions. Sometimes observers conduct **participant observation studies**, studies in which they pretend to be participants in the ongoing activity. For example, a researcher may pretend to be a migrant worker or religious convert in order to examine social interactions within the group being studied.

Observations can be structured or unstructured. **Unstructured observations** are made by researchers who attempt to record everything of importance. They make notes that are later analyzed. Such research tends to be qualitative, rather than quantitative, with conclusions about general phenomena. For example, researchers may observe family interactions and conclude that children appear to be more self-confident if parents allow them to make their own decisions. Such conclusions generally are further tested in more structured studies. **Structured observations** are recorded using a prearranged scheme that focuses observations on specific behaviors. Recorders may use a checklist to record specific activities that occur within a preset timeframe. Box 6.2 shows a rating form that could be used to analyze parent-child interactions. Family pairs could be observed in the laboratory by presenting each pair with the same problem (such as agreeing on a dinner menu), and one-minute intervals of their interaction could be evaluated with this form.

Structured observations require careful planning as the data recording scheme is developed, and data collectors must be trained to use the same criteria. For example, imagine we are developing a study of aggression among prisoners, and we are allowed to make our observations in a prison dining hall. What acts will be recorded? How will they be classified? Are verbal insults recorded differently from physical confrontations? Shall we count an exchange of verbal insults as one event or a series of separate events? How do we handle "accidental" bumping that appears to be intentional? Do we focus on one inmate or one table, or do we attempt to record events throughout the whole room? If there are multiple observers, how do we ensure they use the same criteria?

Behavioral therapists use behavioral observations in their research and to evaluate clients. Behavioral measures are used to define the severity of problems, to create treatment plans, and to monitor progress. Antecedent and maintaining behaviors also may be measured. For example, spousal battering incidents may be preceded by alcohol use and followed by apologies and forgiveness. Knowing the antecedent behavior (drinking) and maintaining behavior (reconciliation), the therapist can target changes in these behaviors, indirectly affecting the battering.

Box 6.2

Child-Parent Interaction Rating Form

Ratings are for the one-minute interval that began at _____ during a _____ minute interaction.

The _____ child _____ parent is rated here.

Check all behaviors that occur during this one-minute interval.

_____   States an opinion
_____   Agrees with other person's opinion
_____   Disagrees with other person's opinion
_____   Makes a request of the other person
_____   Grants a request of the other person
_____   Denies a request of the other person
_____   Suggests a solution to a problem
_____   Agrees with the other's suggested solution to a problem
_____   Disagrees with the other's suggested solution to a problem
_____   Uses humor in a positive way
_____   Uses sarcasm or humor in a negative way
_____   Ignores the other person

Behavioral problems of interest to therapists and researchers typically involve behavioral excess, deficit, or inappropriateness. **Behavioral excess** involves too much of a behavior, such as overeating, smoking too much, or compulsive handwashing. **Behavioral deficits** involve too little of a behavior, such as withdrawal from social contacts or failure to study. **Inappropriate behaviors** are socially unacceptable acts, such as bedwetting or public sexual displays. Researchers need objective measures that quantify the extent of problems and that identify situations under which problems are displayed. Observations may be made by therapists or others, such as clinic staff, teachers, or clients' family members. Sometimes data are collected by clients, who are asked to keep diaries or other systematic records of crucial events. Specific tests also have been developed for this purpose, such as the Behavior Problems Checklist and Fear Survey Schedule.

Behavioral observations should have demonstrated reliability and validity. If multiple observers are employed, their scores can be examined for **interrater reliability**, the extent of their agreement, by correlating their scores or by calculating percentage agreement. Stability of scores can be checked by reobserving subjects, and other aspects of reliability can be examined by rating behaviors in multiple ways, such as recording several aspects of the behavior separately. The validity of the ratings also is important if data are analyzed to infer intentions or to indicate underlying constructs, such as psychological diagnoses. Behavioral therapists generally are less concerned about the validity of their measurements because they focus only on treating observable behaviors. They are less interested in inferring underlying theoretical constructs.

Tests and Surveys

Many psychological tests have been developed, including the Beck Depression Inventory mentioned earlier. These tests can be classified in a number of ways. Tests can measure maximum or typical performance. A **maximum performance test** measures the upper limit of capabilities, and a **typical performance test** measures normal behavior. Maximum performance tests generally have right and wrong answers, and typical performance tests generally measure differences in style. Intelligence tests are maximum performance tests, and personality and interest tests generally measure typical performance. They are not created to discover whether a person knows how to be popular, neurotic, or interested in mechanical objects. Rather, they attempt to uncover whether a person typically has these characteristics. Social skills tests (such as tests of assertiveness or interpersonal empathy) may combine aspects of maximum and typical performance.

Ability tests are further divided into aptitude and achievement tests. **Aptitude tests** measure potential to do something never done before, and **achievement tests** measure what one is competent to do now. General intelligence tests are aptitude tests, and school examinations generally are achievement tests. Teachers are more interested in grading students on what they have learned than on what they could have learned. The distinction between achievement and aptitude tests is not always clear because any ability test measures some aspects of previously learned skills (Kaplan & Saccuzzo, 1989).

Another distinction is between performance and nonperformance tests. **Performance tests** require overt, active responses, such as hand movements, and **nonperformance tests** generally involve written or oral responses to questions. For example, a researcher interested in measuring leadership skills with a performance test could put people in groups, ask them to solve problems, then assess the leadership shown by each participant. Scoring could be made objective by counting indicators of leadership, such as the number of minutes each person talked, the number of ideas each person suggested that were accepted by the group, and the number of times each person yielded to an interruption. A nonperformance test of leadership might be a paper-and-pencil test asking questions about one's leadership history, such as being elected or appointed to administrative positions and feelings of competency about decision-making and people management. Although performance tests may have greater face validity, they are not necessarily better and may involve complicated, time-consuming administration and scoring. Sometimes a nonperformance test can serve as an acceptable substitute for a performance test. For example, multiple-choice tests of English usage (nonperformance measures) correlate highly with ratings of written essays (performance measures) and are much easier to administer and score.

A major distinction among personality tests is between objective and projective tests. **Objective tests** require answers that are easily scored. A typical objective test item would ask for a True or False response to statements such as "I generally sleep well." A scoring key might add one point to an Anxiety score for people who indicate False. **Projective tests** present ambiguous stimuli and test-takers are asked to react to them. One of the best-known projective tests is the Rorschach Inkblot Test. Subjects are asked to describe what they see in a series of inkblots. Various scoring systems have been developed, and they are complex and require extensive training. Although a clerk can be trained to score objective tests, skilled professionals must score projective measures.

Some tests require individual administration, and others can be taken in groups. **Group tests** are given to multiple people simultaneously. They tend to be objective and to require little supervision. **Individual tests** are administered to one person at a time. They frequently require ongoing professional judgments. For example, when administering an individual IQ test, the administrator must monitor responses to determine whether further questions must be asked (e.g., "Please tell me more") and to determine which item to give next. Structured interviews, such as those conducted by opinion pollsters (e.g., Gallup, Harris, and Roper), generally are individual tests that are administered orally by trained interviewers. These interviews are tests and should be subjected to the same reliability and validity standards as any other test.

Another distinction involves the test's interpretation. Scores on **norm-referenced tests** are interpreted by comparing an individual's score to those of a norm group. The conclusion may be that the individual is above, at, or below average on the test compared to the norm group. The norm group may be a cross section of the population or may be a specialized group, such as college graduates. Scores on **criterion-referenced tests** are interpreted as having met or as not having met a criterion. For example, students either pass or do not pass a writing competency examination that is required for graduation. Scores are not compared with each other, but with a specified criterion. Most widely used tests are norm-referenced, but criterion-referenced tests are becoming increasingly popular in schools so that conclusions about student skills can be explicit, such as "This student has mastered the present tense with regular verbs in Spanish, but has not mastered the past perfect tense with regular verbs in Spanish."

CREATING A TEST

Often researchers can use measurement techniques developed by earlier researchers. For example, studies of depression may use the Beck Depression Inventory. Researchers learn how earlier studies defined important variables when they conduct literature reviews, and often use or adapt earlier techniques. This facilitates the integration of new findings into the ongoing research literature.

There are times, however, when researchers must develop their own measurement procedures, and they should demonstrate that new procedures are reliable and valid. The day when psychologists could sit down, pencil in hand, and simply write a psychological test of publishable quality is long gone. Test creation requires considerable effort and insight, but is worth the effort when existing techniques are unsatisfactory.

The first important step is to carefully define what the test will measure. This definition should be based on a thorough review of the literature and often involves a specific theoretical perspective. Tests such as the Beck Depression Inventory also may be based on years of clinical experience and discussions with colleagues. Many decisions must be made. Is the test to be a measure of maximum or typical behavior? Shall it be performance or nonperformance, objective or projective, group or individually administered, norm-referenced or criterion-referenced? If there will be specific items, an item format must be selected. Will the items be closed-ended or open-ended? **Closed-ended questions** require selection among preset responses, and **open-ended questions** require the test-taker to develop responses. Closed-ended items include

---

Box 6.3

Examples of Item Formats

Dichotomous Format

1. I have trouble sleeping.   True   False
2. Doctors should spend more time with patients.   Agree   Disagree
3. Which career would you prefer?   Pilot   Accountant

Multiple Choice

4. Wrong answers for multiple-choice items are
   a. bifurcated
   b. redundant
   c. attractors
   d. distractors

Likert Scale

5. Jury members should be paid minimum wage.
   _____ Strongly agree
   _____ Moderately agree
   _____ Mildly agree
   _____ Mildly disagree
   _____ Moderately disagree
   _____ Strongly disagree

Semantic Differential

6. Lawyers
   Honest   __ __ __ __ __ __ __   Dishonest
   Greedy   __ __ __ __ __ __ __   Generous
   Friendly __ __ __ __ __ __ __   Not friendly

---

questions requiring true-false, multiple-choice, or marked answers along a continuum; open-ended items may require fill-in or essay answers. Box 6.3 shows items with a number of different formats. Alternatively, items may require physical responses, such as manipulating cards or objects.

Dichotomous items require choosing between two answers, such as Yes/No or True/False. **Multiple-choice items** generally present a set of 4 or 5 responses from which to choose. For ability and achievement tests, one response is accurate, and the others are **distractors**, incorrect answers that are designed to appeal to test-takers who do not know the answer. **Likert scales** require subjects to indicate their degree of agreement with a statement. Likert-scale items frequently are used to measure attitudes. **Semantic differential items** (Osgood & Tannenbaum, 1955) are used to measure attitudes toward stimuli by requiring ratings on a number of dimensions. Ratings of multiple stimuli can be obtained to make comparisons among them, such as

Visual Continuum

7. American politicians generally are honest.
   Agree _____ Disagree
8. The national debt should receive the highest priority from government leaders.

   |⎿_____|_____⏌|
   Strongly   Uncertain   Strongly
   disagree   agree

Fill-In/Incomplete Sentences

9. A _____ test has stable scores.
10. My dreams _____ .

Checklist

11. Check each of the adjectives that describes how you generally feel.
    _____ Happy
    _____ Anxious
    _____ Lonely
    _____ Confident

comparing opinions about police officers, judges, and politicians. Ratings can be made along a **visual continuum**, with one or more points along the continuum defined. **Fill-in questions** can require single words or whole phrases. The latter type of item generally is referred to as an **incomplete sentence blank**, a format for projective tests with simple stems designed to elicit important information about test-takers. **Checklists** provide lists of items, and subjects are required to check those that apply. They frequently are used on personality tests to obtain self-descriptions.

Professional test developers create more items than will be needed. They try out items on a sample, then conduct **item analysis**, statistical analysis of item characteristics, in order to select, refine, and discard items (Allen & Yen, 1979). Items also may be examined for gender or ethnic differences that suggest bias. Test instructions must be carefully worded to avoid ambiguity; the reading level of the test must be evaluated for its appropriateness; and scoring criteria must be developed and tested. Reliability

---

Box 6.4

Creating a Survey

1. Avoid compound items. (*Do you like swimming and tennis?* What about people who enjoy one sport, but not the other?)
2. For closed-ended questions, be sure to include all possible response categories. (This may require the use of an "Other" category.)
3. Avoid vague questions. (*Have you recently felt angry?* How recently? How angry?)
4. Avoid confusing wording. (*I rarely feel depressed. True False* Does a False answer mean that the person never feels depressed, often feels depressed, or always feels depressed?)
5. Sometimes you have to allow subjects to not answer questions. (*How old is your third child?*)
6. Avoid biased wording. (*Should parents punish children who don't clean their rooms?* vs. *Should parents beat children who don't clean their rooms?* vs. *Do you agree with experts that children who don't clean their rooms should receive some punishment?*)
7. Avoid questions that threaten or alienate your subjects. (*How prejudiced are you against hiring the handicapped? Do you become sexually aroused at X-rated movies?*)
8. Be careful of order effects, when the response to one question influences the response to a later question. (*Have you ever jaywalked?* followed by *Have you ever broken the law?*)
9. Consider specifying a time frame. (*How many aspirin tablets have you consumed in the last week?*)
10. Avoid negative wording. (*I am not a Communist. True False* Some subjects become confused about what their answers mean.)
11. Remember cultural differences. (*Have you ever consulted a priest over a personal problem?* What about a rabbi, minister, parson, elder, mullah, or other representative of a religion?)
12. Be able to justify each question on your survey. Don't just ask anything that you can think of, and don't ask for personal information unless there are legitimate research hypotheses involving it. Each item on the survey should perform a specific and important function.

---

and validity studies should be conducted. Appropriate norm group data must be obtained for norm-referenced interpretations of test scores, and cutoff scores for criterion-referenced tests should be empirically established.

Let's consider the creation of a simple survey. Box 6.4 gives some pointers. Beginners sometimes get overzealous and forget about the last suggestion. You should be able to explain the importance of every item in your survey. Examine the questions in the Watton Absolutely Sad Test Evaluation (WASTE). Try to identify any problems with these questions.

It is important to remember that the purpose of a test is to obtain variability. Items that all people answer in the same way provide no useful information and waste

---

THE WATTON ABSOLUTELY SAD TEST EVALUATION (WASTE)

---

1. Sex _____
2. Age _____ 0–20 _____ 21–40 _____ 40–60 _____ 60 or higher
3. How old were you when you stopped beating your dog? _____
4. Are your brothers and sisters married? _____ Yes _____ No
5. I am physically fit. _____ True _____ False
6. Have you recently seen a movie at a theater? _____ Yes _____ No
7. Are you not a vegetarian? _____ Yes _____ No
8. Oxymorons blight dialects. _____ True _____ False
9. My mother and father are still living. _____ True _____ False
10. How do you react when someone bullies you into doing something against your will that you really didn't want to do, but you do it anyway because that person has bugged you about doing it for so long and you feel that you might owe this person a favor for something he did for you in the past, but it pisses you off, anyway, because you didn't want to do it? _____

Some problems with the WASTE items:

1. This item may or may not work. Some test-takers can't resist answers such as "As often as I can" and "Yes."
2. Age is easily measured on the ratio level of measurement. Why reduce its measurement to an ordinal scale? In addition, the categories are not mutually exclusive. How would a 40- or 60-year-old person respond?
3. This is an old joke, but points out that test-writers sometimes make assumptions that are not warranted.
4. This is a compound question that assumes that the respondent has brothers and sisters and that all of them have the same marital status.
5. This is vague. How physically fit should one be to say True or False?
6. Another vague question. How recent is recent? A time frame should have been used.
7. Negatives should be avoided because they may confuse some subjects.
8. Vocabulary level appears a bit high for this question. It also does not make sense.
9. This is a compound question that assumes both parents have the same state. Questions about family members also are vague for some respondents. How would adopted children answer this? How would people with stepparents answer this?
10. This question is too long, too wordy, and too confusing.

---

everyone's time. This problem also exists for items that most people answer in the same way. Such items have little variability, so they contribute little to test score variance. However, if the test developer is trying to isolate a rare phenomenon, most test questions will have little variance. You might have to administer the test to thousands of cases before you can isolate someone with the rare syndrome the test is measuring. Such tests would have little value in research based on small random samples from the population.

Test-writers also should be aware that test-takers may have **response sets**, tendencies to respond to questions in stereotypical ways. Box 6.5 lists some response sets that might reduce a test's validity.

Box 6.5

Response Sets

Acquiescent	The tendency to answer "Yes" or "True" to questions.
Nay-saying	The tendency to answer "No" or "False" to questions.
Social desirability	The tendency to present oneself in a socially acceptable light.
Faking bad	The tendency to present oneself in a socially unacceptable light.
Extremity	The tendency to select extreme alternatives (e.g., "Never" or "Very strongly agree").
Cop-out	The tendency to select neutral alternatives (e.g., "Don't know").
Inconsistent	The tendency to give careless or capricious answers.
Fabrication	The tendency to "make up" answers to questions, even when unaware of the issues involved.

Box 6.6 is part of a survey developed by some students in a Research Methods class (Brown, Silvas, & Allen, 1993). They were interested in measuring religiosity, the importance of religion in subjects' lives, and they planned to correlate religiosity scores with scores on another survey. The students adapted items from two sources (Kemmick & Cardwell, 1980; Koenig, Kvale, & Ferrel, 1988) to create their own religiosity questionnaire. Analyze this survey using the information in Boxes 6.4 and 6.5.

Box 6.7 is another example of a data collection form developed by students. This student team wanted to measure student attitude toward a woman with AIDS, and they developed four different scenarios, in which Marsha, a fellow student, contracted AIDS through a blood transfusion, sex with her husband who had contracted AIDS through an extramarital affair, unsafe sex, or drug use with a dirty needle. Although the scenarios differed, the rest of the data collection form was constant. The survey measured two aspects of support for a woman with AIDS: relatively passive, private support indicated by signing a petition and relatively active, public support indicated by circulating a petition. Students were more likely to offer private than public support, and women students offered less support to Marsha when she was infected by risky behavior (Allen & Gutierrez, 1989). Notice that the research team avoided the cop-out response set by not including a "maybe" response category on the survey.

Spector (1992) provides a detailed description of the step-by-step development of the Work Locus of Control Scale, including his item analysis, reliability and validity studies, and norming. You might like to read his account for additional advice on test construction.

CHAPTER SUMMARY

Researchers frequently measure variables. Measurement is assigning numbers to objects in a systematic way to reflect properties of those objects. Systems of measurement

---

Box 6.6

Religiosity Scale

How often do you participate in the following? Please respond using the following scale:

   0 = I never do this.
   1 = I do this less than once a year.
   2 = I do this at least once a year.
   3 = I do this at least once a month.
   4 = I do this at least once a week.

_____   1. Attend formal religious services
_____   2. Attend religious-oriented programs (such as Bible Study)
_____   3. Practice religious rituals at home (such as prayer before meals)
_____   4. Contribute financially to a religious organization
_____   5. Watch or listen to religious programs on TV or radio
_____   6. Pray or worship privately
_____   7. Devote time to religious literature

---

have four properties (distinctiveness, ordinality, equal unit size, and absolute zero), and these properties determine the level of measurement (nominal, ordinal, interval, or ratio). Level of measurement affects which mathematical operations and which statistical analyses are reasonable for a set of scores, but strict rules may be broken because standard parametric statistics are robust.

All measurements must be reliable (stable) and valid (meaningful). Reliability can be assessed as test-retest reliability, parallel or alternative forms reliability, and internal consistency reliability. The latter includes split-half reliability and coefficient alpha. Validity can be assessed as content validity (including face and sampling validity), criterion-related validity, and construct validity. Reliability and validity are psychometric properties of tests that are empirically examined.

Psychologists use many types of measurement. They make physical measurements (such as GSR, EMG, and EEG recordings). They make behavioral observations that may be structured or unstructured. Behavioral excesses, behavioral deficits, and inappropriate behaviors are examined by behavioral therapists. Inter-rater reliability can be assessed for behavioral observations. Psychologists also use psychological tests and surveys. There are many different types of tests, including maximum or typical performance tests, aptitude and achievement tests, performance and nonperformance tests, objective and projective tests, group and individual tests, norm- and criterion-referenced tests, and state and trait tests.

Creating a test involves defining the test's purpose, writing items, and analyzing items. There are many types of items, including closed-ended and open-ended questions, dichotomous items, multiple-choice items, Likert scales, semantic differential items, items with visual continua, fill-in questions, incomplete sentence blanks, and checklists. Test-writers try to write items that avoid response sets. The finished test should be normed, and its reliability and validity should be examined.

Box 6.7

Example of a Scenario Questionnaire

Please read about the following situation and answer two questions about it.

Five years ago Marsha, currently a student at this campus, had an appendectomy, and she received a blood transfusion. Recently, she discovered that the blood transfusion gave her AIDS. Some students have asked the president to ban Marsha from campus. A group of students feel this is unfair and ask you to sign a petition that supports Marsha's right to attend school.

1. How likely are you to sign this petition supporting Marsha?
   _____ Definitely would sign it
   _____ Probably would sign it
   _____ Probably would not sign it
   _____ Definitely would not sign it

Extra petitions are available for those students who wish to volunteer to get more signatures supporting Marsha.

2. How likely are you to volunteer to circulate this petition supporting Marsha?
   _____ Definitely would volunteer
   _____ Probably would volunteer
   _____ Probably would not volunteer
   _____ Definitely would not volunteer

Key Concepts

absolute zero	distractor
achievement test	electroencephalogram (EEG)
acquiescent response set	electromyograph (EMG)
alternate forms reliability	equal unit size
aptitude test	extremity response set
behavioral deficit	fabrication response set
behavioral excess	face validity
checklist	faking bad response set
closed-ended question	fill-in question
coefficient alpha	galvanic skin response (GSR)
construct validity	group test
content validity	inappropriate behavior
cop-out response set	incomplete sentence blank
criterion-referenced test	inconsistent response set
criterion-related validity	individual test
dichotomous item	internal consistency reliability
distinctiveness	interval level of measurement

interrater reliability	psychometrics
item analysis	ratio level of measurement
levels of measurement	reliability
Likert scale	response set
maximum performance test	robust statistic
measurement	sampling validity
multiple-choice item	semantic differential item
nay-saying response set	social desirability response set
nominal level of measurement	social distance scale
nonperformance test	Spearman rank-order correlation
norm-referenced test	coefficient
objective test	split-half reliability
open-ended question	state (vs. trait)
ordinal level of measurement	structured observations
ordinality	test-retest reliability
parallel forms reliability	trait
participant observation study	typical performance test
performance test	unstructured observations
polygraph	validity
projective test	visual continuum

Review Questions

1. What is the level of measurement for each of these measurements?

   a. At a dog show, Chihuahuas are "1," collies are "2," and bulldogs are "3."

   b. The newspaper reports that the temperature was 68 degrees yesterday.

   c. Carlos has a score of 7 on the Attitude Toward Martians scale.

   d. Jane has $2.35 in her purse.

2. Jason has two speeding tickets, and Shawn has four speeding tickets. Jason claims that he is twice as safe a driver as Shawn, and Shawn claims that he drives twice as fast as Jason. Describe the level of measurement of their data and the appropriateness of their conclusions.

3. We can examine relationships between two variables with chi square tests, Pearson correlations, and Spearman correlations. What is the level of measurement of data that are appropriately examined using each of these techniques?

4. The Yen Appetite Test (YAT) has a five-week test-retest reliability of .30 and a parallel forms reliability of .80. Its coefficient alpha is .90. Is this acceptable reliability if the YAT measures a trait? Is this acceptable reliability if the YAT measures a state?

5. Applicants claim the city's employment screening test for gardeners is unfair because it places too much emphasis on the names of esoteric flowers and too little emphasis on actual skills required in the job (such as planting and pruning trees). What type of validity is being questioned?

6. A company uses the Abbott Programming Test to decide which computer programmers to hire. What type of validity is most important for this use of the test?

7. a. Create a set of items for a Shyness test. Use at least five different item formats from Box 6.3 and label the format of each of your items.

    b. Describe two construct validity studies that could be conducted to analyze your Shyness test. What other psychometric properties should be examined?

8. You want to classify children as pre- or post-puberty. What physical characteristics could you measure to determine this classification? Briefly describe the reliability and validity of the measures you would use.

9. You want to better understand dating behaviors in American adolescents. How could you do this using unstructured observations? How could you do this using structured observations?

10. A team of behavioral therapists is interested in studying eating disorders. What types of behavioral observations would they make?

11. Consider the final exam you took in your Introductory Psychology course. Was it a test of maximum or typical performance? Was it an aptitude or achievement test? Was it a performance or nonperformance test? Was it a group or individual test?

12. Dr. Jones grades student exams on the following scale: 0–59% = F, 60–69% = D, 70–79% = C, 80–89% = B, and 90–100% = A. Dr. Smith grades exams on a curve. The top 10 percent of students receive an A, the next 20 percent receive a B, the next 40 percent receive a C, the next 20 percent receive a D, and the bottom 10 percent receive an F. Are they using norm-referenced or criterion-referenced interpretations?

13. What response sets could reduce the validity of the Attitude Toward Martians Scale? Briefly explain your answer.

14. Create two tests with scenarios created to evaluate attitudes toward Martians. Describe how your tests will be used to uncover information about attitudes.

Research Planning

Suppose one of your classmates, Nelson, asked a research question: Is there a relationship between the onset of puberty and conflicts with parents? He conducted a literature review that made him aware of earlier research findings, and he developed criteria for measuring his two variables. He decided to measure the onset of puberty by examining growth spurts and to measure conflict level by applying a set of criteria (child refuses to cooperate in family activities, child challenges parental authority, and so on).

Nelson must make many more decisions. How many subjects will he study? How will he obtain his sample? He could measure the same group of families twice: before and after the child reaches puberty. He could compare two sets of families, matched except for the puberty status of the child. He could examine case records of families seen by family therapists or school counselors. He could sample adults and ask them to remember their age of puberty and changes in their relationships with parents. Many studies could be designed to answer his research question.

The operational definitions for his variables must be fully developed. If he opts to study children and their parents, he may measure family conflict by interviews, surveys, or family observations. If he examines case records, he must develop ways to analyze data in the files. If he examines adults instead of families, he probably will develop a survey or interview to collect self-reports of puberty age and conflict level.

Researchers must make many decisions, and they must understand the implications of their decisions in order to select effective strategies. Their goal is to select strategies and measures that allow them to uncover the truth about research questions. In this chapter we will consider some general factors that affect research planning.

SAMPLING STRATEGIES

Imagine a room with twenty students. If we measure each student's extraversion, we can calculate the mean, a parameter for this small population. But what if we have only enough time to measure six students? If we test the six who are most extraverted, the sample mean will overestimate the population mean. If we test the six who are least extraverted, the sample mean will underestimate the population mean. These samples yield biased estimates of the parameter, so they are **biased samples**. In contrast is a **representative sample**, selected to yield an unbiased estimate because the sample adequately represents the population. What is the best strategy for picking a six-student representative sample?

On the assumption that each of the twenty students is willing to be tested, should we select the first six who volunteer, the six who sit in the front or back row, the six who are available to be tested at 8 A.M. on Tuesday, or six students selected at random? The answer, of course, is to select a random sample. A **random sample** is drawn in such a way that each element in the population is just as likely to be included. For this study, an element is a student. For other studies, elements may be families, corporations, social clubs, cities, or nations. Random samples are likely to be representative samples, especially if they are large enough that the full range of possible scores are found. Random sampling is the basis for **probability sampling**, using random selection to avoid bias and to obtain representative samples.

What if we have another piece of information? The set of twenty students is made up of two groups; half are members of social clubs known to attract extraverts and half are attending workshops designed to reduce shyness. Our sample is more likely to be representative if we include three students selected at random from each of the two groups. This is a stratified random sample. A **stratified sample** has a specified percentage from each target group. For example, we could specify that 50 percent of the sample will be social club members and 50 percent will be students in the shyness workshop. A **stratified random sample** is a stratified sample composed of subjects selected at random from each group.

Now imagine our population is larger. Rather than confining our interest to twenty students, we are interested in the population of all registered university students in the United States. Obtaining a random sample would be difficult. In fact, just obtaining a list of our population would be a challenge. Assuming that we have the cooperation of university personnel and students, however, we could pick three states representing different areas of the country, select two universities within each state, and then study twenty students from each of the six universities. This is **multi-stage sampling**, in which the final sample is obtained through a series of selection decisions that eliminate potential subjects. This example had three stages: picking the states, picking the campuses, and picking the students.

What if our goal is to select a sample of people from the New York City phonebook? We could obtain a random sample by putting all the names in a hat and drawing our sample or by using a table of random numbers (the first few digits of the random number would identify the page of the book, the next digits would identify the person on the page to be included in the sample). But it would be easier to select one page position at random (e.g., the eighth name in the second column), then take that name from every fiftieth page of the phonebook. Because we picked the page position at random, we are unlikely to generate a biased sample in this way. **Systematic samples** are selected through a systematic process; they are **systematic random samples** if the process follows an original random selection.

Much research is done in intact classrooms, perhaps sections of Introductory Psychology, or by using data from local clinics. **Convenience samples** are selected because access is convenient. Convenience samples are examples of **nonprobability sampling** because subjects are not selected by a random process. Another type of nonprobability sample is a **purposive sample** in which available subjects who meet a specific criterion are included. For example, psychologists may want to study EEG recordings among people with schizophrenia and may test every cooperative person with schizophrenia who is available. Only subjects with a diagnosis of schizophrenia are included. Perhaps these psychologists want to study ten people with schizophrenia and ten people with bipolar disorder. If they test the first ten people of each type and turn away subsequent potential subjects, they are using **quota sampling**, in which subjects in specified groups are added to the sample until prespecified quotas are met. Samples obtained through nonprobability sampling methods may or may not be biased.

Within-subject and between-group variables were contrasted in Chapter 5. Within-subject variables are created by repeated measures or matching; and the effects of between-group variables are examined by comparing groups of subjects that are on different levels. The sampling designs are different. Say we are studying the effects of practice on typing speed. We could study practice as a within-subject variable by repeatedly measuring a group of typing students (measuring their typing speed in the first, sixth, and sixteenth week of the semester), or we could study practice as a between-group variable by comparing the typing speed of students who practice a few minutes a week with the speed of students who practice a few hours a week. For the first design we recruit one sample of subjects and measure them repeatedly; for the second design we select samples from distinct groups of subjects who are at different levels of our independent variable. This could be done through stratified, purposive, or quota sampling.

Special sampling strategies are used when age or time is the independent variable. For example, a developmental psychologist may want to examine the effect of age on abstract reasoning. Two basic strategies exist: cross-sectional and longitudinal designs. For **cross-sectional sampling**, stratified samples are selected from designated age groups, and age is studied as a between-group variable. The researchers may compare the abstract reasoning of twenty three-year-olds, twenty four-year-olds, twenty five-year-olds, and so on. **Longitudinal sampling** involves repeatedly measuring a single sample of subjects so the effect of age or time can be examined. For example, a single sample of children would be measured repeatedly in a longitudinal study, with age studied as a within-subject variable. The same group of children would be tested at age three, four, five, and so on. Each child would be tested annually for the course of the study.

Trend and cohort studies are used to study the effect of time. **Trend studies** compare different samples of the population that are measured at different times in order

---

Box 7.1

Sampling Strategies

Cohort sampling: A subset (cohort) of the population is sampled at different times so the effect of time can be examined.

Convenience sampling: The sample is selected because access is convenient.

Cross-sectional sampling: Stratified samples are selected from designated age groups so the effect of age can be examined.

Longitudinal sampling: A single sample of subjects is measured repeatedly so the effect of age or time can be examined.

Multi-stage sampling: The sample is selected through a series of decisions that eliminate groups of potential subjects.

Nonprobability sampling: Subjects are not selected by a random process.

Probability sampling: Random selection is used to avoid bias and to obtain a representative sample.

Purposive sampling: The sample is formed by including available subjects who meet a specific criterion.

Quota sampling: Subjects in specified groups are added to the sample until specific quotas are met. Sampling is not random.

Random sampling: The sample is drawn in such a way that each element in the population is just as likely to be included.

Stratified random sampling: The sample is randomly selected from target groups and is composed of a specified percentage of subjects from each target group.

Stratified sampling: The sample is selected to have a specified percentage from each target group.

Systematic random sampling: The sample is selected through a systematic process that follows an initial random selection.

Systematic sampling: The sample is selected through a systematic process.

Trend sampling: Different samples of the population are measured at different times so the effect of time can be examined.

---

to identify changes over time. For example, a trend study could be used to examine changes in drug use or sexual behavior in college students over a fifty-year period by comparing data from college samples drawn at different times. Some data were collected in 1930, other data were collected in 1940, and so on. A **cohort study** identifies a **cohort**, a subset of the population with an identifiable characteristic, and analyzes this cohort over time by taking different samples. For example, post-traumatic stress symptoms of Viet Nam veterans may be examined in 1975 from one sample, in 1980 from another sample, and in 1985 from a third sample. If each sample is representative of the cohort of Viet Nam veterans, inferences about the effect of time on the cohort can be made.

The various sampling strategies are summarized in Box 7.1. To practice these concepts, identify the sampling strategies in the studies described in Box 7.2.

POWER CONSIDERATIONS IN RESEARCH PLANNING

How many subjects should be included in the sample? For most studies one case is too few and the whole population is too many. Some data collection is relatively inexpen-

---

Box 7.2

Sampling Examples

Label the sampling strategy used in each of the following studies. Use the most descriptive name for the sampling technique, e.g., *convenience sampling* rather than *nonprobability sampling*. Answers are at the bottom.

1. A team selects homes for a door-to-door survey by picking four neighborhoods, six blocks in each neighborhood, and three homes in each block.
2. Children who were first measured in 1950 are reexamined in 1960 and 1970.
3. Subjects for a study at a university are randomly selected from each of its three schools, with their representation proportional to the enrollment in the three schools.
4. A university administers a battery of personality tests to each year's incoming doctoral students to examine changes in student characteristics.
5. A computer randomly picks 100 people from a list of all registered voters in the community.
6. An Alzheimer's researcher gives a test battery to volunteers at a local senior citizen's center.

7. The sample includes the first twelve men and the first twelve women who volunteer at a PTA meeting.
8. Doctors refer newborn deaf infants to researchers for their study.
9. The third caller to a radio talk show and every tenth caller thereafter are included in the sample. (The third caller was picked through a random process.)
10. Japanese researchers annually examine the health records of samples of people born in 1945. Different samples are studied each year.
11. The physical development of groups of 10-, 20-, and 30-year-olds is compared.

Type of Sampling

1. Multi-stage
2. Longitudinal
3. Stratified random
4. Trend
5. Random
6. Convenience
7. Quota
8. Purposive
9. Systematic random
10. Cohort
11. Cross-sectional

---

sive, such as studies that mail surveys to national samples; but some data collection is very expensive, such as studies that involve individual testing by highly trained professionals or lengthy interventions, such as applications of long-term therapy. Sampling considerations must be made with respect to two criteria: representativeness and power. A huge, biased sample may not lead to valid conclusions about the population. A moderately sized, representative sample may be much more desirable.

As described in Chapter 5, power is the probability of correctly rejecting the null hypothesis. Researchers want to design studies that are likely to uncover the truth. They want to have tests with low alpha and high power. Low alpha protects against Type I error; high power protects against Type II error.

Researchers generally want significant results, so they require powerful studies. Power is affected by many aspects of the study, including effect size, sample size, alpha, the choice of one- or two-tailed tests, the choice of between-group or within-subject variables, the relative sizes of groups being compared, the choice of statistical technique, and the precision of the study.

Effect Size

As defined in Chapter 5, effect size is how strongly the independent variable influences the dependent variable, or the strength of the relationship between the variables. For example, gender has a larger effect size when men and women are compared on height than when they are compared on intelligence; and the relationship between height and weight is stronger than the relationship between height and intelligence. If there is a larger effect size and we calculate a statistical test on the data, we expect our groups to be more different or our variables to be more strongly related, so a larger effect size makes extreme outcomes of the test statistic more likely. This increases the chance of rejecting the null hypothesis, so it increases power. Research with larger effect sizes has more power than research with smaller effect sizes.

If researchers are planning a study that lacks sufficient power, they may be able to increase power by increasing effect size. For example, if they want to prove that different birds lay eggs of different sizes, they can compare chickens to ducks (a small effect size) or they can compare hummingbirds to ostriches (a large effect size). The latter study would be more powerful. A psychologist who wants to demonstrate that a new type of therapy is effective could have a large effect size by comparing clients treated for a long time with the new therapy to untreated subjects. This would be more powerful than comparing clients barely exposed to the therapy with untreated subjects or comparing subjects treated under the new therapy with subjects given other types of effective treatment. Of course, the results would be interpreted differently for each of these studies, but researchers who want to examine something new should begin by using large effect sizes to avoid finding nonsignificant results that could lead to the abandonment of promising lines of research.

Sample Size

Statistics tend to be more stable for larger samples. For example, a sample mean generally would be quite unstable for samples of 2 or 3 subjects, but would be more stable for samples of 200 or 300 subjects. Increasing the sample size allows us to make more precise estimates of parameters, making it more likely that we will reject the null hypothesis when relationships exist. This is power, so power is higher when larger samples are used. In general, research with very small samples lacks power unless the effect size is very strong. Researchers can have sufficient power with relatively small samples if they are studying large effect sizes, but must use larger samples when they are studying small, subtle effects. Research with very large sample sizes may even have too much power. For example, studies using national census data may have millions of subjects. They may uncover statistically significant, trivial results.

Alpha

Generally, researchers are conservative; they don't allow the risk of a Type I error to exceed .05. There may be times, however, when power is so important that increasing alpha is justified. This occurs when a Type II error is very bad, and increasing the risk of a Type I error is less serious. For example, a research team is conducting a pilot study on a new therapy for severe depression. Their conclusion will determine if the new treatment will be dropped or studied further. Their null hypothesis is that the therapy is not effective, and the alternative hypothesis is that the therapy is effective. Research subjects may be difficult to obtain and expensive to treat, so increasing the sample size or effect size may not be feasible ways to increase power. The researchers may decide to use an alpha of .10, rather than an alpha of .05. This increased level of alpha makes rejecting the null hypothesis more likely, which increases power. Researchers seldom increase alpha because the .05 convention is so strong, but this strategy may sometimes be justified. Researchers who increase alpha must recognize that they are increasing the risk of a Type I error, making their test less conservative and more likely to result in a false claim that the alternative hypothesis is true.

One- and Two-Tailed Tests

A one-tailed test, when feasible, is more powerful than a two-tailed test for the same alpha because the rejection region is formed differently. The two-tailed test must split alpha in half, placing half of alpha in each tail. The effect of splitting the alpha between two tails is to use a smaller alpha on each side, and smaller alphas mean reduced power. A one-tailed test has more power than a two-tailed test because it is equivalent to having a higher alpha in the appropriate tail.

Why don't researchers always do one-tailed tests? Self-protection. If the actual result occurs at the wrong tail, the one-tailed test will not reject the null hypothesis. Two-tailed tests are used when results could go in either direction; one-tailed tests are used when results could occur only in one direction. For example, if a new teaching technique could result in superior or inferior performance, its effectiveness should be examined with a two-tailed test. If it is inconceivable that the new technique could be worse than the old technique, the test could be conducted with a directional hypothesis and a one-tailed test.

Researchers generally have more power when they can justify directional hypotheses, but they risk failing to discover that the opposite of their expectations actually occurred. One-tailed tests can be justified by theory, logic, or the history of results documented in the literature review. For example, if a new teaching method includes all the techniques in the old method, plus some extra practice, it is inconceivable that students could learn less under the new method than under the old method, so a directional hypothesis would be reasonable.

Between-Group and Within-Subject Variables

Variables such as age, time, and the amount of practice can be studied as between-group or within-subject variables. Experimenters who expose subjects to various stimuli also can use between-group or within-subject designs. For example, researchers studying the effect of illumination on visual acuity could test different subjects at each illumination level (a between-group design) or could examine each subject at every level (a within-subject design). The choice can affect the study's power. Within-subject designs are more powerful if there are large differences between subjects but small differences within subjects.

Suppose we are analyzing the effect of age on vocabulary size. We could study age as a within-subject variable using a longitudinal design, or we could study age as a between-group variable using a cross-sectional design. To decide which design would be more powerful, we consider the variability of vocabulary scores. Say the standard deviation of vocabulary scores is 250 words for people of the same age (differences between subjects), but the standard deviation is only 50 words when vocabulary is measured in the same subject over the span of the study (within-subject variability). In this case, a longitudinal design would be more powerful.

Larger within-subject variability reduces the power superiority of within-subject designs. One easy way to check for within-subject consistency is to correlate the paired scores. Higher correlations suggest higher within-subject consistency and higher power for within-subject designs.

Although within-subject designs may be more powerful, they may be inconvenient, time-consuming, and expensive. For example, a lifespan longitudinal study requires repeated subject cooperation and contact for decades. In addition, repeatedly measuring the same subjects may affect their behavior, invalidating research conclusions.

Relative Group Size

Researchers using between-group variables compare groups of subjects measured at each level. In general, the best power is attained for **balanced designs** in which the number of subjects at each level is the same. For example, if we compare men to women by examining 97 men and 3 women, the male mean is measured with more precision than the female mean. The comparison of the two means is weakened because the female mean is imprecise. If 100 subjects will be tested, it is more powerful to examine 50 men and 50 women, so that both means are adequately measured. The use of unequal group sizes also can complicate the interpretation of analysis of variance results when there are interactions. If the effect of one variable depends on another variable and these effects are not evenly distributed, results can be misleading. This will be discussed in more detail in Chapter 13.

Sometimes researchers cannot balance group sizes. For example, epidemiological studies of random samples collected to compare rare groups of individuals to others must include many subjects. Many subjects must be examined to get information on the few people with the rare condition and to offset the weak power associated with the enormous inequality in group size. Purposive sampling strategies, with a quota on non-rare subjects, may allow the researcher to avoid some of these problems, but this requires an adequate referral network to obtain a reasonable sample of those with the rare condition.

Choice of Statistical Technique

There are a variety of statistical techniques that can be used to analyze a set of data, and these techniques differ in power. In general, parametric tests are more powerful than nonparametric tests, so they should be used when appropriate. The test for a main effect in a multi-way analysis of variance is more powerful than a corresponding t test if its error term is smaller, which occurs when the independent variables explain much of the variance in the dependent variable. A complete discussion of this topic is beyond the scope of this book, but you should be alert to information on the relative power of tests you learn in subsequent courses.

Box 7.3

Ways to Increase the Power of a Study

1. Increase the effect size.
2. Increase the sample size.
3. Increase alpha.
4. Switch from two-tailed tests to one-tailed tests.
5. Switch from between-group to within-subject variables (or vice versa).
6. Have equal sample sizes for each level of the independent variable.
7. Switch to more powerful statistical tests.
8. Increase the precision of the study.

Precision of the Study

Sloppy research yields sloppy results. Precise research yields precise results. Researchers who do not carefully control independent variables or who are unreliable in their measurement of variables are less likely to reject the null hypothesis because their sloppiness masks the effect being examined. Researchers try to be precise in order to have greater power to detect true alternative hypotheses.

Powerful research requires reliable measurements. Unreliable data have too much random variability. Imagine we want to compare heights of men and women, and we have two ways to measure height. We can use the instrument available in physicians' offices, place a scaled bar on top of subjects' heads, and carefully measure subjects with their shoes off; or we can take a one-foot ruler and, placing the ruler next to subjects' bodies, estimate their height. The former technique would be much more reliable. Scores would be more stable. Our *t* test comparing men and women would be more powerful because of greater precision of measurement. This is one reason reliability of measurement is important to researchers.

Ways to Increase the Power of a Study

Eight ways to increase power are summarized in Box 7.3. Researchers concerned about power may use one or all of these techniques. Sometimes a technique is not appropriate. For example, increasing the sample size may be impossible for a purposive sample composed of rare individuals, and alternative effect sizes may be unavailable. However, each possibility should be considered. The correct time to worry about power is when the study is being planned, not after nonsignificant results are found. Studies with insufficient power should not be conducted.

CHOOSING A SAMPLE SIZE

How many subjects is enough? Table 7.1 gives the approximate sample size needed for several basic types of studies. Calculations were based on formulas presented by Kraemer and Thiemann (1987) and were rounded off to the nearest five subjects, with

TABLE 7.1 APPROXIMATE TOTAL SAMPLE SIZE NECESSARY FOR DESIRED POWER

	DESIRED POWER											
	.90				.70				.50			
Number of Tails	2	2	1	1	2	2	1	1	2	2	1	1
Alpha	.05	.01	.05	.01	.05	.01	.05	.01	.05	.01	.05	.01
Type of Test **Size of Effect**												
One-sample *t*												
Small	270	385	220	335	160	250	125	210	100	175	70	140
Medium	45	65	40	60	30	45	20	45	20	30	15	25
Large	20	30	20	25	15	20	10	20	10	15	10	15
Independent groups *t* (two groups of equal size)												
Small	1045	1480	855	1295	615	960	470	810	385	665	270	540
Medium	180	250	145	220	105	160	80	140	65	110	50	95
Large	75	100	60	90	45	70	35	60	30	45	20	40
Independent groups *t* (one group four times the size of the other)												
Small	1640	2320	1335	2030	965	1500	735	1270	600	1035	425	845
Medium	260	365	210	320	155	235	120	200	95	165	70	135
Large	110	155	90	135	65	100	50	85	40	70	30	60
Dependent sampling *t* (correlation between scores is .20)												
Small	405	575	330	500	240	370	185	315	150	255	105	210
Medium	70	100	60	90	45	65	35	60	25	45	20	40
Large	35	45	30	40	20	30	15	25	15	20	10	20
Dependent sampling *t* (correlation between scores is .80)												
Small	110	160	90	140	65	105	50	85	45	70	30	60
Medium	20	30	20	30	15	20	10	20	10	15	10	15
Large	15	15	10	15	10	10	10	10	10	10	10	10
Correlation coefficient												
Small	260	365	210	320	155	235	120	200	95	165	70	135
Medium	40	55	30	45	25	35	20	30	15	25	10	20
Large	10	15	10	15	10	10	10	10	10	10	10	10

a minimum of ten subjects required for any study. Effect sizes were classified as small, medium, or large, as suggested by Cohen (1977). Small mean differences are 20 percent of a standard deviation, medium differences are half a standard deviation, and large differences are 80 percent of a standard deviation. For example, Wechsler IQ scores have a standard deviation of 15. A small difference would be 3 points (.2 × 15 = 3), a medium difference would be 7.5 points (.5 × 15 = 7.5), and a large difference would be 12 points (.8 × 15 = 12).

Six sets of analyses are summarized in the table. The one-sample *t* test is used to compare a sample mean to a known population mean. For example, this test would be used to see whether children given vitamins have higher-than-average IQs. The population mean is 100. If the IQs of children given vitamins average 103, vitamins have a small effect; averages of 107.5 and 112 are medium and large effects, respectively. The independent groups *t* test is used to compare the means of two separate groups. Two cases are summarized in the table: a balanced design in which the two samples are the same size, and a design in which one sample is four times as large as the other sample. The table gives the total number of subjects, i.e., the number of subjects in *both* groups. The dependent sampling *t* test is used to compare two means for a within-subject variable, such as data collected before and after some intervention. Two cases are summarized in the table: one in which the two sets of scores correlate .20 and one in which they correlate .80. The table gives the total number of subjects, and matched subjects are counted as one person. The independent groups *t* test and dependent sampling *t* test compare two means. If the means are IQ scores, the effect is small if the two means differ by 3 points, medium if they differ by 7.5 points, and large if they differ by 12 points.

The last set of entries in the table is for a test of the significance of a Pearson product-moment correlation coefficient, to see if the correlation is significantly different from zero. Correlations of .20, .50, and .80 were arbitrarily considered small, medium, and large. The squared correlation is the proportion of variance in one variable accounted for by the other. Small, medium, and large correlations, as defined for Table 7.1, occur when one variable accounts for 4 percent, 25 percent, or 64 percent of the variance in the other, respectively.

Minimal sample sizes to achieve powers of .90, .70, and .50 are provided for one- and two-tailed tests using alphas of .01 and .05 for each of the three effect sizes. Numbers are approximate because they are based on rounding and estimating values within tables. Studies conducted with a power of .50 have a 50 percent chance of rejecting the null hypothesis when the alternative hypothesis is true. Remember that the alternative hypothesis is based on the research hypothesis, and researchers hope to find significant results supporting research hypotheses. Entries in the .50 power columns can be considered minimum sample sizes because smaller samples would have powers below .50. Usually researchers want to have powers above .70, and powers in the .90s make accurate conclusions about true research hypotheses quite likely. Powers less than .50 are unreasonable because research conclusions are more often wrong than correct when the alternative hypothesis is true.

Use the appropriate statistical procedure, effect size, power level, test direction (one- or two-tailed), and alpha to estimate the required sample size. For example, a one-sample *t* test with a one-tailed alpha of .05 requires a sample size of 20 in order to have a power of .70 for a medium effect size, but this study requires 125 subjects if the effect size is small. Researchers who cannot estimate effect sizes may decide to be conservative by assuming that effect sizes are small when planning sample size requirements. This estimate may be reevaluated after a pilot study is conducted.

We can use Table 7.1 to demonstrate points made in previous discussions of power. Compare corresponding entries for small, medium, and large effect sizes. Studies with larger effect sizes require fewer subjects because large effect sizes are associated with more powerful tests. Compare the entries in corresponding columns for alphas of .05 and .01. Smaller samples are required for alphas of .05 because larger alphas are associated with more powerful tests. Compare corresponding entries for one- and two-tailed tests. One-tailed tests require fewer subjects because one-tailed tests are more powerful. Compare corresponding entries for the two independent-groups *t* tests.

Balanced designs, with the same number of subjects in each group, require fewer subjects, because balanced designs are more powerful. Compare corresponding entries for the two dependent-sampling t tests. Fewer subjects are required when the correlation between measurements is higher because this implies higher within-subject consistency and more power. Compare corresponding entries for the independent-groups and dependent-sampling t tests. Even when the two scores correlate only .20, the use of a within-subject variable instead of a between-group variable reduces the required number of subjects, and this advantage is even stronger when the two scores correlate more highly.

Table 7.1 indicates that there is no magic number for the ideal number of subjects for all studies. The appropriate number depends on a complex interaction of a number of factors, including the type of independent variables (between-group or within-subject), effect size, desired power, type of test (one- or two-tailed), relative number of subjects in each group, correlations between measurements, and alpha level. Kraemer and Thiemann (1987) provide instructions for calculating the required sample sizes for other tests and for powers other than those reported here.

PLANNING VALID RESEARCH

Designing studies with low alpha and high power is one aspect of research planning. However, low alpha and high power do not guarantee that research conclusions are valid. Researchers try to design and to conduct studies that lead to unambiguous conclusions about causal relationships. They are aware of threats to validity; and they introduce, if possible, techniques to reduce or eliminate the risk of making errors. Many factors can threaten the validity of a study, and these threats may operate singly or together to undermine the accuracy of research conclusions.

Research validity concerns the accuracy of research conclusions. Cook and Campbell (1979) defined four types of research validity for experiments, and they correspond to four questions asked by researchers.

1.   *Are there relationships among variables in the experiment?* Significant results from statistical analyses lead to the conclusion that variables are significantly related, and nonsignificant results lead to the conclusion that variables are not significantly related. If depression and self-esteem are related, a study of these variables should result in the conclusion that they are significantly related; if depression and intelligence are unrelated, a study of these variables should result in the conclusion that they are not significantly related. If these results occur, Type I and Type II errors have been avoided. Experiments have **statistical validity** if statistical evidence leads to accurate conclusions about relationships.

2.   *Did changes in the independent variable cause changes in the dependent variable?* If researchers find more attitude change in the cognitive dissonance condition than in a control condition, was the observed attitude change caused by the experimental manipulation or some other variable, such as subtle cues offered by researchers? Experiments have **internal validity** if changes in the independent variables cause observable changes in dependent variables.

3.   *Are causal inferences about underlying theoretical constructs accurate?* If children of professional parents have higher career aspirations than children of working-class

parents, is the underlying relationship between imitation and modeling, between ambition and reinforcement contingencies, or between some other pair of theoretical constructs? Experiments have **construct validity for causal conclusions** if underlying theoretical constructs for causes and effects are identified correctly. We learned about the construct validity of tests in the measurement chapter. Construct validity for causal conclusions will not occur if measurements are invalid.

4. *Can causal conclusions be accurately generalized to other situations?* For example, if researchers are studying American children and find that partial reinforcement schedules lead to slower extinction than continuous reinforcement schedules, will these results be found for American adults? Would the same results be found among Asian children or at different times? Experiments have **external validity** if causal conclusions generalize to other subjects, settings, and times.

Suppose a research team is studying gender differences in aggression. They observe children on a playground and record all aggressive acts on a checklist (e.g., hitting or grabbing a ball from another child), and they find that boys are more aggressive. This is a quasi-experiment because researchers did not randomly assign children to be girls or boys. The experiment would have statistical validity if gender and aggression really are related. To evaluate the internal validity of this study, we ask if gender caused boys to be more aggressive than girls. Could other factors explain the results? Perhaps more girls in the study were sensitive to adult observers' opinions, so they behaved unusually well during the study. Perhaps more boys in the study became aggressive because they were being observed; they wanted to show off. Perhaps the observers had biases that led them to ignore aggression in girls and to notice aggression in boys. These possibilities threaten the internal validity of this study's conclusion because they identify different causal variables: sensitivity to adults' opinions, showing off, and observer bias.

The causal conclusions have construct validity if the underlying theoretical constructs are measured accurately. We must consider the construct validity of the cause and of the effect. It is difficult to determine what theoretical construct gender represents. The theoretical construct causing the differences in aggression might be a genetic factor, or it might be some factor related to differential socialization of girls and boys. It is possible that results were caused by researchers' gender-based biases; researchers may have responded differently to male and female subjects. The independent variable is gender, but the theoretical construct causing the gender difference may be identified incorrectly, diminishing the conclusion's construct validity. The effect in this study is aggression. Does the checklist accurately measure aggression? Perhaps the checklist included items reflecting assertiveness, rather than aggression, threatening the conclusion's construct validity.

We also ask if results can be generalized to other situations. Was the sample biased, containing unusually saintly girls and devilish boys? Would results generalize to other types of children in different settings or to children studied at different times? If not, the external validity of the study is weak.

Let's consider a second example, a true experiment. If you have visited a zoo, you may have noticed that some caged animals pace. They repeatedly retrace the same walking pattern. A research team may theorize that pacing reduces tension. In order to test the theory that tension causes pacing, they randomly select animals and tease them by holding tempting foods outside their cages. They find that teased animals pace more than animals that have not been teased, so evidence supports their theory. This study would have statistical validity if the two variables actually are related. It would have internal validity if teasing the animals caused the pacing. If some other variable caused the pacing, the internal validity is threatened. For example, if teased animals were more bored than unteased animals, boredom may have caused increased pacing. The construct validity for causal conclusions would be high if the observed relationship actually concerned the theoretical constructs of tension (the cause) and tension reduction (the effect). If boredom caused the pacing, the theoretical constructs for the cause and the effect were incorrectly identified. The cause was boredom, and the effect was to increase, rather than to decrease tension. The study has external validity if results generalize to other situations. Do animals in the wild show increased pacing when tensions are high? Do children show more repetitive behaviors when they're under stress?

Notice that the four types of validity are not independent. For example, many factors that threaten internal validity also threaten construct validity for causal conclusions. If the examined variables are not causally related in ways specified by the theory, it is unlikely that the theoretical constructs underlying the relationship have been correctly identified. Statistical validity and internal validity will be discussed more fully in Chapter 8; and construct validity for causal conclusions and external validity will be discussed more fully in Chapter 9.

THE USE OF COMPUTERS IN RESEARCH

Research planning may involve anticipating the use of computers. Just twenty or twenty-five years ago, researchers relied on slide rules, desktop manual calculators, and cherished computer time on giant computers that were carefully maintained in controlled environments. They keypunched decks of computer cards and learned to program data collection computers in binary codes. The giant computers of the past had less capacity than today's notebook computers, which are so compact and sturdy that they can be carried in a suitcase or briefcase.

Computers have revolutionized how academics and researchers conduct their business. *Computer Use in Psychology* (Stoloff & Couch, 1992) lists nearly 900 programs that are specifically designed for psychologists, including academic, clinical, testing, and research programs. Academic programs include computer simulations of psychological phenomena that faculty can assign as homework or use as in-class demonstrations. Most clinical programs fall into one of two categories: teaching modules for rehabilitating clients with brain injuries and programs that offer career guidance. No human could be as patient, tolerant, and ever-present as a computer that drills rehabilitation clients through tedious exercises necessary to recover functioning. Testing programs administer and score a variety of psychological tests, including most of the tests frequently used by professional psychologists. Research programs are available that control laboratory equipment and collect data, that analyze data using general procedures (such as *t* tests), and that offer special analyses (such as survey analysis).

There are two aspects of any computer work: hardware and software. **Hardware** is the machinery: the computer, printer, and other devices. **Software** is the programming, such as programs that do word processing, graphics, or data analysis. Hardware and software must be **compatible**; the software must work on the hardware being used. For example, a program written for one brand of computer may not run on another. Large computers that are shared by many users are **mainframe computers**, and small computers that generally have one user are **personal computers**. **Midsize computers** have characteristics of both large and small computers. Personal, midsize, and mainframe computers may be **networked** so that information can be electronically exchanged between machines.

Each computer has an **operating system**, the software that allows the user to read and save files and to activate specific software packages. **Software packages** perform specific functions, such as word processing; they generally are purchased from software developers, such as Microsoft or Claris. Many software development companies exist, and the industry is constantly changing. Most psychological programs are **interactive**, the user and computer have an ongoing dialog of questions, answers, and instructions.

The manuscript for this book was prepared using the software package Microsoft WORD, and many competing word processing software packages exist. Each document is a **file**; for example, the text of each chapter in this book was stored as a separate file. Each file has a unique **file name**, an identifier that allows the user to locate files to edit, use, or print them. For example, the file name for this chapter was *Ch. 7 Research Planning*. Other files for this book were called *Box 7.1, Table 5.3*, and so on.

Most computers and software are **user-friendly**, relatively simple for the novice to use. This is in contrast to earlier computers and computer programs that required extensive training. Programs frequently have built-in **Help functions**, which serve as manuals for users with questions. If you forget how to do some operation, you can turn to the Help function for advice and examples. Each computer and software package has its own idiosyncrasies, but once you have mastered any computer program, you will find other computers and programs easier to learn. Each application is like a game, such as Monopoly. You just need to learn the rules for playing it.

Your teacher will decide whether computers will be used in this course and, if so, which programs you will learn. Too many alternative programs and computers exist to be covered here, so we will describe a simple application of the Statistical Package for the Social Sciences (SPSS) to illustrate computer data analysis.

We will use SPSS to calculate descriptive statistics for the age of our subjects, a *t* test comparing men to women on Test X, and a correlation between Test X and Test Y. First, we need to collect the data. Box 7.4 shows the data for our study, the coding scheme, the data file, and the command file. The **coding scheme** is a plan for how data are arranged in the data file. The **data file** contains the data that will be analyzed by the computer program. Each subject is coded on one line of the data file. The **command file** contains the commands that read the data file and calculate the desired statistics.

Notice that each subject's data are coded in the same way in the same columns. Each subject's age is in columns 4 and 5, for example. Also notice that zeroes are entered in some columns, so that scores line up appropriately. For example, the first subject's score on Test Y is coded 090 in the last three columns, so that the score is read correctly. The SPSS command file has four lines. The first line identifies the data file (CH7.DAT) and its location (on the Macintosh hard disk drive), then gives the variable names and locations. The second line asks for descriptive statistics (mean and standard

---

Box 7.4

Sample SPSS Analysis

Data:

Subject	Gender	Age	Text X	Test Y
1	Male	25	10	90
2	Male	30	15	94
3	Male	31	12	106
4	Male	25	10	90
5	Male	19	8	70
6	Female	18	20	100
7	Female	26	24	128
8	Female	34	18	95
9	Female	26	15	82
10	Female	30	21	116

Coding Scheme:

Variable	SPSS Variable Name	Columns	Notes
Subject Number	ID	1-2	IDs range from 1 to 10.
Gender	Gender	3	1 = Male, 2 = Female
Age	Age	4-5	
Test X	X	6-7	
Test Y	Y	8-10	

Data File:

```
0112510090
0213015094
0313112106
0412510090
0511908070
0621820100
0722624128
0823418095
0922615082
1023021116
```

Command File:

```
DATA LIST FILE="Macintosh HD:CH7.DAT"/ID 1-2,GENDER 3,AGE 4-5,X 6-7, Y 8-10.
DESCRIPTIVES /VARIABLES=AGE /STATISTICS=MEAN STDDEV.
T-TEST /GROUPS=GENDER/VARIABLES=X.
CORRELATIONS /VARIABLES=X Y.
```

deviation) for age. The third line specifies an independent-groups t test comparing men to women on Test X scores. The last line requests the Pearson correlation between scores on the two tests. SPSS creates an **output file**, the file that contains the requested analyses. For your information, the average age was 26.40 ($SD = 5.10$); the t test was significant, $t(8) = 4.50$, $p < .005$ ($M = 11.00$, $SD = 2.65$ for men and $M = 19.60$, $SD = 3.62$ for women); and the correlation of .79 was significantly different from zero, $p < .01$.

There are other versions of SPSS with slightly different commands, but the basic structure of all SPSS command files is the same, with a series of lines that identify data and specify desired analyses. Many data analysis programs require you to submit a data and command file in order to generate an output file, but some programs have a single file that integrates data and commands. Requesting sophisticated data analyses is relatively easy using statistical packages. Computer-based statistical packages have removed most of the tedious arithmetic from data analysis, but they also make unwarranted analyses possible. The real chore is knowing what to ask and how to interpret results.

CHAPTER SUMMARY

Many alternative research strategies can be used to answer most research questions, and many decisions must be made when designing a study. A variety of sampling strategies exist, including probability sampling, random sampling, stratified sampling, stratified random sampling, multi-stage sampling, systematic sampling, systematic random sampling, nonprobability sampling, convenience sampling, purposive sampling, quota sampling, cross-sectional sampling, longitudinal sampling, trend sampling, and cohort sampling.

Power considerations are important. Effect size, sample size, alpha, the choice of one- or two-tailed tests, the choice of between-group or within-subject variables, the relative sizes of groups being compared, the choice of statistical analysis, and the precision of the study affect power. Techniques for estimating necessary sample size exist. Table 7.1 gives approximate sample sizes for several types of research studies.

Research validity concerns the accuracy of causal conclusions. Four types of research validity have been identified: statistical validity, internal validity, construct validity for causal conclusions, and external validity. Experiments have statistical validity if statistical evidence leads to accurate conclusions about relationships. Experiments have internal validity if independent variables cause observed changes in dependent variables. Experiments have construct validity for causal conclusions if underlying theoretical constructs for causes and effects are identified correctly. Experiments have external validity if causal conclusions generalize to other subjects, settings, and times.

Computers have revolutionized how academics and researchers conduct their business. Psychologists use mainframe, midsize, and personal computers for teaching, clinical work, testing, and research. Software and hardware must be compatible. Most computers are user-friendly, and software packages offer Help functions and interactive use. Before conducting a statistical analysis, researchers must code their data and write data and command files. The computer program produces an output file with the desired analyses.

Key Concepts

balanced design
biased sample
coding scheme
cohort
cohort study
command file
compatible software
construct validity for causal conclusions
convenience sampling
cross-sectional sampling
data file
external validity
file
file name
hardware
help function
interactive program
internal validity
longitudinal sampling
mainframe computer
midsize computer

multi-stage sampling
networked computers
nonprobability sampling
operating system
output file
personal computer
probability sampling
purposive sampling
quota sampling
random sampling
representative sample
research validity
software
software package
statistical validity
stratified random sampling
stratified sampling
systematic random sampling
systematic sampling
trend study
user-friendly

Review Questions

1. Manuela wants to study the effect of ethnicity on self-esteem in children. How could she conduct her study with random sampling, stratified sampling, stratified random sampling, multi-stage sampling, systematic sampling, systematic random sampling, convenience sampling, quota sampling?

2. Paul wants to study the effect of aging on social network size (the number of people one regularly interacts with), and he wants to examine ages from 30 to 80. How could he do this as a cross-sectional study? How could he do this as a longitudinal study?

3. William is studying American trust in politicians over the period from 1940 to 1990. Describe how he could do this as a trend study.

4. Tasha is interested in studying the effects of aging on people's memories of the day President Kennedy died. How could she do this as a cohort study?

5. Ruby wants to demonstrate that children become more independent of their parents as they grow older. Initially, she planned to compare 10 third-graders with 20 fourth-graders, and she anticipated a small effect size because the children were similar in age. She planned to use a two-tailed t test with an alpha of .01. Preliminary calculations suggested that her power would be too low. Describe all the ways that Ruby could increase the power of her study.

6. Mike plans to test the significance of the correlation between anxiety and depression. He estimates that the correlation is .20, and he plans to do a one-tailed test with an alpha of .05. Approximately how many subjects should be in Mike's

study if he wants a power of .70? If the population correlation was .50, how many subjects would he need?

7. Scores on the Jacobs Risk-Taking Test have a mean of 60 and a standard deviation of 25. Bill hypothesizes that members of the campus skydiving team score above average on this test, and he estimates their average is 80. He plans to collect a sample of skydivers and to use a one-tailed test with an alpha of .05. Approximately how many subjects should Bill examine if he wants a power of .90? If the population mean for skydivers is 65, how many subjects would he need?

8. Ethel plans to test an equal number of men and women in order to see if there is a gender difference in musical talent. Scores on the musical talent test have a mean of 85 and a standard deviation of 20. Ethel will use a two-tailed test with an alpha of .01, and she wants power to be at least .50. How many subjects should be in her study if the gender difference is 10 points? How many subjects should she include if she switches to an alpha of .05?

9. Pat wants to demonstrate a significant improvement in assertiveness among clients who participate in her assertiveness training program. Assertiveness scores have a mean of 50 and a standard deviation of 10. She estimates that scores taken before and after participation in her program correlate .20 and that participants should improve by 8 points. She plans a one-tailed test with an alpha of .05. Approximately how many subjects should Pat examine to have a power of .70? How many would she need if the scores correlate .80?

10. Judy is confused about the relationship between effect size and power. Explain effect size to her; and, using information from Table 7.1, demonstrate the relationship to her. Repeat this process for sample size, one- vs. two-tailed tests, and alphas of .05 vs. .01.

11. Joshua plans to compare two groups using an independent groups t test, and he asks your advice on group sizes. What advice can you offer? Use information in Table 7.1 to support your answer.

12. Bill and Beth plan to do studies with the same number of subjects. Each study will examine the effectiveness of their math tutoring. Bill's tutoring strategy is to give the same help to all students, so he anticipates that all his students will increase their scores by about the same amount (10 points). Beth gives individualized tutoring, so she believes that some of her students will improve a great deal and others will show less improvement. On average, her students should improve 10 points. Whose study should have higher power? (*Hint*: If all of Bill's students improve by the same amount, the correlation between scores taken before and after tutoring will be very high.)

13. Do effect size and sample size influence statistical validity? Explain your answers.

14. Weisz, Weiss, and Donenberg (1992) found that results for the effectiveness of therapy in experimental laboratory clinics did not generalize to practicing clinics. Does this conclusion involve the internal or external validity of research conducted in laboratory clinics?

15. Carmen wrote a computer program that runs on the operating system of her computer, and she is willing to sell it to you. You have a different brand of computer. Should you accept Carmen's offer?

16. Sam tries to print his term paper and is dismayed when nothing happens. How could this be a hardware problem? How could this be a software problem?

17. How would the command file in Box 7.4 be different if

    a. we wanted descriptive statistics for Test X, rather than age?

    b. we wanted to compare men to women on age, rather than on Test X?

    c. we wanted to correlate age with Test Y, rather than Test X with Test Y?

18. Here are data for a study on actual and ideal weights for a group of people at a gym. Each subject is classified as a novice or expert exerciser.

Subject	Level	Age	Actual Wt.	Ideal Wt.
1	Novice	56	214	185
2	Novice	35	189	180
3	Novice	8	59	85
4	Expert	45	178	146
5	Expert	9	88	94
6	Expert	26	124	135

    a. Develop a coding scheme and data file.

    b. Use Box 7.4 as your guide to write the command file to analyze these data. Pretend your data file is stored on a Macintosh hard disk drive, as discussed in this chapter. Write commands to calculate the mean weight of your subjects, to compare the ages of novices and experts, and to correlate actual and ideal weights.

Statistical Validity and Internal Validity

Researchers examine research hypotheses by analyzing data. They conclude that variables are significantly related (significant results) or that they are not significantly related (nonsignificant results). Experiments have statistical validity if their statistical evidence leads to accurate conclusions about relationships. If a relationship has been established, researchers ask if changes in the independent variable caused observable changes in the dependent variable. Experiments have internal validity if researchers arrive at accurate conclusions about causal relationships among variables being examined. In this chapter, we examine threats to statistical validity and internal validity.

THREATS TO STATISTICAL VALIDITY

Data analyses are conducted to support or falsify research hypotheses. Appropriate inferential statistics are applied, such as t tests or tests to see if correlations are significantly different from zero. Researchers who conduct hypothesis tests run the risk of concluding there is a relationship when one does not exist (a Type I error) or of concluding there is no relationship when one does exist (a Type II error). Research that avoids Type I and Type II errors has statistical validity. If we conduct research with low alpha and high power, our results are likely to have statistical validity. If alpha is .05, however, we expect to commit a Type I error 5 percent of the time when the null hypothesis is true; and if power is, say, .80, we run a 20 percent risk of a Type II error, so we expect to commit this error 20 percent of the time when the alternative hypothesis is true. These unlikely events could happen at any time. This is irritating, especially to beginning researchers who want to believe that these unlikely events always happen to someone else. Chapter 7 reviewed a number of strategies for designing research with high power, such as using large effect sizes, large sample sizes, and balanced designs. These strategies increase the statistical validity of research conclusions.

Fishing for Significant Results

Sometimes researchers conduct many statistical tests within a single study, **fishing** for some significant results. The fishing analogy is used because if people are fishing and throw many hooks in the water, they're more likely to catch some fish than if they throw only one hook in the water. Researchers on fishing expeditions are trying to catch something, but do not anticipate what might be caught. The problem with fishing is that Type I errors are likely. For example, say researchers examine correlations among 25 variables. There are 300 different pairwise correlations (variable 1 with variable 2, variable 1 with variable 3, etc.). [The formula for the number of pairs selected from n objects is n times $(n - 1)$ divided by 2. If $n = 25$, the number of pairs is $(25 \times 24)/2 = 300$.] If an alpha of .05 is used and if population correlations are zero, one would expect to find 15 significant results by chance ($.05 \times 300 = 15$). If the researchers find about 15 significant correlations, there is good reason to suspect that they uncovered only Type I errors. Their conclusions would have limited statistical validity.

Lack of Precision

Statistical validity also is threatened when independent or dependent variables are imprecisely manipulated or measured. If levels of the independent variables are not carefully controlled, the imprecision may mask actual differences that should have been found. Suppose a research team is studying the effect of noise on subjects' ability to learn a list of paired associates (arbitrarily paired words, such as house-rope, car-needle, and bicycle-book). Subjects are randomly assigned to three conditions, with noise levels ranging from silence to loud music. However, classes in the room across the hall from the laboratory sporadically make loud noises (such as scraping chairs, laughter, and movie soundtracks), and these noises sometimes occur during the silent or moderate-noise conditions. This lack of control over conditions reduces the effect size of the experimental manipulation because actual noise levels in the three conditions are not as different as researchers planned. As we saw in Chapter 7, research with small effect sizes is less powerful, so the lack of precision in the independent variable reduces statistical validity.

Unreliable dependent variable measurements also reduce statistical validity. Subjects' scores are unstable when measurements are unreliable, so scores are measured less precisely. In effect, unreliability adds random variation to the dependent variable, making estimates of the means for the different levels of the independent variable less precise. This reduces the study's power and statistical validity. Precise research is more likely to have statistical validity.

Attenuation Due to Restriction of Range

Cook and Campbell's (1979) concept of statistical validity concerns experiments, but we can also ask about the accuracy of conclusions in correlational studies. Researchers examining correlations must be aware of the effect of **restriction of range**, reduced

ATTENUATION DUE TO RESTRICTION OF RANGE **FIGURE 8.1**

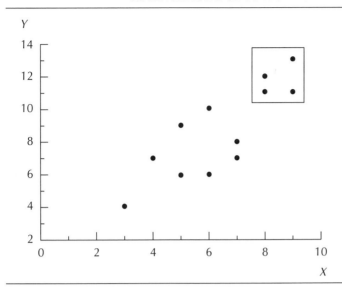

variability of the variables being correlated. Restriction of range **attenuates** (reduces) the size of observed correlation coefficients. This phenomenon is referred to as **attenuation due to restriction of range**. The effect is easy to understand if you remember that the size of correlations indicates how tightly the points in the scatterplot surround a line. Scatterplots that look like cigars have higher correlations than scatterplots that look like squares. Look at Figure 8.1. The two variables plotted in this scatterplot have a correlation of .83. If we restrict our observations to X values of 8 or more, though, we observe the points in the upper-right corner box. The correlation calculated on these values is only .30, a substantial attenuation in the observed correlation because we restricted the range of our variables.

Researchers observe smaller correlations when the range of variables is restricted, even when variables are substantially correlated in unrestricted populations. For example, the correlation between IQ and grades in medical school is low. Does this mean that someone with an IQ of 40 should do as well in medical school as someone with an IQ of 140? Of course not. The range of IQs is restricted substantially among medical students, attenuating the observed correlation. We observe small correlations in restricted samples under two circumstances. The variables may be uncorrelated or their correlation may have been attenuated. Studies in unrestricted samples must be conducted to determine which condition has occurred.

Attenuation due to restriction of range reduces the power of a correlational study. Remember that correlations indicate effect size, as discussed in Chapter 7. Reducing the range of the variables reduces the correlation, which reduces the effect size, power, and statistical validity. If restricted samples must be studied, sample sizes should be larger to compensate for this power loss. If variables are restricted so greatly that variability is lost, even large sample sizes cannot improve statistical validity. Researchers cannot examine relationships if variables do not vary.

Statistical Validity and Replications

Statistical validity may explain failed replications. Perhaps the original study lacked statistical validity, or perhaps the replication suffers from this problem. Researchers are suspicious of replications that are too consistent because this should not happen, especially when small, subtle effect sizes are examined in smaller samples. We expect more sampling fluctuation in our test statistics under these circumstances, and failure to replicate would not be surprising. On the other hand, if effect sizes or sample sizes are large, we expect to replicate results; failure to replicate in such cases suggests the phenomenon is questionable, rather than the result of simple problems with statistical validity.

THREATS TO INTERNAL VALIDITY

A study has internal validity if identified independent variables actually cause changes in identified dependent variables for the specific subjects, location, time, and data collection methods used. Many factors threaten the internal validity of a study.

Causal Ambiguity and Extraneous Variable Confounds

Causal ambiguity is the inability to make unambiguous causal inferences. Causal ambiguity is an especially severe problem for correlational studies. Correlation does not imply causation. If X and Y are correlated, X may cause Y or Y may cause X. If there is a relationship between loss of sleep (X) and anxiety (Y), it could be that loss of sleep (X) causes anxiety (Y), or it could be that anxiety (Y) causes loss of sleep (X). It is also possible that X and Y are caused by a third variable, Z. There may be a strong correlation between ice cream consumption (X) and pool drownings (Y), but both are probably caused by people's reactions to hot weather (Z). When it's hot, people eat more ice cream, and people spend more time in pools. The correlation between ice cream consumption and drowning should not lead to banning ice cream to prevent drownings. The two variables are related, but they are not causally related.

Another possibility is **reciprocal causation**, which occurs when two variables cause each other. Alcohol consumption and depression may be reciprocally causative. Some people drink because they're depressed and become more depressed because they drink.

Causal ambiguity also exists in studies of naturally occurring phenomena. Some research finds a relationship between Super Bowl Sunday and wife battering (Henry, 1993). Women's shelters may see a 40 percent increase in clients on Super Bowl Sunday and the subsequent Monday. Does watching this football game cause family violence? Do violent men watch football? Do men drink too much alcohol while watching the game, and become drunk and violent? Do wives complain about the game, so husbands become provoked and violent? The game occurs at the end of January. Is frustration over Christmas bills the real culprit? When two naturally occurring variables are related, the causal link is not clear.

Some of this ambiguity may disappear if observations are temporally ordered. Suppose we find a positive relationship between traumatic history during childhood (as indicated by parental divorce) and mental health problems in adulthood. Because the variables are ordered in time, it is easier to believe that childhood trauma causes later adult mental health problems, rather than that adult problems cause traumas in childhood. Even in this example, however, the causal link is ambiguous. Perhaps, as children, the adults with adjustment problems developed symptoms that led to parental conflict and divorce. Perhaps a third variable, such as parental alcoholism, caused parents' marital problems and precipitated the children's eventual mental health problems. Even reciprocal causation is possible. Early signs of mental illness in the children may have caused parental marital problems, and the added trauma of the parents' divorce may have exacerbated the child's long-term adjustment problems.

Causal ambiguity is a problem for quasi-experiments that lack random assignment of subjects to conditions. Quasi-experiments frequently compare intact groups, such as classrooms. One level of the independent variable is assigned to each classroom, but subjects are not randomly assigned to the classes they're in. Differences between the groups may have been caused by the independent variable or may have been caused by preexisting differences. For example, the two teachers may attract different types of students.

Suppose a research team wants to compare the effectiveness of behavioral therapy and psychoanalysis for the treatment of phobia. Dr. Williams uses behavioral therapy, and Dr. Perez uses psychoanalytic therapy. The researchers examine a sample of clients with phobias who have been treated by each therapist for six weeks, and they compare the extent of their phobic symptoms. If Dr. Williams' clients have fewer symptoms, they conclude that behavioral therapy is more effective; and if Dr. Perez's clients have fewer symptoms, they conclude that psychoanalysis is more effective. The researchers are comparing two intact groups: clients of each of the therapists. They did not randomly assign subjects to conditions. Their conclusions are suspect because of this lack of control.

One of the most serious problems with studies using intact groups is **self-selection bias**, which occurs when the groups differ in ways not specified by the independent variable. Perhaps clients who selected each therapist initially differed in symptom severity. Perhaps clients with mild symptoms were referred to the behavioral therapist, and clients with severe symptoms were referred to the psychoanalyst. Perhaps clients who could attend therapy sessions only twice a month were seen by the behavioral therapist, and clients who could attend sessions twice a week were seen by the psychoanalyst. Perhaps the two therapists charge different rates, motivating clients seeing the more expensive therapist to cooperate and recover more quickly. Perhaps the behavioral therapist was a woman and the psychoanalyst was a man, and clients selected therapists based on gender. Perhaps more women than men saw one of the two therapists, so differences between the effects of therapies may be caused by gender differences in clients' symptoms or responsiveness to therapy. Perhaps one of the therapists had more extensive training and experience with phobic clients than the other, so differences between their clients were due to differences in therapist competence. Any of these **extraneous variables** (variables that are not independent variables that are causally related to the dependent variable) might have affected results. The extraneous variables are **confounded** with the independent variable; they are mixed with the independent variable in ways that do not allow us to separate their effects on the dependent variable.

Demographic variables (such as age, gender, ethnicity, geographical location, and income) frequently are examined in quasi-experiments. Because researchers do not randomly assign subjects to these groups, extraneous variable confounds may explain results. For example, women tend to score higher than men on tests of verbal fluency (the ability to string words together to communicate meaning). Perhaps men and women differ in genetic predisposition to develop language skills, but there probably are socialization differences. Perhaps greater encouragement is given to girls' language development, or perhaps early identification with female caretakers (mothers, teachers) gives girls a head start in language development. Perhaps women develop greater verbal fluency than men because they have less muscle mass. They learn to handle confrontations verbally, rather than physically. The causal link between gender and verbal skills is hard to understand because many variables are confounded with gender.

Time-series designs involve repeated measurements of subjects and include natural or planned interventions. For example, in a **pretest-posttest design** each subject is tested before and after some intervention, such as a lecture on drug abuse to adolescents arrested for substance abuse crimes. The lecture would be considered effective if attitudes about drugs on the posttest are more negative than attitudes on the pretest. However, other events may have occurred between the two testings which affected the subjects, such as media coverage of an athlete who died from drug overdose. This extraneous event is confounded with the independent variable, so changes in attitude could have been caused only by the lecture, only by the death of the athlete, by both events, or by some other influence, such as fear of incarceration.

Time-series designs can be used with manipulated interventions, such as the drug abuse lecture, or with nonmanipulated interventions that occur naturally, such as earthquakes or graduations. For example, researchers may examine public opinion polls before and after an election outcome is announced. The outcome of the election is not under experimenter control. Some extraneous variable may occur simultaneously with the election, such as an increase in international tension, and this change could alter people's opinions about political issues. The extraneous variable threatens the internal validity of the study because an incorrect conclusion could be made about the causal influence of election results on public opinion.

Even true experiments can have confounded variables that create causal ambiguity. Say subjects are randomly assigned to two conditions: one in which they wait in groups and one in which they wait alone for test results. The study is designed to examine the effect of social support on anxiety. The large waiting room may be on the first floor, and researchers cannot justify tying up this room for the wait-alone condition, so they use small cubicles on the third floor. Subjects are randomly assigned to conditions and are treated identically, except for the room in which they wait for results. If subjects who wait alone report more anxiety, results suggest that social support causes people to become more comfortable with stress. However, the independent variable is confounded with room size and location. Perhaps subjects who wait alone are more uneasy because of claustrophobia in the cramped cubicle or fear of heights or elevators associated with being on the third floor. Perhaps other confounds exist, such as differences in room color. If the cubicles were grey and the waiting room was pink, differences in the dependent variable may be due to the relaxing effect of pink walls. Perhaps the cubicles are in a less-traveled section of the building, so subjects waiting alone become anxious over personal safety. These possible confounds would not exist if all subjects waited in the same room. Experiments are less likely to have extraneous variable confounds if conditions are identical in all respects except for the independent variable.

Studies involving changes in extreme groups are subject to the regression effect. The **regression effect** is the tendency for extreme groups to score less extremely when they are retested, even without intervention. Many factors that could have influenced the original extreme score (such as fatigue, ill health, inattentiveness, high or low levels of motivation, and good or bad luck guessing answers) are unlikely to operate at the second testing, so extreme people tend to look more average (less extreme) when retested.

The regression effect is likely under two circumstances: when unreliable tests are used and when tests measure states. Tests with poor test-retest reliability and tests that measure states (rather than traits) are least likely to be stable. Extreme scores on unreliable tests and state tests probably are exaggerated by temporary factors, so people who are selected because of extreme scores are unlikely to be as extreme at retesting, making research results difficult to interpret.

For example, imagine the dependent variable is depression as measured by the Beck Depression Inventory. People who score as highly depressed are identified, given therapy, then retested to see if depression was reduced. Significantly lower depression scores suggest the therapy was effective. However, some of the people who originally scored as highly depressed may have just faced a personal crisis (e.g., the death of a family pet), and have been temporarily depressed, and others may have scored extremely because of other factors, such as lack of sleep or ill humor. On retesting, their scores will show them to be less depressed, but this change is caused by the regression effect, not the therapy. Similarly, a study showing that preschool programs lead to improved test scores in low-scoring children may have results that are inflated because the score improvement is due to regression.

It is doubly hard to demonstrate the effects of treatments designed to improve scores in subjects who were selected because of high scores. For example, to show the effectiveness of programs for gifted students (identified by tests), researchers must demonstrate changes that compensate for regression because regression will cause subjects to score lower at posttest, not higher. The intervention program must compensate for this reduction, plus increase the scores beyond the pretest level in order to show program effectiveness. The Head Start program that demonstrates increased scores may be taking credit for the regression effect, and the Gifted Student program must be very effective to increase scores because it is going against the regression effect.

Randomly assigned control group subjects can be used to uncover regression effects. Changes in control subjects' scores allow researchers to measure the regression effect, and these changes can serve as a basis for comparison of score changes among experimental subjects. There is evidence for the efficacy of treatment if experimental subjects change more than control subjects.

Subject Reactivity

Subject reactivity occurs if subjects respond differently because they know they're being observed. For example, subjects may be more likely to volunteer to help if they know they're being observed. The observer, rather than the independent variable, may cause changes in the dependent variable.

Box 8.1

A Classic Case of Subject Reactivity

Orne and Scheibe (1964) examined the effects of subject reactivity in sensory deprivation studies. Earlier studies showed dramatic effects for volunteers subjected to extreme sensory deprivation by immersion in tanks of body-temperature water or by isolation in silent rooms with restricted movement, translucent goggles, and cardboard covers over their hands. Subjects reported hallucinations, loss of concentration, spatial and temporal disorientation, and impaired mental functioning. Orne and Scheibe postulated that the demand characteristics of these studies created these effects by setting the stage for bizarre experiences.

Orne and Scheibe's subjects were twenty male volunteers, divided into two groups of ten volunteers. Experimental subjects were greeted by a researcher in a white lab coat who took their medical history in a room where an emergency table with a tray of drugs and medical equipment was prominently displayed. They were told they would be kept under constant observation and a physician was on call for their protection; and they were given a microphone to report "any visual imagery, fantasies, special or unusual feelings, difficulty in concentration, hallucinations, feelings of disorientation, or the like," experiences which were "not unusual" (p. 5) in this experiment. They were also provided a panic button for emergency escape and were told, "Try to stick it out if you can" (p. 5). Although these instructions sound

extreme, they were typical of those used in earlier sensory deprivation studies. Prior researchers, concerned about the welfare of their subjects, took extensive precautions to protect them from harm. Control subjects were treated identically, except that they were not given any suggestions or cues that unusual or dangerous things might happen.

Each subject was put in a 6×7×8-foot isolation chamber for four hours. Beige drapes covered a small outside window, and subjects were observed through a 2×4-foot window. A desk, two comfortable chairs, ice water, and a sandwich were provided. Movements were not restricted, lighting was sufficient for subjects to explore the room, and subjects were able to hear footsteps in the hallway and birds singing outside.

Experimental subjects were much more likely to display the bizarre reactions noted in sensory deprivation studies, including perceptual aberrations, intellectual dullness, unpleasant affect, restlessness, and irritability. For example, one experimental subject reported that "objects on the desk are becoming animated and moving about" (p. 9) and others reported strange changes in room color and size. Observations, self-reports, and scores on a battery of tests confirmed the effect of subject reactivity. Orne and Scheibe concluded that sensory deprivation results from earlier research are in part an artifact of subject reactivity to the strongly framed demand characteristics created by their procedures.

Demand characteristics are overt or subtle cues to subjects on how they should behave. Subject reactivity can occur when subjects change their behaviors in response to demand characteristics. These changes may be deliberate, or they may be unconscious efforts to cooperate with or undermine the research. A classic study of subject reactivity (Box 8.1) involved the reactions of volunteers to sensory deprivation.

Several strategies have been developed for reducing the effects of demand characteristics. One way is to conduct **blind research**, in which subjects are not aware of the treatment condition they are in. The use of placebos for control groups is an example of a blind research strategy, as long as subjects are not aware they are in the placebo group.

Observations can be obtrusive or unobtrusive. Subjects are aware of **obtrusive observations**, but are not aware of **unobtrusive observations**. Obtrusive observers are in clear view and may hold clipboards and other note-taking tools. Unobtrusive observers are hidden from view or blend into the background. For example, unobtrusive observations of adolescents at a shopping mall could be made from a coffee shop window. Unobtrusive observations are less likely to invoke subject reactivity. Obtrusive observers may decrease subject reactivity if they allow subjects to acclimate to their presence before data collection begins.

Another strategy to reduce demand characteristics is to separate data collection from the manipulation. For example, data collection may be conducted in a separate room by different researchers or may be conducted unobtrusively in the waiting room while subjects are not aware they are being observed.

Reactivity may take many forms. Control group subjects frequently are given more boring experiences. They may become demoralized and perform at abnormally low levels, a problem called **resentful demoralization**. This may exaggerate the effects of intervention programs. On the other hand, control group participants may demonstrate **compensatory rivalry**: striving harder than usual to make up for their weaker treatment. This could mask the positive effects of the experimental treatment.

Subject reactivity may be caused by **treatment contamination**, which occurs when members of different treatment groups discuss their experiences and undermine the effect of the independent variable. For example, research clinic clients may discuss their treatment in the waiting room, and student subjects may discuss their experiences during recess. All subjects may be exposed to some aspects of all treatments, and control subjects may become demoralized or may develop compensatory rivalry. Subjects may try to figure out what the independent and dependent variables are or may become suspicious of researchers' intentions when they become aware of other treatment conditions. If subjects react to treatment contamination, they may change their behaviors; and it is difficult for researchers to determine if these changes deflate or inflate group differences.

Subject reactivity may be in response to characteristics of the data collectors. For example, Galla, Frison, Jeffrey, and Gaer (1981) found that subjects' responses on a sex-role attitude questionnaire were more conservative if data were collected by male researchers, even when subjects were told their answers would not be scored until hundreds of surveys were collected. Research conducted by male research teams finds sex-role attitudes more conservative than research conducted by female teams.

If researcher gender is confounded with the independent variable, results may be incorrectly attributed to the independent variable. For example, a study on the effect of different types of arguments for women's rights in which some subjects hear one type of argument from a man and other subjects hear another type of argument from a woman could incorrectly conclude that the type of argument influenced opinion. To avoid this confound, arguers' gender could be held constant (all arguments are presented by one gender or, to handle other possible confounds, all arguments are presented by the same person) or the gender of the arguers could be balanced, so that half the subjects under each condition hear the arguments presented by each gender.

Other aspects of the data collectors, including their friendliness, status, and age, may affect subjects. If some, but not all subjects are affected or if subjects are affected in different ways, subject reactivity adds random variance to the dependent variable, reducing the study's power and statistical validity; or this reactivity may be confounded with the independent variable. Depersonalization of the data collection process, such as collecting data with written surveys, administering recorded instructions, or using unobtrusive observations, may reduce subject reactivity to data collector characteristics.

The **Hawthorne effect** occurs when subjects' responses reflect their reaction to the novelty of participating in a study and their awareness that someone is interested in observing them. The Hawthorne effect also is known as the **placebo effect** or **novelty effect**. This phenomenon was suggested when a research team at a Hawthorne assembly plant conducted a series of studies and found that worker productivity increased regardless of experimental condition (Roethlisberger & Dickson, 1939). Workers were exposed to a number of changes, such as changes in illumination, rest periods, and work hours. Productivity increased in unpredictable ways. For example, productivity increased when lighting was enhanced and when lighting was unchanged. One interpretation is that the novelty of participating in the research motivated subjects to excel because it improved morale. [Alternative explanations have been offered. For example, Parsons (1974) suggested that changes in the recording system to measure the dependent variable gave productivity feedback to the workers, and they learned to perform better. The term "Hawthorne effect" is reserved for the novelty explanation.] Control groups allow researchers to identify the Hawthorne effect when it occurs.

The positive impact of the Hawthorne effect exemplifies the **good subject effect**: good research subjects try to figure out and to provide what the researcher wants. This effect sometimes is called the **Orne effect** because Martin Orne (1962) examined its influence on research results. Unfortunately, good subjects may undermine research validity. Orne conducted a series of studies demonstrating the good subject effect. For example, he (1959) suggested to one class of students that hypnotized people have rigid dominant hands; then, in a separate experiment, he compared students from that class to other students in a hypnotism experiment. As expected, the majority of students from the experimental class and none of the students from the control group demonstrated a rigid dominant hand when hypnotized. In effect, the students were good subjects; they behaved in the way they thought was appropriate for people in hypnotic states.

Not all subjects are good subjects. Some ignore the demand characteristics of the study and behave normally. These are subjects that researchers want to examine because they provide valid data. There also are **bad subjects** who deliberately undermine the study. The **screw-you effect** is observed when subjects deliberately behave in ways that invalidate research. For example, bad subjects may make jokes of their answers to questionnaires (such as writing "seldom" in response to a question asking their sex), may mark answers at random, and may be inattentive to experimental conditions or instructions. These responses may be more likely in volunteers who feel coerced and who prefer not to participate or in volunteers who believe the research is frivolous. Luckily, most subjects do not deliberately attempt to ruin research endeavors.

Bad data also may be provided because of **evaluation apprehension**, which occurs when subjects become uncomfortable about exposing personal information to data collectors, so they answer evasively or with social desirability response sets. Researchers who stress anonymity, confidentiality, and privacy and who present materials in nonthreatening ways probably are less likely to elicit evaluation apprehension.

People who take many tests may learn to be good test-takers. These **test sophisticated subjects** are aware of subtle cues to correct answers and ways to falsify desired response patterns, so scores may reflect their sophistication. Much research is conducted on college student subjects, and college students (especially psychology majors) may figure out aspects of their assessment in studies. Their sophistication can undermine the validity of their answers. For example, you probably would recognize items on a social distance scale (like the Attitude Toward Martians Scale in Chapter 6); and this realization may affect your answers, invalidating your test score.

Subjects also might have **research sophistication**: They may guess the nature of experiments involving deception. Subjects may decide that researchers are studying how neurotic, helpful, or disobedient they will be under varying conditions; and this realization (correct or not) might affect their responses. Randomly assigning subjects to control conditions may allow researchers to uncover these problems, and researchers who keep subjects engaged with credible activities are less likely to encourage subjects to second-guess the purpose of the study.

Some problems are particularly relevant to time-series designs in which the dependent variable is assessed repeatedly in the same subjects. **Memory** or **practice effects** occur when subjects remember previous responses or improve with practice, affecting their performance on later tests. If subjects improve with practice in time-series studies and all subjects are given treatments in the same order, differences between conditions reflect practice effects, rather than condition. Researchers can counterbalance conditions to spread this effect evenly. Conditions are **counterbalanced** when equal numbers of subjects receive each possible ordering. For example, if there are two treatment conditions, A and B, half the subjects receive A first and half the subjects receive B first. Researchers can analyze resulting data to see if presentation order significantly affected responses.

Subjects take pretests and subsequent posttests in simple pretest-posttest or other time series designs. **Pretest sensitization** occurs when subject reactivity is created by taking the pretest. For example, simply taking a test that measures attitudes toward some social issue may spark introspection and change in subjects; this change is confounded with the influence of the independent variable. In addition, pretest sensitization may operate by providing demand characteristics that cue subjects to the purpose of the study. Randomly assigned control group subjects who take the same pretest provide data that allow researchers to estimate this effect.

Pretest sensitization may have differential impact on different types of subjects. Rosnow and Suls (1970) found that volunteer subjects who had been pretested were more receptive to attitude change, but nonvolunteer subjects who had been pretested were more resistant to attitude change. This has implications for the statistical validity of conclusions, as explained in Box 8.2.

Researchers may eliminate pretest sensitization by collecting only post-intervention data. This eliminates the within-subject comparison, so may weaken the power of the statistical analysis. Another strategy is to conduct a **Solomon four-group design**, in which two groups of subjects are treated just like the pretest-posttest subjects, but without the pretest, as shown in Figure 8.2. Groups 1 and 2 are the standard pretest-posttest subjects; and Groups 3 and 4 are treated identically, but without the pretest. Rosnow and Suls' study (Box 8.2) used this research design. Data from this design allow researchers to examine the impact of pretest sensitization and to determine the effect of the independent variable with and without pretesting.

Box 8.2

Pretest Sensitization

Rosnow and Suls (1970) investigated the effects of pretest sensitization in an attitude change experiment. Their major goal was to determine whether pretest sensitization operates differently for volunteer and nonvolunteer subjects.

Subjects were 146 introductory psychology students, including volunteer and coerced research participants. Coerced subjects were "captive undergraduates" (p. 339) who were required to participate as a course requirement, and volunteer subjects were recruited by an appeal for research volunteers.

About half the subjects in each group were given a pretest measuring attitudes toward nuclear research. Experimental subjects were given a purported *New York Times* editorial on the dangers of nuclear research, and control subjects were given a purported *New York Times* editorial on sexual promiscuity. All subjects then were given the attitude survey on nuclear research.

Pretesting had contrasting effects in the two groups. Pretested volunteers in the experimental group changed their opinion in the direction of the editorial; and pretested nonvolunteers in the experimental group changed their opinion in the direction opposite that of the editorial. This has important implications for research. Studies on pretested volunteer subjects overestimate the influence of the intervention on attitude, and studies on pretested nonvolunteer subjects underestimate this effect. In addition, the type of subject affects statistical validity. Type I errors, rejecting a true null hypothesis, are more likely with volunteer subjects; and Type II errors, not rejecting a false null hypothesis, are more likely with nonvolunteer subjects. Typical research studies on attitude change that uses only volunteer subjects are not as conservative as their statistical results suggest and may reach overly optimistic conclusions about the effectiveness of attitude change manipulations.

Extraneous Variables

Subject characteristics that are related to the dependent variable may lead researchers to invalid conclusions. Suppose researchers want to compare two training methods for teaching tennis. If subjects differ in tennis skill before training, and if more experienced subjects end up in one of the two training conditions, these subject characteristics are confounded with the independent variable. These problems could be reduced or eliminated if researchers randomly assign subjects to conditions or apply stratified sampling strategies that balance the characteristics of subjects in conditions.

Many variables can be confounded with the independent variable in quasi-experiments. For example, ethnicity may be confounded with income, housing quality, school funding, and teacher and community expectations. These confounds introduce interpretation problems. Are ethnic group differences due to genetic differences, confounded variables, or both? One way to handle such identified confounds is to eliminate them (e.g., by studying only college graduates or only individuals with specific incomes) or to include them as additional independent variables for analysis.

CONDITION

	Experimental	Control
Pretested	Group 1	Group 2
Not Pretested	Group 3	Group 4

Studies examining the effects of age are subject to **generational effects**, which occur when differences between generations are confounded with the independent variable. This affects cross-sectional and longitudinal designs. Cross-sectional studies compare people of different ages, but age is confounded with generational differences. Generations who survived depressions and wars may be different from generations who were raised without such catastrophes, and these differences are confounded with age. Standard of living, education, parental practices, and many other variables also are confounded with age. Researchers conducting longitudinal studies of one generation may incorrectly attribute changes to age, rather than to historical circumstance. For example, studies on the development of sexual knowledge in children exposed to adult movies on cable television may attribute changes to age, rather than to environment.

The reactivity of other interested parties may undermine the influence of the independent variable. For example, control group teachers in classrooms without special grant-funded computers and teaching assistants may be aware of the extras provided to experimental classrooms and may perform more poorly than usual. This would magnify the effect of the treatment condition. The opposite effect also could occur: **compensatory equalization**, improving control conditions to be more fair to control subjects. Sometimes government agencies or other funding organizations feel sorry for subjects in control conditions, so they compensate by providing extra support. For example, teachers of control groups may, through other channels, receive computers and teaching assistants already provided to experimental classrooms.

Although the funders may feel justified in their attempts to be fair to all children, their efforts can invalidate research findings.

Long studies may be confounded with subject mortality or maturation. **Mortality** refers to loss of subjects due to refusal to continue, relocation, or death; such losses may invalidate research conclusions. **Differential mortality** occurs when subjects in one condition are more likely to drop out than subjects in other conditions, so mortality is confounded with the independent variable. For example, subjects may drop out of experimental conditions that involve electric shocks or difficult training sessions. Consequently, the effect of the treatment becomes less clear. Perhaps only masochistic subjects stayed in these groups, and these subjects may be different on the dependent variable from subjects in other groups, regardless of treatment. Would you be convinced that training is effective if only 10 percent of subjects complete the program?

Maturation is a threat to studies when subjects change during the research in ways not related to the independent variable. For example, children may become wiser, more coordinated, or more test-sophisticated over the course of a long experiment. Later performance may reflect these changes, rather than the independent variable. Similar threats affect shorter studies. Subjects can become bored, tired, or hungry over the course of a study, so their responses later in the study may reflect these changes. Researchers sometimes can counterbalance conditions to spread this effect evenly across conditions, or they may use matched subjects to take advantage of the power of within-subject comparisons while avoiding the confound. Alternatively, control group subjects could be used for comparison, or the independent variable could be studied as a between-group variable, with different subjects tested under each condition.

Another problem that can occur in repeated measures designs is **confounds with history**: events occurring during the experiment that cannot be separated from the independent variable. Many things may occur between initial and final testing in addition to experimentally planned interventions. There could be riots, wars, power outages, parties, or holidays that influence the dependent variable. Control groups are useful to detect such confounds.

Experimenter Bias

Experimenters can bias research results in a number of ways. Box 8.3 summarizes types of **experimenter bias** described by Rosenthal and Rosnow (1991). Observer, interpreter, and intentional effects can be discovered by checks of interrater reliability. Research suggests that raters are more accurate when they know that reliability checks will be conducted (Romanczyk, Kent, Diament, & O'Leary, 1973), so such checks are recommended for all studies, especially for those involving subjective or complicated ratings. Biosocial, psychosocial, situational, and modeling effects may cause subject reactivity or extraneous variable confounds.

Experimenter expectancy effects bias results because of experimenters' beliefs or attitudes. These effects have received much attention. Experimenter expectancy effects also are called **self-fulfilling prophecies** or the **Rosenthal effect** (because Robert Rosenthal has contributed substantially to our understanding of this phenomenon). Data collectors may create demand characteristics that produce subject reactivity,

---

Box 8.3

Experimenter Bias

Observer effect: Systematic observation errors, such as always starting the stopwatch a few seconds early when timing subjects.

Interpreter effect: Systematic interpretive errors, such as labeling an assertive act aggressive.

Intentional effect: Deliberate dishonesty or sloppiness in data collection, such as faking data or introducing extensive random measurement error.

Biosocial effect: Demographic characteristics of data collectors affect subjects' responses, or demographic characteristics of subjects affect data collectors' behavior (for example, researchers who smile more at female subjects may obtain different responses from male and female subjects).

Psychosocial effect: Data collectors' interpersonal styles affect subjects' responses, such as when anxious, warm, and authoritarian data collectors obtain different responses from subjects.

Situational effect: Results are unique to the situation under which data are collected, such as when teachers collect data on students in their classes or researchers study their friends.

Modeling effect: Researchers who offer sample answers or who demonstrate equipment inadvertently introduce idiosyncrasies that are mimicked by subjects.

Experimenter expectancy effect: Data collectors' expectations influence subjects to behave in ways consistent with these expectations or bias data collectors' observations.

Adapted from Rosenthal and Rosnow (1991, pp. 125–130)

such as unconsciously rewarding responses or behaviors consistent with predictions; or they may allow expectations to systematically affect their observations, such as being more aware of outcomes that support predictions. For example, spectators at sports events may be more sensitive to referees' "errors" in rulings against their team, especially if spectators believe a history of bias exists. An interesting early study of experimenter bias is the analysis of Clever Hans (described on page 152).

Rosenthal, his colleagues, and others have conducted hundreds of studies on experimenter expectancy effects, and have found these effects in a broad range of studies of both humans and animals. Expectancy effects have been found in studies of animal learning, reaction time, inkblot interpretation, person perception, student performance, and client behavior in therapy (Rosenthal & Rosnow, 1991). For example, teachers who expect students to do well probably treat students differently from teachers who expect students to fail, and these differences can create self-fulfilling prophecies.

One way to reduce experimenter bias is to conduct **double-blind research,** studies in which data collectors and subjects are unaware of the treatment condition. For example, placebo medication may look identical to experimental medication, and only the pharmacist who dispenses pills to data collectors knows which type of pill is given to each subject. This is more difficult for demographic variables because data

CLEVER HANS

Shortly after the turn of the century, Europeans traveled to see a German horse, Clever Hans, who was famous for his arithmetic skills. Hans was able to tap out dates and answers to mathematical questions. Testimonials by experts were widely published, and Hans was toasted as a genius. Pfungst (1911), doubting Hans' talent, studied Hans for six months to discover the secret of his accuracy. Hans was inadvertently being instructed by his questioners. For example, they might lean forward while counting his strokes, then begin to straighten when answers were complete. Hans had learned to stop striking based on these subtle cues, and his accuracy was destroyed if his questioners did not know the answers themselves. Pfungst's review, although not using today's language, probably was the first recorded case of an experimenter expectancy effect.

collectors generally can observe the gender, age, and ethnicity of research subjects. To promote objectivity, typed transcripts of responses may be scored by **blind raters**, raters unaware of subject or condition characteristics. Experimenter bias also is less likely when very standardized instructions are used, so research conducted with taped or written instructions and little interaction between subjects and data collectors is less likely to have this problem.

There may be **experimenter drift**: gradual changes in the treatment of subjects as the study progresses. For example, data collectors may read instructions more quickly or may become more confident or bored as the study progresses, or they may become tired or irritable near the end of a long day of seeing subjects. Such behaviors may blur distinctions among treatment conditions or may alter their characteristics. Raters may drift in their application of scoring criteria, becoming more lenient or more strict as the study progresses. If this happens, scores on early subjects may not be comparable to scores on later subjects; e.g., a score of ten aggressive acts may mean that the observed child was a hellion if the child was observed early in the study, but a normal child if observations were made late in the study. Such changes undermine the reliability and validity of scores. Researchers must train data collectors and raters to avoid drift.

The Nature of Internal Validity

Studies with high internal validity have accurate conclusions about the causal relationship between independent and dependent variables. In general, true experiments (with carefully controlled conditions, control groups, and random assignment of subjects to conditions) have high internal validity because extraneous variables are controlled or eliminated; however, even these studies may suffer from subject reactivity, measurement and statistical problems, and experimenter bias. When researchers consider threats to internal validity, they identify rival hypotheses about the study's results. For example, results may be affected by treatment contamination, pretest sensitization, or experimenter expectations. Strategies that allow researchers to discard these rival hypotheses offer greater internal validity.

CHAPTER SUMMARY

Two aspects of validity are statistical validity and internal validity. Research that avoids Type I and Type II errors has statistical validity. This is threatened when researchers fish for significant results or when they conduct studies with imprecise independent or dependent variables. Attenuation due to restriction of range also reduces statistical validity. Statistical validity may explain failed replications.

Studies have internal validity if identified independent variables actually cause changes in identified dependent variables. Many factors threaten the internal validity of a study, including threats due to subject reactivity, extraneous variables, and experimenter bias.

Statistical threats to internal validity include problems with causal ambiguity and the regression effect. Subject reactivity may be in response to demand characteristics in the study. Resentful demoralization, compensatory rivalry, responses to treatment contamination and characteristics of data collectors, the Hawthorne effect, responses by good and bad subjects, problems due to test or research sophistication, and the effects of memory, practice, and pretest sensitization can create subject reactivity problems.

Extraneous variables threaten the internal validity of studies. These may involve subject characteristics, generational effects, reactivity by other interested parties, subject mortality and maturation, and confounds with history. Experimenter bias may take many forms, including observer, interpreter, intentional, biosocial, psychosocial, situational, modeling, and experimenter expectancy effects. In addition, experimenter drift may occur.

When researchers consider threats to internal validity, they identify rival hypotheses about the study's results. Strategies that allow them to discard these rival hypotheses offer greater internal validity.

Key Concepts

attenuate
attenuation due to restriction of range
bad subject
biosocial effect
blind rater
blind research
causal ambiguity
compensatory equalization
compensatory rivalry
confounded variable
confounds with history
counterbalanced conditions
demand characteristics
demographic variable
differential mortality
double-blind research
evaluation apprehension

experimenter bias
experimenter drift
experimenter expectancy effect
extraneous variable
fishing
generational effects
good subject effect
Hawthorne effect
intentional effect
interpreter effect
maturation of subjects
memory effect
modeling effect
mortality of subjects
novelty effect
observer effect
obtrusive observation

Orne effect
placebo effect
practice effect
pretest-posttest design
pretest sensitization
psychosocial effect
reciprocal causation
regression effect
research sophistication
resentful demoralization
restriction of range

Rosenthal effect
screw-you effect
self-fulfilling prophecy
self-selection bias
situational effect
Solomon four-group design
subject reactivity
test sophistication
time-series design
treatment contamination
unobtrusive observation

Review Questions

1. Sandy has means for 16 experimental conditions, and she plans to conduct a t test to compare each pair of means. Why is this a problem for the statistical validity of her conclusions?

2. Critics claim that college admissions tests (such as the SAT) do not correlate very highly with grades in college. How could attenuation due to restriction of range be involved in this issue?

3. Two alcohol treatment centers are compared. The center in Detroit uses lay counselors, and the center in Boston uses licensed counselors. Analyses show that the Detroit center is more effective. Does this prove that lay counselors are more effective than licensed counselors? Why or why not?

4. Doctors refer hypertensive patients with high concentrations of salt in their blood to therapists who work with them to change their salt intake. Blood tests show reduced salt concentrations after one month of therapy, and researchers conclude the therapy was effective. Why should a control group have been used?

5. A conservatively-groomed young man in a business suit collected survey information about people's attitude toward the John Birch Society in Los Angeles, and a pony-tailed young man wearing a sweatshirt and sandals distributed the same survey in Berkeley. People in Los Angeles had more favorable attitudes toward this organization. What possible factors threaten the internal validity of this study?

6. A school football team with an underfunded program, amateur coach, and old equipment devastates a team with high funding, a professional coach, and new equipment. Does this prove that football teams perform better when given less support? Why or why not?

7. Researchers examine the effect of payment on productivity by paying junior high students either five dollars or five cents for each A they earn in an English class. All subjects are in the same course, and they are asked not to discuss their payment rates with each other. What may threaten the internal validity of this study?

8. Experimental results for early teaching machines were promising, but the effect tended to wear off after the children worked with the machines for a while. What subject reactivity threat could explain these results?

9. Professor Johnson states that she prefers not having good subjects in her research studies. Why would she state this?

10. A research team plans to do a deception study on upper-division college students and decides to exclude psychology majors. Why would they do this?

11. Calvin examined the test-retest reliability of his attitude test by having subjects take the test twice in a one-hour period. His results led him to conclude his test is very reliable. What may threaten the internal validity of his study?

12. Lydia has created a comic book designed to make children look less favorably upon drug use. She used a pretest-posttest design with volunteer subjects in an experimental or control group and demonstrated that the book did cause children to change their attitude in the expected direction. She is seeking help from your agency to mass-produce the book and to distribute it to children who have been arrested for drug-related behaviors. One of your colleagues suggests that Sylvia should conduct a Solomon four-group design study before you review her request. Another colleague suggests that her suggested program may backfire, citing Rosnow and Sul's (1970) study (Box 8.2). Explain your colleagues' reasons for their suggestions.

13. Compared to longitudinal studies, cross-sectional studies show an earlier and more severe decrement in intelligence test scores as people age. How might generational effects influence the internal validity of the two types of studies?

14. Subjects were asked to read a list of words first under bright lighting, then under medium lighting, and then under weak lighting. Results led to the conclusion that people read best under weak lighting. A critic argues that researchers should have counterbalanced conditions. Explain the critic's reasoning.

15. Is double-blind research designed to combat subject reactivity, experimenter bias, or both? Explain your answer.

16. Why do true experiments generally have higher internal validity than quasi-experiments, correlational studies, and descriptive studies?

9

Construct Validity for Causal Conclusions and External Validity

Researchers conduct experiments to examine theories defining causal relationships between hypothetical constructs. They must apply operational definitions of these constructs in order to conduct research. If variables in the study are causally related (i.e., if the study has internal validity), researchers infer that the corresponding theoretical constructs are causally related. This inference is accurate if the study has construct validity for causal conclusions. Researchers make further predictions from supported theories, and they expect to obtain results that support these research hypotheses. They expect findings to generalize to new subjects, settings, and times. If these expectations are met, conclusions based on the original study have external validity. Construct validity and external validity deal with generalizations. Construct validity involves generalizations about causal relationships between theoretical constructs, and external validity involves generalizations of theories to new subjects, settings, and times. In this chapter we will explore both of these types of validity.

CONSTRUCT VALIDITY FOR CAUSAL CONCLUSIONS

A study has construct validity for causal conclusions if underlying theoretical constructs for causes and effects are identified correctly. Researchers operationally define causal variables and manipulate or measure them as independent variables, and they operationally define effects and measure them as dependent variables. Independent and dependent variables may be defined too broadly, too narrowly, or inaccurately.

Independent Variables

Independent variables must have construct validity. Suppose researchers are analyzing the effect of laughter on autonomic nervous system arousal. They show experimental subjects a funny movie and control subjects a neutral movie and measure autonomic arousal with physical indicators, such as GSR and heart rate. What if the "funny" movie is boring for most subjects? If this were to occur, researchers would incorrectly attribute differences in autonomic arousal to laughter.

One way to see if the independent variable is perceived in ways that were planned is to conduct a manipulation check, as Croyle and Cooper (1983, Box 2.1) did. Researchers interview or survey subjects at the end of the experiment to verify the construct validity of the independent variable. For example, subjects are asked their emotional response to the movie that was supposed to make them laugh, or they are asked questions about the stimulus materials to verify that key variables were salient. If a few subjects give aberrant answers to the manipulation check, researchers may decide to omit these subjects from the data analysis or to analyze them separately. If many subjects give inappropriate answers to the manipulation check, the entire study may be invalid.

Complex interventions often are hard to define, and it may be difficult to unravel specific causal aspects within the intervention. Therapists using the same theoretical model may focus on different aspects of their approach. They have defined the independent variable differently, and subtle differences may undermine the correct determination of underlying theoretical constructs.

Independent variables may be operationalized in many ways. For example, the effect of distraction on learning could be studied by distracting people with noise, lights, smells, interpersonal conflict, hunger, or fireworks. Construct validity for this causal variable would be high if results are consistent across these distractors. Cook and Campbell (1979) suggest that researchers have more confidence in the construct validity of causal variables if they avoid a **mono-operation bias** (the tendency to have only one exemplar for an independent variable). Suppose a research team is studying the effect of physical attractiveness on perceptions of intelligence. Do we believe that attractive people are more or less intelligent than unattractive people? Researchers could examine the effect of attractiveness by having subjects rate the intelligence of people in two photographs: one photograph of an attractive person and one photograph of an unattractive person. This strategy shows the mono-operation bias. To avoid this bias, researchers could use multiple exemplars of attractive and unattractive people. In this way they could be more confident that the causal variable is the general construct of physical attractiveness, rather than some aspect specific to the single exemplar, such as ethnicity. In addition, researchers could systematically vary aspects of exemplars in order to better understand the limits of their theory. The effect of physical attractiveness on ratings of intelligence may be different for male and female models or for models with and without glasses.

Dependent Variables

Invalid dependent variable measurements also lead to invalid conclusions about the hypothetical constructs involved. If a prejudice test really measures the social desirability response set, results are interpreted incorrectly. In Chapter 6, we reviewed a number of other response sets that could undermine test validity. Moreover, what people say they do on self-report questionnaires and what they actually do in their private lives may be different, so self-report data may be questionable. Data from **retrospective accounts** (reports based on memory, such as, asking parents to remember the ages at which their children began to walk) may be unreliable and invalid. Anecdotal evidence always is questionable unless supported by other sources of information. In Chapter 6, we looked at ways to examine the content, criterion-related, and construct validity of measurements.

Construct validity does not require that dependent variables in experimental studies have operational definitions identical to those in the outside world. What is important is that processes common to both settings are measured. Experiments in which pilots find shapes embedded in complex designs may measure the same cognitive processes as those required to locate airport markers during actual flights.

Sometimes the dependent variable is measured in multiple ways. For example, Darley and Latane (1968) studied the effect of diffusion of responsibility on bystander apathy. They simulated emergencies and led subjects to believe that they were the only ones aware of the problem or that others were also aware of the problem. They hypothesized that subjects tested alone are more likely to offer help than subjects who believe other possible helpers are available. Darley and Latane measured people's willingness to help in two ways: whether they offered help and how long it took for help to be offered. They found significant and consistent results for both ways of assessing the dependent variable. Inconsistent results would have cast doubt on conclusions about the causal link between diffused responsibility and bystander apathy. Researchers who use multiple measures of the dependent variable and who find consistent results across measures have more confidence in the construct validity of their dependent variable. Results from the various measures are said to **triangulate** when they are consistent, because they converge on the same conclusion.

Sometimes tests measuring the dependent variable lack sufficient discrimination to demonstrate change or group differences. For example, if most people obtain very high scores, the instrument has a **ceiling effect**. This type of test will not allow researchers to demonstrate score improvement if pretest scores already are near-perfect; also, differences between groups cannot be demonstrated if both groups score at the top end of the scale. For example, adult experimental subjects may be mathematically superior to control subjects, but a simple arithmetic test may be too easy to demonstrate their superiority; all subjects may do well.

The opposite is a **floor effect**, in which most people obtain very low scores. This type of test will not allow researchers to demonstrate that treatment decreases scores or that two low-scoring groups are different. For example, if all clients score at the low end of a psychosis scale, the effectiveness of therapy cannot be demonstrated using this test; they already score at the low end of the scale at pretest. Groups of small children differing in verbal skills will not demonstrate differences on a test designed for college graduates; the test is too difficult and all children will score at the low end. Floor and ceiling effects illustrate this axiom: Variables must vary to be useful in research. Measures with floor and ceiling effects are not valid indicators of hypothetical constructs at required levels, so they weaken construct validity.

Another possible problem with measurements is **instrument drift**: finely tuned data collection devices may gradually change in accuracy. For example, batteries may run low or settings may need periodic adjustment. Instrument drift threatens the validity of studies because measurements are not uniformly reliable and valid. Experimenter drift, described in the last chapter, creates a similar problem. When drift occurs, measurements are not valid indicators, so construct validity is reduced.

Researcher Effects on Construct Validity for Conclusions

Each researcher or research team is unique. Experimenter bias effects that threaten internal validity also threaten construct validity for conclusions because researchers may be investigating different constructs, even when they apply the same labels. Researchers are not unbiased, disinterested parties. They are deeply involved in their projects, and they have biases toward some results and against others. Double-blind research strategies and other techniques described in the previous chapter may make generalizations about underlying theoretical constructs more trustworthy.

Subject reactivity to researcher characteristics threatens internal validity. Researchers may combat this threat by holding variables constant, such as by having all data collected by a single research assistant. Unfortunately, this may threaten the construct validity of the independent variable because results may be affected by characteristics of this single data collector, a variation of mono-operation bias. A better strategy might be use multiple data collectors or to balance their characteristics so that characteristics are not confounded with the independent variable. Researchers also can analyze the effect of data collectors and combine data with confidence if no differences are found.

A paradigm is a conceptual framework that encompasses a set of assumptions about the nature of the discipline and how research questions should be examined. For example, behavioral and psychoanalytic psychologists look at people differently, ask different types of questions, use different types of research strategies, and interpret results from a different framework. Barber (1976) argues that there is a pervasive **investigator paradigm effect**: "the prevailing paradigm determines not only what questions are asked but also what kinds of data are considered relevant and how the data will be gathered, analyzed, interpreted, and related to theoretical concepts" (p. 5). Researchers may not identify actual causes and effects; but, if they have only one paradigm, they may be unable to suggest alternative constructs. The investigator paradigm effect can produce **conceptual bandwagons**, ideas that are popular fads, and riding one may be "more a political than an intellectual event" (Mednick, 1989, p. 1118).

A major problem with the investigator paradigm effect is that psychologists who are overly enmeshed in one paradigm may not see the world accurately; they may misperceive evidence against the paradigm and may selectively notice or seek out evidence that supports their position. Journal editors who subscribe to paradigms may censor or discredit researchers who bring in new perspectives, and they may encourage researchers with studies conforming to their model. This biases the accumulated published research record.

Paradigms tend to outlive their usefulness. Early researchers found evidence for phrenology, the practice of inferring psychological characteristics from the shape of the skull. For example, Gall, the father of phrenology, believed that people with bulging eyes had good memories (Reuder, 1984). Although their theories have since been discredited, phrenologists established a paradigm that examined relationships between head shape and personality, and they developed the first concepts of brain localization.

This paradigm was used to make comparisons of head shapes to "prove" that Africans were genetically inferior to Europeans; and these conclusions were considered facts by many nineteenth-century scientists (Gould, 1981). A more recent conceptual bandwagon took one aspect of brain localization (laterality) and advocated treatments to "free" the creativity of the right brain to enhance athletic, artistic, and psychic abilities (Harrington, 1987). The efficacy of such treatments is "exceedingly doubtful" (Gleitman, 1991, p. 55).

Researchers must closely examine their own assumptions, make them explicit, and consider new ideas with open minds. They also should use the same open-minded, but critical, attitude when considering others' claims and paradigms. Multiple paradigms exist because no single paradigm explains all psychological phenomena. For example, most psychotherapists use an **eclectic** (multi-theory) **approach**, borrowing relevant ideas from various therapeutic perspectives to conceptualize and treat clients. Researchers who consider only one paradigm are like carpenters who only own a hammer. When the only tool you have is a hammer, everything looks like a nail.

Internal Validity and Construct Validity for Causal Conclusions

In the previous chapter, we reviewed threats to internal validity. These threats also jeopardize construct validity for causal conclusions. If an extraneous variable confounded with the independent variable actually caused changes in the dependent variable, there would be little construct validity for the hypothesized causal variable. Similarly, if evaluation apprehension or test sophistication undermined the measurement of the dependent variable, the construct validity for the effect would be weakened.

EXTERNAL VALIDITY

Research has external validity if causal conclusions generalize to other subjects, settings, and times. A major concern is whether results generalize to the real world. We ask questions such as "For which populations, settings, and times are conclusions accurate?" Each of these apects involves special considerations.

Subjects

Suppose a study is done in a Chicago classroom. Do subjects represent children in this school, all children in Chicago, all children in Illinois, all American children, or all children worldwide? Are results equally applicable to children varying in gender, ethnicity, social class, age, and geographical location? Would findings be true for children who are deaf, blind, or in single-parent homes, or for children who have English as a second language? Researchers address such questions as they examine external validity.

External validity across subjects usually is analyzed through literature reviews of studies conducted with different types of samples and through replications that extend the type of sample originally studied. Another strategy is to begin with a diverse sample; Cook and Campbell (1979) suggest deliberate **sampling for heterogeneity**. Sampling for heterogeneity may increase external validity because results reflect a wide variety of subjects. Sampling for heterogeneity generally decreases statistical validity, however, because it adds random variation (variation among subjects in the same condition), making the determination of group means less precise. In addition, this strategy may lead to inaccurate conclusions if groups differ substantially and only combined data are analyzed. For example, if outcomes are reversed in women and men and a diverse sample is examined, results for the two groups may cancel each other out. Findings for the heterogeneous sample would lack external validity when applied to each group separately. Researchers conducting large-scale studies can conduct subgroup analyses when subgroups of sufficient size are available. In this way, they can identify group differences. The use of stratified samples facilitates this process.

The population being examined may not be clear when nonprobability samples are studied. Considerable research is conducted with convenience samples, such as students taking introductory psychology courses. The accuracy of generalizations to other subjects depends on what is being studied. There is little reason to suspect that introductory psychology students have sensory systems, memory systems, or autonomic nervous systems that differ markedly from the rest of the population. Research on basic processes in college students probably generalizes well to any human population. Lack of random sampling does not necessarily threaten external validity. Because college students may be unlike other segments of the population in intelligence, motivation, and attitude toward social issues, however, results for these variables may not generalize well.

Sampling for heterogeneity may be useful for research involving nonprobability samples. If convenience samples are used, researchers can deliberately select quite different groups and examine external validity issues. For example, if two corporations will participate, researchers can select two that differ in size, product, managerial style, and location. If results are consistent, external validity is more certain; but if results are inconsistent, conclusions lack external validity. Researchers then can systematically examine the effects of corporate characteristics on findings.

Most research is conducted on volunteers, and volunteers may have unique characteristics that threaten external validity. Volunteers tend to be from higher social classes and to be better educated, more intelligent, more sociable, and in greater need of social approval than nonvolunteers. Research also suggests that women and people from small towns volunteer more often, and that volunteers may be younger and more arousal-seeking, unconventional, nonauthoritarian, altruistic, self-disclosing, maladjusted, and nonconforming than nonvolunteers (Rosenthal & Rosnow, 1991).

Volunteers also may have ulterior motives. Volunteers who return surveys may have unusually strong opinions, and they may be motivated to make political statements. Students who volunteer to participate in faculty's research may hope to earn higher grades. Prison inmates who volunteer may expect to be "paid" by early parole or special privileges, and they may not represent prisoners in general. This is further complicated by the fact that prisoners have been caught, found guilty, and incarcerated, so results for this group may not generalize to criminals who have not been caught.

Results may not generalize across demographic groups. For example, research conducted on Asian-American women may not generalize to African-American women or to men. Research conducted on adults may not generalize to children. Research conducted in Florida may not generalize to Alaska, and research conducted in England may not generalize to Japan. The need for replications across age, gender, ethnic, and geographical boundaries is clear.

Demographic groups may be defined too broadly. For example, Asian-Americans include groups of people with few cultural ties, such as those with roots in Tibet and the Philippines. New immigrants and fifth-generation Americans are combined, but they may have major differences in primary language, command of English, and cultural experiences. Results for one type of ethnic sample may not generalize to other samples from the same broadly-defined population. Immigration patterns also may influence findings. Studies conducted on ethnic minorities on the East Coast may not generalize to studies conducted on the West Coast. For example, East Coast Latinos probably include more people with roots in the Caribbean, and West Coast Latinos probably include more people with roots in Mexico. Their cultural traditions may be so different that results do not generalize, limiting external validity.

Pretest sensitization and repeatedly measuring the dependent variable can affect external validity in studies with repeated measurements. For example, suppose we are evaluating the effectiveness of a drug created to eliminate heroin addiction. We recruit a sample of heroin addicts, give them the experimental drug, and regularly monitor their urine for evidence of heroin use. Positive results suggest the drug is effective. Would you expect these results to generalize to heroin addicts who are not monitored? It is possible that simply monitoring their blood has produced the decrease in heroin use because subjects fear criminal prosecution or public detection of their habit. Testing and the independent variable are confounded, threatening the internal and external validity of conclusions.

Psychologists frequently conduct research with animal subjects. Generalizing results to humans or to some other species may not be important. For example, when bats' echo location skills are studied, researchers may not be interested in generalizing to other species. However, sometimes processes are studied and results are generalized to other animals. For example, Pavlov's work on classical conditioning was conducted with dogs, Selye's work on stress and his development of the general adaptation syndrome were primarily conducted with rats, and much work on the functioning of the central nervous system has been conducted with rats, cats, and monkeys. The external validity of such studies for generalizations across species must be empirically demonstrated.

Settings

Research is conducted in particular settings, such as university laboratories or city streets. Would the same results be obtained if studies were replicated in different settings? Situational variables confounded with the independent variable may lead to conclusions that are invalid in other settings. For example, altruistic (helping) behaviors are more likely when subjects are alone than when they share the call for help with other bystanders (Darley & Latane, 1968). Findings in one setting will not generalize to the other.

Concerns about volunteers also apply to organizations. Businesses, schools, hospitals, and other facilities that allow researchers to use their organizations' space, records, and personnel may be atypical. Cook and Campbell (1979) conclude that volunteer organizations often are more "progressive, proud, and institutionally exhibitionist" (p. 74) than facilities that decline to participate. Replications and subgroup analyses allow researchers to examine generalizations across settings.

One criticism of carefully controlled experiments is the artificial nature of the research environment. Critics argue that true experiments lack **ecological validity**, generalizability to the real world. Subjects may react in unusual ways to white-coated scientists, pristine laboratory conditions, and carefully controlled situations, and these reactions may undermine generalizations to complicated real-life settings. For example, Weisz, Weiss, and Donenberg (1992) found that experimental results on the effectiveness of therapy for children in research laboratories do not appear to generalize well to typical mental health clinics that treat children.

Laboratory experiments do have ecological validity if they examine processes important outside the laboratory. Laboratories need not have **surface realism**, precise duplication of the real world. The question is not if laboratories are the same as the rest of the world; they lack surface realism. The question is if phenomena studied in the laboratory also operate in other environments (Berkowitz & Donnerstein, 1982). Many laboratory findings have strong ecological validity. For example, antidepressant medications developed in laboratory settings function effectively in humans' day-to-day lives, and behavioral therapists routinely and effectively apply learning principles developed in human and animal experiments. Box 9.1 summarizes Mook's (1983) argument that psychologists have overestimated the importance of external validity for theory-based experimental research.

Time

Are research conclusions applicable today, to the past, and to the future? This may be hard to judge because each generation faces different challenges (e.g., wars, moon landings, nuclear threats, and economic crises). Researchers can have more confidence generalizing across time if present results confirm findings from previous research.

Sometimes the independent variable is confounded with history. The cause of change in the dependent variable is not the stated independent variable, but events that occur when the study is conducted. For example, work training programs for the unemployed may be successful during times of full employment (when new employees are hard to recruit) and may fail during times of recession (when many skilled employees are looking for work). The state of the economy at the time of the program's functioning may be the major causal variable. Results on the program's effectiveness will not generalize across time if periods of full employment and recession are studied, so they will not have external validity.

Replication

The basis for evaluating external validity is replication across subjects, settings, and times. Working in the 1960s, Horner (1969) developed a theoretical construct called fear of success, and she used her theory to explain gender differences in achievement. Box 9.2 describes attempts to replicate her findings. Results show limited external validity. Psychologists develop an understanding of the limits of their theories by discovering when they are not applicable, and they are challenged to develop new theories when evidence for external validity is weak.

Replications across subjects, settings, and times may require adaptations of operational definitions. Researchers must translate questionnaires to use them cross-culturally, and stimulus materials may have to be altered. Researchers conducting

---

Box 9.1

Is Research That Lacks External Validity Invalid?

Mook (1983) argues that psychologists have overestimated the importance of external validity for experiments. Experiments most often are designed to test deductions made from theories, rather than to find results that generalize to the real world. Psychologists generalize from the theory, rather than from the experiment. Mook argues that experiments apply only indirectly to the real world, through their contributions to theory development. Experimental psychologists "are not *making* generalizations, but *testing* them" (p. 380). They ask, "Under these specified conditions, are theoretical predictions accurate?"

Tightly controlled experiments offer "pure" investigations of a theory's limits. A valid theory should hold true for any population, so the exact population sampled is not necessarily important. If diffusion of responsibility leads to bystander apathy, this should be true for college sophomores in an introductory psychology course, nuns in a convent, and pedestrians on a street corner. If the theory is not confirmed, it is amended to account for what has been found.

Carefully controlled conditions may have no analogue in the real world. The real world doesn't have cloth and wire monkey mothers, tachistoscopes that flash stimuli to the left vi-

sual field, or electrodes that measure brain waves; but psychologists have used these devices to develop important theoretical understandings of attachment, brain localization, and information processing. Psychologists conducting research in "artificial" laboratory settings are interested in uncovering what "can" happen. Biofeedback technology and associated biofeedback therapies would never exist had psychologists restricted their research settings to what happens naturally in the real world. Moving into the laboratory, psychologists could ask previously unthought-of questions, such as "Can people control brain waves?"

Mook does not discount the importance of external validity for some studies. Research conducted to create generalizable results clearly requires external validity. For example, survey research conducted to predict the outcome of an upcoming election is designed to have direct, real-world application. Representative samples are essential to avoid biased results, and the survey must contain questions that validly reveal citizens' actual behavior in the voting booth. Mook argues that the real test of a theory is its eventual usefulness, but experiments designed to examine a theory should not be judged on the direct external validity of their findings.

learning experiments might have fish swim, birds fly, and rats walk through mazes, and these mazes must be fabricated differently. Materials appropriate for children may be inappropriate for adults, and vice versa. For example, cognitive tests for young children require them to demonstrate their vocabularies by pointing at pictures, but cognitive tests for older children and adults require them to generate abstract definitions. Major personality, interest, and ability tests are revised periodically because items become obsolete or take on different meanings. These adaptations threaten the construct validity of causal conclusions because new operational definitions may not measure the same theoretical constructs. Researchers also may deliberately adapt materials to test alternative explanations. For example, Horner's subjects (Box 9.2) responded to same-gender cues, and results did not generalize when other researchers presented opposite-gender cues.

Box 9.2

Fear of Success

Horner (1969) speculated that the achievement gap between women and men is caused by women's fear of success. Everyone fears failure; it's embarrassing. However, Horner speculated that women also fear success because they equate success with unpopularity and loss of femininity. Because women fear success and also fear failure, they strive to be average—good, but not excellent. Men, she speculated, do not fear success because competitiveness and ambition are masculine characteristics. Horner's ideas received wide distribution by the popular media. Articles appeared in *Psychology Today* and *The New York Times*, and a popular book and tape designed to help women overcome fear of success (Friedman, 1980, 1985) were published. Horner's ideas became a conceptual bandwagon because she offered an explanation of male dominance in the work force.

Horner measured fear of success by administering a projective test to college undergraduates. Women were asked to respond to Anne, a first-year medical student at the top of her class, and men were asked to respond to John, a first-year medical student at the top of his class. Horner assumed that subjects would project personal attitudes toward success onto Anne and John. As she predicted, Horner found many more fear-of-success responses among women, who reported that Anne faced social rejection and loss of femininity and that Anne was ugly and would never find a man. In addition, women were more likely to give bizarre responses, such as the suggestion that Anne would be beaten up by her classmates, that Anne would drop out to become a nurse, or that Anne was a fictitious person created by a group of male students who took tests in her name. Men described John as successful and as having a productive future in medicine.

The external validity of Horner's study is in doubt. Results using Horner's technique did not generalize across subjects or time. Replications found reversed or no gender differences, and no trends across time were apparent (Paludi, 1984; Tresemer, 1977; Zuckerman & Wheeler, 1975). Results also did not generalize to African-Americans, where no gender difference was found (Paludi, 1984). Results did not generalize across different operational definitions of fear of success. For example, Cherry and Deaux changed "medical school" to "nursing school" and found both men and women wrote fear-of-success stories for Anne in medical school and for John in nursing school (Hyde, 1991). Horner's study confounded subject and stimulus gender. Monahan, Kuhn, and Shaver (1974) and others (Nash, 1979) also found that men give fear-of-success responses to Anne. Results suggest that Horner's test measures cultural stereotypes about women in nontraditional occupations (Hyde, 1991).

Work continues on fear of success. Researchers are seeking more effective measures and more thorough understanding of when people will exhibit fear of success and how fear of success affects behavior. After reviewing the accumulated evidence, Mednick (1989) concludes that fear of success is a concept that "refuses to be buried" in spite of its "problematic scientific status" because it "survives on intuitive appeal" (p. 1119), and Hyde (1991) concludes that fear of success probably exists in some people, but "there is not much scientific evidence for it" (p. 169).

As Barber (1976) states, "There are so many pitfalls in any one experimental study that we should not take any one study too seriously" (p. 87). Literature reviews can be used to search backward, and subsequent studies can extend results forward. Meta-analyses (See Box 9.3) examining the effects of subjects, settings, and times can be

---

Box 9.3

Meta-Analysis

Meta-analysis, a summary of the results of multiple studies, allows researchers to systematically examine external validity by investigating consistency of results across subjects, settings, and times. Meta-analysis formalizes and quantifies the review of accumulated research on specific relationships. Traditionally, researchers conduct literature reviews by qualitative analysis, and they produce narrative summaries. Results from multiple studies can provide data, however, and these data can be analyzed quantitatively. Meta-analysis is becoming increasingly popular because it provides quantitative summaries of accumulated research on specific relationships. For example, Smith and Glass (1977) analyzed hundreds of studies to examine the efficacy of therapy and found that treated clients fared better than subjects in untreated control groups. The overall effect of therapy was to increase clients' functioning by about 70 percent of a standard deviation. Therapy had larger effect sizes for treating fear, anxiety, and self-esteem problems (average effect sizes close to 1.0) than for treating general adjustment or achievement problems (average effect sizes of .56 and .31, respectively).

Two approaches to meta-analysis have been developed: combining studies and comparing studies (Rosenthal, 1984). Researchers can combine results from multiple studies to create a single summary statistic that estimates an overall significance probability or effect size, and they can ask if studies have

homogeneous or heterogeneous significance probabilities or effect sizes. Heterogeneous results suggest problems with external validity because findings are inconsistent. If results are heterogeneous, researchers can focus attention on explaining these differences. For example, if studies of gender differences in aggression use behavioral or self-report data, the meta-analyst may ask if the type of data influences the relationship between gender and aggression. Effect sizes or significance probabilities found using behavioral data are compared to corresponding statistics found using self-report data to see if results are significantly different. The meta-analyst is checking to see if results have external validity across studies.

Meta-analysis has proven useful for the analysis of many psychological phenomena, including the effectiveness of therapy and medical treatment for mental health problems; the effect of school desegregation, class size, tutoring, computer-assisted instruction, and ability grouping on learning; and gender differences in cognitive and interpersonal functioning (Mullen & Rosenthal, 1985). Meta-analysis can produce more powerful tests of relationships by combining results of multiple studies.

Rosenthal (1984) reports a meta-analysis of nearly 350 studies examining the effects of self-fulfilling prophecies on data collection. Results suggest that self-fulfilling prophecies have stronger effects in animal studies than in human studies. Whether subjects are

---

used to examine external validity. Literature reviews also may uncover gaps in the accumulated literature, suggesting useful studies that examine variables in unexplored ways. Extending results through replication is crucial for a complete understanding of psychological phenomena. Novice researchers, by carefully analyzing previous findings, may discover opportunities for important contributions through well-conceived replications.

human affects the influence of self-fulfilling prophecies. Similarly, Eagly (1978) analyzed trends in the literature on gender differences in influenceability. She compared results from studies conducted prior to 1970 to results of studies conducted since 1970, and she found that older studies are four times more likely to show that women are more easily influenced than men. Results suggest that social changes in the late 1960s and early 1970s may be responsible for this change in gender's effect size. Conclusions did not have external validity across time.

Critics have pointed out some problems with meta-analysis. One problem that affects both traditional and meta-analytic reviews is the **file drawer problem**. Research with significant results is more likely to be published than research without significant results; so, presumably, researchers have file drawers stuffed with unpublished nonsignificant findings. This biases the accumulated literature. Another problem involves "combining apples and oranges." Meta-analysts combine studies that identify the independent and dependent variables using different operational definitions, and this may be like combining apples with oranges (Rosenthal, 1984). Proponents of meta-analysis argue that all literature reviews involve such combinations, and that combining data is the essence of research. Just as researchers average data from individual subjects to achieve unbiased estimates of parameters, meta-analysts combine data from different studies to achieve unbiased estimates of effect sizes. They use meta-analysis to distinguish between phenomena with strong effect sizes over a variety of studies and phenomena that do not generalize well across studies.

Other critics argue against a single-number summary of effect size or significance level. Meta-analysts are not prohibited from describing the richness of their literature review in traditional narrative form, and they systematically examine possible variables that might affect results. Perhaps a more reasonable criticism is that a unique summary statistic has yet to be agreed upon. Formal meta-analysis is relatively new to psychology, and procedures are evolving. Different meta-analytic procedures use alternative summary statistics for effect sizes. Time will tell which, if any, of the presently suggested statistics will predominate in future meta-analytic reviews. In addition, further development is needed for objective ways to weight research varying in quality, to estimate computational values from incomplete research reports, and to weight groups of results from the same study, laboratory, or research team. As Rosenthal (1984) concludes, "Our procedures are not perfect, we can use them inappropriately, and we will make mistakes. Nevertheless, the alternative to the systematic, explicit, quantitative procedures is even less perfect, even more likely to be applied inappropriately, and even more likely to lead us to error" (p. 17).

PRIORITIZING THE FOUR TYPES OF VALIDITY

Researchers must make many decisions when they plan experiments. As Cook and Campbell (1979) point out, sometimes strategies designed to enhance one type of validity threaten another type of validity. For example, statistical and internal validity are higher when conditions are carefully controlled, but external validity may be higher when naturally occurring variables are examined; and statistical validity generally is strengthened by the use of within-subject variables, but repeated measures may create subject reactivity threats to the other types of validity. Researchers attempt to maximize all types of validity, but sometimes they must make compromises in one type to enhance another.

Cook and Campbell suggest that the top priority for researchers who conduct experiments to test theories is internal validity, followed by construct validity of the cause, statistical validity, construct validity of the effect, and external validity. As Mook (1983, Box 9.1) argued, external validity is not high priority for theory-based researchers. Causes are the independent variables in theoretical research, and these are carefully manipulated and controlled. Croyle and Cooper (1983, Box 2.1) conducted a pilot study just to demonstrate the construct validity of their manipulated independent variable because this type of validity was crucial for testing Festinger's theory.

Cook and Campbell suggest that applied researchers who conduct experiments frequently place top priority on internal validity, followed by external validity, construct validity of the effect, statistical validity, and construct validity of the cause. External validity is much more important to them than to basic researchers because they are examining real-world problems, and their goal frequently involves finding solutions to these problems. Construct validity for effects is more important to them because they are seeking ways to produce these effects. For example, an applied research team may examine causes of adolescent depression. They focus on the issue of adolescent depression, and this issue is the dependent variable in their research. They are not interested in finding causes for other dependent variables, so construct validity of their measurement of the effect is crucial.

Cook and Campbell placed internal validity at the top of both lists because they were prioritizing validity issues for experiments. "The unique purpose of experiments is to provide stronger tests of *causal* hypotheses than is permitted by other forms of research" (1979, p. 84). Internal validity is necessary to make any inferences about *causation*. Researchers conducting descriptive or correlational studies may have less interest in examining causal relationships. For example, correlational research may be conducted to analyze relationships among personality or cognitive variables. The goal is to document these relationships, and researchers may hope to make predictions based on documented relationships. For example, an issue-based research team may examine characteristics related to recidivism in prison inmates (subsequent arrests, convictions, and returns to jail). This information may not involve causal relationships, but it may be useful to parole boards when they consider applications for early release from custody. These researchers probably have external validity as their top priority. Are predictions accurate in the samples, settings, and times under which decisions are made?

All four types of validity are important. Research with statistical, internal, construct, and external validity will satisfy every researcher. Nevertheless, sometimes tradeoffs are necessary. Research planners should recognize that there are four types of research validity, and they should thoughtfully consider their own priorities in order to design studies that meet their objectives.

CHAPTER SUMMARY

Research has construct validity for causal conclusions if underlying theoretical constructs for causes and effects are identified correctly. Researchers may examine the validity of causal variables studied in experiments by conducting manipulation checks, and they may determine the validity of dependent variables through triangulation of multiple measures of the dependent variable. Mono-operation biases may lead to incorrect identification of causal variables. Measurement problems, such as floor and ceiling effects and instrument and experimenter drift, threaten the construct validity of dependent variable measurements. Researchers and journal editors may be biased by the paradigms they share, limiting the construct validity of their conclusions and the range of constructs considered.

Research has external validity if causal conclusions generalize to other subjects, settings, and times. A major concern of applied researchers is whether results generalize to the real world.

Replications can be used to examine generalization to other subjects, and researchers may decide to sample for heterogeneity to obtain results descriptive of a broad population. Lack of random sampling, the use of volunteers, pretest sensitization, and lack of generalizability across and within levels of demographic variables and across species may threaten this aspect of external validity. In addition, simply monitoring the dependent variable may weaken generalization to subjects that are not so carefully monitored.

Results may not generalize to other settings. Research in volunteer organizations may not generalize to other organizations. One criticism of laboratory experiments is their lack of ecological validity. Surface realism is not required for an experiment to have ecological validity, but experiments do have to examine phenomena that operate in other environments.

Researchers have more confidence generalizing across time if present results confirm findings from previous research. Research may not generalize if results are confounded with historical phenomena.

The basis for evaluating external validity is replication. Literature reviews, perhaps involving meta-analyses, and replications can be used to estimate the extent of external validity and to identify opportunities for further research.

Sometimes researchers must compromise some types of validity to insure that other types are high. Cook and Campbell have suggested priorities for theory-based and applied experiments.

Key Concepts

ceiling effect	investigator paradigm effect
conceptual bandwagon	mono-operation bias
eclectic approach	retrospective accounts
ecological validity	sampling for heterogeneity
file drawer problem	surface realism
floor effect	triangulate
instrument drift	

Review Questions

1. Box 6.5 contains a scenario questionnaire used in a study of people's reactions to a hypothetical woman with AIDS who was infected in different ways (through a blood transfusion, unsafe sex, sex with her husband, or drug use). Design a brief survey that could be used as a manipulation check for this study.

2. Earl wants to examine the effect of perceived expertise on attitude change. He plans to randomly assign subjects to one of two conditions. In one condition arguments are given by a person introduced as "Dr. Goldstein, a renowned expert on this topic," and in the other condition the same arguments are given by the same person, but she is introduced as "Mrs. Goldstein, a cashier at a drugstore." Comment on the construct validity of Earl's independent variable.

3. Denise is discouraged because her dependent variables did not triangulate. Why is this a problem?

4. Dorothy examines altruism by dropping a box of pencils in a shopping mall and observing people's responses. Sam examines altruism by giving pairs of children three pieces of candy and observing how the candies are shared. What aspects of construct validity are relevant when their studies are compared?

5. Brittanie is a behaviorist, and Jim has a psychoanalytic perspective. Each is asked to conduct a literature review on dreams. How might their paradigms affect their analyses?

6. Gene's attempt to demonstrate that motivational lectures can increase children's accuracy on *New York Times* crossword puzzles has failed. How might a floor or ceiling effect have threatened the internal validity of his study?

7. Can the concept of sampling for heterogeneity be applied to settings and times to increase the external validity of results? Explain your answers.

8. Davina conducts a study of attitudes toward capital punishment by collecting data in an introductory psychology class. Are results likely to have external validity in the general population? Explain your answer. When do convenience samples yield biased results?

9. Vernon analyzed data for a sample of volunteers and found that most people were willing to donate blankets and food to earthquake victims. Are results likely to have external validity in the general population? Explain your answer.

10. Frances conducts a literature review and discovers that studies on the East Coast find that Protestants are more conservative than Catholics, but studies on the West Coast find that Catholics are more conservative than Protestants. How might these findings be explained?

11. Female cats have estrus cycles (with periods "in heat" and infertile periods without sexual activity). Can studies of cats' sexual activity be generalized to humans? Why or why not?

12. Studies conducted in a prestigious bank found that salaries of middle managers are not related to productivity. Are results likely to generalize to other businesses? Why or why not?

13. David disregards all findings from laboratory studies. He claims they lack ecological validity. Describe Mook's perspective on this issue. Do you agree with David or Mook? Explain your answer.

14. Eagly (1978) compared results from studies conducted prior to 1970 to results of studies conducted since 1970. She found that older studies are more likely to show that women are more easily influenced than men. How can you explain this lack of external validity across time?

15. Micah and Carey are required to conduct a senior thesis. Micah hopes to design one big study that will answer all questions ever asked by psychologists. Carey plans to conduct several studies that replicate and extend results into new subjects, settings, and times. Which student is more likely to make lasting contributions to the discipline? Why?

16. A key phrase for understanding internal validity is *rival hypothesis*; and a key word for understanding external validity is *generalization.* Explain internal and external validity using these terms.

17. Consider Cook and Campbell's (1979) validity priorities for theory-based and applied experiments. Describe an experiment that you are familiar with or that you might like to conduct. How would you prioritize the validity requirements for this experiment?

18. Meta-analysts have been accused of inaccurate results because of the file drawer problem and because they combine apples with oranges. Are these criticisms also relevant to traditional literature reviews? How serious are these problems? How can psychologists address them?

10

Descriptive Studies

Four types of research will be described in Chapters 10 through 14: descriptive studies, correlational studies, experiments, and applied research. Each can be used for multiple purposes, but each has a unique major purpose. Descriptive studies summarize characteristics of some person or group. Their major purpose is to describe phenomena of interest. Correlational studies examine relationships among naturally occurring variables. Their major purpose is to discover which variables are related. Experimental studies systematically evaluate the effects of independent variables on dependent variables. Their major purpose is to demonstrate causal relationships. Applied research is designed to meet practical needs. Its major purpose is to answer immediate, practical questions.

Although Cook and Campbell's (1979) four types of research validity were developed to evaluate experiments, the same criteria can be relevant to nonexperimental studies. Statistical validity is important whenever hypothesis testing is used or relationships are concluded. Narrative descriptive studies that include discussions of relationships should document evidence that these relationships really exist. Causality is an important aspect of Cook and Campbell's other three types of validity, but descriptive and correlational studies may be used to examine noncausal relationships. The general notions of construct validity and external validity (without causal requirements) are relevant to any study. If researchers claim to be examining theoretical constructs measured by observed variables, they should provide evidence that their operational definitions have construct validity. Results that generalize across subjects, settings, times, and operational definitions of variables, even if cause-and-effect relationships are not examined, have generality that exemplifies external validity.

There are two major types of descriptive studies: case studies and archival research. **Case studies** are in-depth analyses of specific individuals or groups. **Archival research** is the analysis of records and artifacts.

CASE STUDIES

Uses of Case Studies

Case studies can be used to illustrate a phenomenon of interest, to demonstrate the effect of some intervention, or to provide evidence to develop or to examine a theory.

Psychologists frequently develop case studies of individuals with unusual characteristics. For example, Thigpen and Cleckley, in *The Three Faces of Eve* (1954), describe a woman with three personalities: Eve White, Eve Black, and Jane. Eve White was a demure, controlled, and conventional woman who suffered from headaches and blackouts. After several months of treatment, Eve Black appeared during a therapy session. This Eve was outgoing and flirtatious. Later, the more integrated Jane appeared. *The Three Faces of Eve* is a classic description of a woman with multiple personality disorder. More recently published was *The Man Who Mistook His Wife for a Hat* (1985). In this book Oliver Sacks describes cases with unique neurological problems, including a man who reached for his wife when he intended to get his hat. Yalom, in *Love's Executioner* (1989), describes ten clients' progress in therapy and gives us insight into their lives and the therapy process they shared. Peters and Waterman (*In Search of Excellence,* 1982) offered case studies of American corporations known for excellence. Each of these books provides useful descriptions, and each reached a relatively wide audience, educating the public. Roger Sperry's case studies on the psychological effects of having a split brain are summarized in Box 10.1.

Case studies frequently are reported in order to illustrate therapeutic techniques. For example, Neale and Liebert (1969) described a technique for increasing speech volume. They were working to develop speech in a mute, psychotic woman. When she began to talk, she was almost inaudible. The therapists rigged a device that lit up when she spoke loudly enough, and she was encouraged to make the light go on. She soon was consistently audible.

Collections of case studies also are available. For example, Wedding and Corsini (1989) edited a book with twelve therapeutic case studies that illustrate different therapy styles, including cases presented by Carl Rogers, Albert Ellis, Rollo May, and Aaron Beck. Readers can see how these therapists put their theories into action with actual clients.

Psychology faculty share case studies of teaching strategies in the journal *Teaching of Psychology.* For example, Wilson and Marcus (1992) describe how they teach the anatomy of sheep brains by requiring students to make three-dimensional PlayDoh sculptures, and Benn and Gay (1992) describe their interdisciplinary honors course on

---

Box 10.1

Case Studies of Split-Brain Patients

Roger Sperry (1968) joined two neurosurgeons, Philip Vogel and Joseph Bogen, to evaluate the psychological characteristics of split-brain patients. The brain is divided into two major hemispheres that are in constant communication through connective tissue, the corpus callosum. The corpus callosum can be surgically severed, isolating the two hemispheres. This has been done to eliminate debilitating seizures in patients with severe epilepsy that could not be controlled with medication.

Their first analyses were done on one split-brain patient, but eventually more than a dozen were studied. The first patient was a middle-aged veteran who had been struck in the head repeatedly in a concentration camp, leading to severe, uncontrollable seizures that occurred a dozen or more times a day.

Sperry and his colleagues flashed visual stimuli on a screen. Subjects were asked to fixate their eyes on a central dot, and two words were flashed, such as KEY on the left and CASE on the right. KEY was transmitted to the right brain, and CASE was transmitted to the left brain. The left hemisphere, which specializes in language, would report that the word CASE was read; but if the subject was asked to use the left hand (directed by the right hemisphere) to pick up the designated object, a key would be picked up. Split-brain patients had split minds. Some reported anecdotes confirmed this conclusion, such as buttoning a shirt with the left hand, followed immediately by the right hand unbuttoning it.

Sperry and his colleagues also found that the two brains can have different memories. When a group of objects were shown to the left brain, these objects were recognized if displayed again to the left brain, but were viewed as if for the first time if shown to the right brain. Sensations of touch also were not communicated. An object held in the right hand could be named easily by the left hemisphere. An object in the left hand could not be named by the right hemisphere, but could be recognized if touched again by the left hand. (The right brain knew what it felt, but it could not name the object.) An object held in the left hand could not be recognized by the touch of the right hand. Subjects were given an object to hold in each hand, then were asked to find them by touch among a group of objects. The two hands moved independently, each searching for its own object, unaware of the other hand's goal.

Were the split-brain patients running into walls, tripping over their own feet, or having trouble feeding themselves? Not at all. The carefully controlled laboratory conditions prohibited shared information in the two hemispheres by flashing stimuli into one hemisphere or by allowing objects to be manipulated by one hand hidden from view. Under normal circumstance, the two hemispheres are exposed to the same information, so they operate on shared information. Patients also developed tricks to compensate for their split minds, such as "talking to themselves." The left brain would talk out loud to the right brain, and the right brain would point at objects with the left hand to direct the left brain's attention. The left brain controlled language, but the right brain demonstrated its own skills, such as facial recognition.

Sperry's research earned him a Nobel prize in physiology and medicine in 1981. His case studies demonstrated that split brains can produce split minds and that people can adapt to compensate for this bizarre condition (Schwartz, 1986).

children's rights. Faculty who read these articles are encouraged to try these ideas on their own campuses.

Theories have been inspired by case studies. Notable in this area is the work of Jean Piaget, a Swiss psychologist who developed a theory of child development, basing many of his ideas on observations of his own children. Another classic case study involves a little boy named Albert (Watson & Rayner, 1920). The researchers wanted to demonstrate that specific fears can be generalized. A sudden, loud noise was made by experimenters whenever Albert reached for a white rat. Soon Albert cried at the sight of this rat and also when he was presented with similar objects, such as a white rabbit and a Santa Claus beard. (Researchers would have trouble obtaining approval for this study from current ethics review boards.)

Descriptive studies of unusual cases also may be used for theory evaluation. A good theory should be consistent with all facts, including unusual cases. A theory that predicts or explains the usual and fails to predict or to explain the unusual is questionable. For example, theories about the development of sexuality should predict and explain the full range of sexual targets and behaviors found in humans. Theories that cannot account for unusual cases require reexamination because they appear to lack external validity.

Field Research

Case studies of behaviors and social processes in their natural setting are sometimes called **field research** or **naturalistic observations**. Field researchers may observe juvenile delinquent gangs, political groups, prison inmates, or corporate executives in their normal environments. Such research is performed in the field, rather than in the laboratory. Classic field studies include Festinger's (Festinger, Riecken, & Schachter, 1956) examination of a doomsday cult that predicted a cataclysmic flood and Zimbardo's (1969) studies of street vandalism.

Field research may involve structured or unstructured observations of social processes. Structured observations generally involve a rating form, such as the Child-Parent Interaction Rating Form in Chapter 6. For example, Kagan, Reznick, and Snidman (1988) studied shyness in two-year-olds by recording how children responded to strangers. They analyzed the extent to which children clung to their mothers, became quieter, and retreated when introduced to strangers. Unstructured observations generally are collected in a journal of field notes. Notes should be made simultaneously with observations or soon after, to maintain accurate records, and observed behaviors and interpretations should be kept separate. Interpretations should be treated as hypotheses, rather than as facts. These hypotheses can guide further observations or research.

Field researchers must develop sampling strategies for making observations, and some specialized strategies have been developed for this purpose. **Continuous sampling** is observing subjects for a period of time, recording behaviors during the whole time period. When complex behaviors are studied, continuous sampling may be more reliable and valid if the material is videotaped, so researchers can analyze behaviors repeatedly and carefully. **Time sampling** is recording behaviors only at specific times. **Time-point sampling** is recording behaviors at specific points in time, such as recording behaviors that occur at one, five, and ten minutes into the observation. **Time-interval sampling** is recording behaviors during preselected intervals, such as one-minute intervals at ten, twenty, and thirty minutes into the observation. Time-point data are like

---

Box 10.2

Active Listening Skills

1. Ask open-ended questions.
2. Be quiet and listen.
3. Attend to what is said with respect and acceptance.
5. Maintain eye contact and orientation toward the speaker.
4. Be relaxed, warm, interested, and open. Avoid being judgmental or hostile.
5. Keep the conversation flowing with minimum contributions, such as "Mm-hm" and "I see."
6. Avoid trying to fill every second with words. Give the other person time to think. Indicate nonverbally that the other person should continue.
7. Don't abruptly change the topic. Go with the flow of the conversation.
8. Occasionally confirm what you just heard by briefly paraphrasing it. Don't embellish or fabricate details.
9. Occasionally verify your conclusions by phrasing them and allowing the speaker to accept or to reject them.
10. Use closed-ended questions only to obtain specific facts, such as age and marital status.

---

a series of photographs, time-interval data are like a movie with the camera turned on and off during the filming, and continuous sampling data are like a movie made by never turning the camera off during the filming.

Sampling can also be made by individuals or events. **Individual sampling** is recording behaviors for subjects one at a time, such as separately observing each individual for three minutes. Sometimes event sampling is used. **Event sampling** is recording observations only during specific events. For example, researchers interested in vandalism could station themselves in areas with frequent vandalism, then record behaviors only when vandalism occurs. A time-sampling strategy would be less effective for this study because events may not occur when observations are made. Combinations of sampling strategies may be applied, such as observing first the female, then the male behavior (individual sampling) for repeated time intervals (time-interval sampling) when they're dancing (event sampling).

Sometimes observations are augmented by interviews with selected informants. These interviews may be structured or unstructured. **Structured interviews** are oral surveys, with the same questions given to each subject. **Unstructured interviews** are individually tailored; each unstructured interview may involve a unique set of questions. Active listening skills, such as those practiced by therapists, are especially important for conducting unstructured interviews, and many of these skills also are useful for handling open-ended questions on structured interviews. The goal of **active listening** is to understand someone else. It differs from normal communication because it does not stress mutual exchange of information. Some active listening skills are summarized in Box 10.2.

A striking example of field research is Rosenhan's (1973) study of mental hospitals. Rosenhan conducted a still controversial study in which volunteers were **participant observers** (researchers who pretend to be group members) in mental hospitals, viewing the hospital staff and patients from the perspective of a patient. Rosenhan hypothesized that psychiatric diagnoses would be valid if pseudopatients could be quickly recognized, but psychiatric diagnoses would be suspect if pseudopatients were not discovered. This study demonstrates the richness of observations and the controversy surrounding their interpretation. Rosenhan and his confederates originally did not expect to be admitted, and they were surprised by their experiences. Their field study led to unexpected and interesting conclusions.

Case Studies of Animals

Case studies also may involve animals. Jane Goodall's analyses of chimpanzees (1986) and other animals and Dian Fossey's (1972) descriptions of gorillas are well-known case studies of animal behavior that reached a wide audience. Researchers who conduct case studies of animals must be careful to avoid **anthropomorphic thinking**, attributing human motives and characteristics to animals. For example, an insect's buzzing may be the inadvertent sound of its wings moving, not a deliberate attempt to annoy the observing human.

The Observers

All case studies involve observers. The observers may be therapists describing their own clients or may be members of research teams. Field study observers could be actual participants in social organizations being analyzed (such as professors who describe faculty meetings), could be participant observers (pretending to be group members), or could be outside the group. Group members may or may not be aware of the observer's status as a researcher, and informed consent may or may not have been obtained. Critics object to case studies without informed consent because of related ethical problems, but ethics review boards may approve such studies if subjects' anonymity is protected.

Observations can be obtrusive or unobtrusive, and obtrusive observations are more likely to elicit subject reactivity. For example, parents may be more attentive to children when they know observers are present. Sometimes researchers using obtrusive observations try to reduce subject reactivity by not recording behaviors until subjects become accustomed to the researchers' presence. For example, when Addison (1986) conducted a videotaped observational study of preschool children, he waited five days before data collection. By then the children appeared to ignore him and his equipment.

Experimenter expectancy effects occur when results are biased by experimenters. Biases may create selective attention to information that supports experimenters' ideas. For example, Lyons and Serbin (1986) found that observers who expect boys to be more aggressive than girls are less likely to notice girls' disagreements. Biases also may affect interpretations. For example, observers of an abortion clinic may interpret behaviors and intentions differently, depending on their personal views regarding these activities. Participant observers run the risk of creating a self-fulfilling prophecy, unintentionally manipulating subjects to behave in ways previously predicted. For example, participant observers may influence group decisions by suggesting or by arguing for a specific agenda. As Rosenthal and his colleagues (Rosenthal, 1966) demonstrated, these effects threaten research validity.

A problem with descriptive studies is **cultural relativism**: our interpretations are based on our own cultural heritage and may be inaccurate for other cultures. An-

---

Box 10.3

Rosenhan's Study of Mental Hospitals

Rosenhan (1973) and seven confederates (a housewife, painter, pediatrician, psychology graduate student, psychiatrist, and two other psychologists), all without psychiatric history, presented themselves at twelve different public and private mental hospitals in five states and complained of the same symptom. They said they were hearing voices, and although they said most of the language was unclear, they could make out the words "hollow," "empty," and "thud." Except for giving false names and occupations, they behaved normally, gave honest answers to questions, and after being admitted, they reported no more symptoms. All were diagnosed as psychotic.

Their goal was to behave normally in order to see how long they would be retained. On their second day they asked to see the admitting psychiatrist, reported that the symptoms were gone, and indicated they wished to be released. Discharge was more difficult than admission. They were kept in the hospitals from 7 to 52 days, an average of 19 days, and eventually were released with the diagnosis of their psychosis being in remission. (Sometimes spouses or colleagues came to facilitate discharge, and one researcher "escaped" after two months because he could no longer tolerate hospitalization.)

The researchers kept field notes on their observations. Staff did not treat them as individual people with dignity, but as "mental patients." Staff avoided eye contact and ignored their attempts to communicate. Four pseudopatients made careful records of their interactions with hospital staff. They attempted to speak to the psychiatrists a total of 185 times, but were completely ignored on 71 percent of these attempts. The psychiatrists stopped to respond to only 6 percent of their communications. They were even less successful with lower-level staff. They made 1283 attempts to speak to nurses and attendants, and established conversations only 2.5 percent of the time; i.e., 195 out of 200 attempts to speak to the staff failed. Actual encounters were often meaningless, such as this conversation: "Excuse me, Doctor. Could I talk to you this afternoon?" (Physician answers without stopping.) "Good morning, Bill. Nice day, isn't it?"

Actual therapy was minimal. Average daily contacts with professional staff ranged from 3.9 to 25.1 minutes, with a mean of 6.8 minutes, including time spent in the admissions interview and group ward meetings. On the whole, the staff seemed to be caring, committed, and intelligent. However, some attendants, especially when no other staff were around, were cruel to patients. Rosenhan, himself, witnessed staff members beating patients for trying to talk to them, including one patient who approached a staff member saying, "I like you." Staff apparently felt safe behaving unprofessionally when only mental patients were witnesses because the credi-

---

thropomorphic thinking is one example of cultural relativism. Each of us has unconscious beliefs that influence our thinking. Racism, sexism, heterosexism, nationalism, social classism, and other "isms" may be so deeply ingrained that we are unaware of their influence on perceptions. Suppose you were observing people in a public park and noticed two men walking hand-in-hand. How would you interpret it? Was one man helping a disabled friend? Were they long-lost brothers reunited after years of separation? Were they lovers? Were they from an area in which this is typical behavior? Cross-cultural comparisons are especially sensitive to cultural relativism, and these bility of mental patients would be suspect.

Rosenhan and his confederates felt an "overwhelming sense of powerlessness which invades the individual as he is continually exposed to the depersonalization of the psychiatric hospital" (p. 256). As mental patients, they experienced a loss of their legal rights, credibility, freedom of movement, freedom to initiate contact with staff, privacy, confidentiality from staff members, and respect for modesty. They frequently felt invisible because they were openly discussed in front of themselves and others, and staff generally ignored them. For example, Rosenhan described a nurse who unbuttoned her blouse to repair her bra in front of a ward of male mental patients, oblivious of their presence.

Staff interpreted the pseudopatients' normal behavior and histories as symptoms. For example, one volunteer's honest report of his life history led to the conclusion that he had a history of ambivalent close relationships, and his report of normal family life (including occasional disagreements with his wife and the need to spank his children occasionally) was noted as problems controlling emotionality with a history of angry outbursts. Heavy reliance was placed on medication. The pseudopatients were given nearly 2100 pills and frequently found that other patients, like themselves, pretended to take their medication, but flushed it down the toilet.

None of the staff suspected the pseudopatients were sane, but it "was quite common for the patients to 'detect' the pseudopatients' sanity. During the first three hospitalizations where accurate accounts were kept, 35 of a total of 118 patients on the admissions ward voiced their suspicions, some vigorously" (p. 252), with suggestions that the researchers were journalists or professors studying the hospital.

Critics accused Rosenhan and his colleagues of being biased witnesses without sympathy for employees who face budget and staff problems. Employees of mental hospitals simply do not have time to respond to every patient's beck and call, and real mental patients often initiate nonsense conversations and behave in unpleasant and unpredictable ways. Rosenhan acknowledged such problems, but argued that institutions set priorities for their staff. Staff who depersonalize patients apparently were not discouraged from such behaviors.

An interesting second study was conducted. Because so many psychiatrists complained that Rosenhan's study led to the conclusion that they could not distinguish normal from mentally ill people, Rosenhan volunteered to send out more pseudopatients to a few hospitals to see if they would be recognized. Pseudopatients were not sent out, but analyses of admission records for these hospitals revealed that 21 percent of their new admissions had been suspected as being pseudo rather than real patients.

cross-cultural comparisons may be across subcultures of American society or across nations. For example, personal space (a zone surrounding the body that we don't like to share with others) varies with culture, so an American researcher may interpret friendliness as rudeness if conducting observations in South America and as aloofness if conducting observations in England. Travelers frequently are warned that some hand gestures have different meanings in other countries. Observers unaware of these meanings may misinterpret others' responses and behaviors. Researchers can use local informants to ascertain local interpretations of behaviors.

Strengths and Weaknesses of Case Studies

Case studies provide rich information. They may be based on hundreds of hours of observation and interviews with a variety of sources. Multiple hypotheses about histories and beliefs can be explored in depth. The degree of intensity and intimacy in case studies is not found in other research approaches. Psychologists use field research to analyze behaviors and dynamic social interactions in the real world. In addition, field researchers may be able to study populations that would not cooperate with the demands of other research techniques, such as street vandals and drug users. (This does, though, bring up questions of informed consent.)

There are methodological problems with the case study approach. Subject reactivity may undermine the validity of case studies. The very act of conducting a study may change the "facts," because research subjects may be flattered by the attention given them and may respond by embellishing stories. Alternatively, they may censor answers or behaviors that are inconsistent with the image they want to project. Experimenter expectancy effects also may invalidate conclusions. Researchers may be too willing to believe statements that support their hypotheses or theories, they may ignore contradictions or discrepancies, and they may inadvertently manipulate respondents to give inaccurate statements or to display unusual behaviors. Cultural relativism may lead to inaccurate interpretations of others' behaviors. Field researchers also run the risk of "**going native**," identifying with the groups they study and losing scientific objectivity. For example, researchers may become advocates for underprivileged groups they study and slant research findings to serve as propaganda.

Case studies have other limitations. They offer descriptions of individuals or groups that may be uniquely tied to times or places, so other researchers may be unable to replicate or verify results, even with the same subjects. Conclusions may lack external validity. For example, a type of therapy may work for one client, but not for others. A single case can never be used to prove a theory or to demonstrate the general effectiveness of a treatment program.

ARCHIVAL RESEARCH

Archival research, the analysis of records and artifacts, is most often associated with archaeologists who excavate sites to learn about ancient people. But psychologists also use such techniques.

Archival methods usually involve examining two major types of evidence: physical traces and documents. **Physical traces** are remnants of activities, such as worn carpets in front of popular paintings in a museum, graffiti on restroom walls, and beer cans left on beaches. Trash cans at elementary schools provide evidence about what children ate and did not eat, such as uneaten sandwiches and wrappers from desserts. Friedman and Wilson (1975) examined student study habits by examining physical traces on textbooks, such as underlined passages. They found evidence of reduced studying for materials assigned later in the course.

Archival researchers also study documents. Public documents, such as birth and marriage certificates; semi-public documents, such as high school yearbooks; media materials, such as newspaper stories and novels; and private records, such as diaries, can be analyzed. For example, Winter (1987) examined expressed needs of American presidents by analyzing their inaugural addresses.

Conclusions about the subject of study often are obtained through **content analysis**, systematic measurement of information in a communication record. For example, Shneidman analyzed the content of suicide notes and found they often contained strong emotion, forlornness, need for love, specific instructions to survivors, and illogical reasoning (Frederick, 1969).

Archival records allow psychologists to study historical phenomena. An early archival study by Sir Francis Galton (1872) examined the efficacy of prayer to prolong life by comparing the lifespan of royalty (who are prayed for by thousands of subjects) and others. Galton found that royals actually had shorter lifespans than authors and scientists, suggesting that prayer did not increase their longevity. Phillips (1977) used public records to examine copy-cat suicides. He found that well-publicized suicides are followed by increases in suicides and fatal car accidents, suggesting that some car accidents actually are suicides.

Archival records can be used to explore many research questions. For example, cross-cultural comparisons of children's literature can be used to examine values in different cultures. Census data can be used to demonstrate changes in living patterns, such as increases in single-person households. Birth and death data can be tied to natural and manmade phenomena; e.g., an increased birthrate may follow major power blackouts by about nine months, and there may be fewer deaths among people shortly before their birthdays and holidays.

Strengths and Weaknesses of Archival Research

The content of physical traces and documents can be analyzed to describe historical phenomena. Archival data generally are nonreactive. Research subjects were not aware they would be studied, so subject reactivity is less likely. Archival research also can be inexpensive if someone else, such as the U.S. Census Bureau, has already collected the data. Extensive data covering long periods of time may be available, allowing researchers to avoid costly longitudinal designs. Records generally have continued availability, so they can be reexamined if new hypotheses or variables emerge. This is not true for most other data collection strategies.

There are problems with archival research, however. Sometimes subjects' behaviors are reactive, but to a different audience. Politicians' speeches, newspaper articles and editorials, and criteria used to classify crimes may be politically motivated. Diagnostic criteria for mental health records have changed over time, so direct historical comparisons of proportions of clients with specific diagnoses may not be meaningful. Important data may be lost or unavailable. Records may deemphasize reports of some phenomena, such as the internment of Japanese-Americans during World War II. Families may object to public scrutiny of personal documents left by suicide victims or by famous or notorious relatives.

Data quality may vary across time and place if different record-keepers and data collection procedures were used. Even if data are reliable, researchers may impose their own biases in doing content analyses, so experimenter expectancy effects and cultural relativism may undermine the validity of conclusions. Interpretations of historical records may not reflect their meaning at the time they were created because language and customs have changed, and we may have inaccurate understandings of historical conditions and events. For example, Zinsser (1960, originally copyrighted in 1934) provided an interesting reanalysis of history in *Rats, Lice and History*. He demonstrated that traditional historians placed too much emphasis on "great people" and too little emphasis on microorganisms. According to Zinsser, "… soldiers have rarely won wars. They more often mop up after the barrage of epidemics. And typhus, along with its brothers and sisters—plague, cholera, typhoid, dysentery—has decided more campaigns than Caesar, Hannibal, Napoleon, and all the inspector generals of history" (p. 113). Although Zinsser's conclusion may be extreme, his analysis demonstrated that people who analyze historical records may overlook important causal variables, illustrating the investigator paradigm effect.

CONTENT ANALYSIS

Descriptive studies often rely on content analysis of available data. Content analysis involves systematically measuring variables in a communication record. The record could be a written document, tape-recorded conversation, photograph, song, work of art, television program, or any other recorded communication. Specific variables are measured through the careful application of a coding scheme. For example, Etaugh (1980) analyzed trends in child-care advice in popular women's magazines (e.g., *McCalls, Ladies' Home Journal*) by applying content analysis to articles on day care. She found increasingly positive attitudes toward non-maternal child care within the period she studied, 1956–1976.

As with any measurement, the important first step is to define the variables of interest. For example, suppose we want to analyze altruism and violence in Saturday-morning cartoons. First, we must define the variables. Altruism is voluntarily doing something for the benefit of another, and violence is intentionally trying to harm another. As we watch cartoons, we could count acts of altruism or violence. For example, if Casper gives Wendy a flower, we tally one point for altruism; and if Bluto punches Popeye, we tally one point for violence. Alternatively, we could develop an index, such as a four-point scale ranging from slightly violent to extremely violent. After analyzing a variety of shows, we could examine the relative predominance of the two behaviors. Perhaps we would also contrast cartoons targeted at little girls (e.g., "Rainbow Bright"), at little boys (e.g., "GI Joe"), and at all children (e.g., "Bugs Bunny"). To do this, we would have to develop a way to classify cartoons. For example, we could examine the gender ratio of children in advertisements accompanying the cartoons and classify cartoons as gender-identified if one gender predominates in the ads.

Content analyses can be based on manifest or latent content. **Manifest content** is observable and objectively measured, such as the number of adverbs in a passage. **Latent content** is inferred underlying characteristics of communications, such as inferences that the communicator is angry. Analyses of manifest content generally yield more reliable data, but data may be less meaningful. For example, we could count the number of times a passage contains words such as "hate" or "bad" to measure anger, but this technique may misclassify materials that obviously indicate anger but avoid using such language. Examinations of interrater reliability are called for, especially when latent content is being measured.

Box 10.4

A Letter to Mom and Dad

Dear Mom and Dad,

I love going to college. The classes are easier than I thought they'd be. I have my first exams next week and have been studying like mad to do well. I got a D on my first Econ paper, but I know I can do better on the next one.

Colleges have so many fun things to do. The parties have been very quiet and sophisticated: coffee, donuts, and conversation. I only go to them on weekends, so I can study every weekday night. People dress differently here than at high school. You'll love my new look.

My roommate invited me home for the weekend, so don't try to call me this weekend because I'll be away. And I usually study at the library, so don't worry if you don't catch me on school nights. My roommate said you called last night while I was out studying. Oh yes, while I'm thinking of it. Would you please send my skis and boots? The ski lodge just an hour from here has terrific rates for students on weekdays, and my skiing has greatly improved.

Books were more expensive than we thought. Can you send me an extra $100? I ran out buying my books. $200 would be even better because I have to buy bluebooks for exams.

Well, back to the books.

Love,
Pat

Box 10.3 contains a letter written by a first-year college student away from home. Suppose we wanted to conduct a study of honesty in communications with parents. Would you analyze the manifest or latent content of this letter?

We also have to develop a sampling scheme. To conduct the analysis of altruism and aggression in cartoons, we could randomly sample from all Saturday-morning cartoons. We might prefer a stratified sample, with determined portions from cartoons involving animals and involving humans. We also could use multi-stage sampling, picking three Saturdays, two networks, and three cartoons on each network. After selecting the cartoons, we could use continuous, time, individual, and/or event sampling as we measured our variables. Researchers should select sampling strategies that result in representative, manageable samples.

CHAPTER SUMMARY

The major purpose of descriptive studies is to describe phenomena, including interesting cases and interventions. Descriptive studies also may provide information for theory development or evaluation. Descriptive studies include case studies and archival research. Case studies describe interesting individuals or groups, and archival research examines physical traces and documents. Field research studies (naturalistic observations) are case studies of behaviors and social processes in their natural settings. Field researchers make structured and unstructured observations and may interview informants using active listening skills. Several sampling schemes have been developed for observational studies, such as time-point sampling and event sampling.

Researchers also conduct case studies of animals, and in doing so they should avoid anthropomorphic thinking.

Case study observations may be obtrusive or unobtrusive, and subject reactivity is more likely when obtrusive observations are made. Experimenter expectancy effects can bias results through selective attention, biased interpretations, and self-fulfilling prophecies; and cultural relativism may lead to inaccurate conclusions. Case studies can provide rich information about individuals, groups, and social interactions.

Researchers conduct historical studies of physical traces and documents using archival research. Archival data are less reactive to researchers, but may be reactive to other audiences. Archival data may be missing, incomplete, inaccurate, or inaccurately interpreted.

Descriptive studies often rely on content analysis to measure variables. Manifest and latent content can be measured, and interrater reliability can be examined. Sampling schemes for the content analysis must be developed, and many alternatives exist.

Key Concepts

active listening skills
anthropomorphic thinking
archival research
case studies
content analysis
continuous sampling
cultural relativism
event sampling
field research
"going native"
individual sampling

latent content
manifest content
naturalistic observations
participant observers
physical traces
structured interview
time sampling
time-interval sampling
time-point sampling
unstructured interview

Review Questions

1. Classify each of the following as descriptive, correlational, experimental, or applied research:

   a. A health psychologist examines the relationship between stress and health.

   b. A clinical psychologist evaluates the effectiveness of a community mental health clinic.

   c. An industrial psychologist publishes an article describing a corporation's use of flex-time scheduling.

   d. Clients with phobias are randomly assigned to one of three types of therapy to see which approach is most effective.

2. What is the major difference between case studies and archival research?

3. Review the discussion of strengths and weaknesses of case studies. Which of these can be applied to Sperry's and Rosenhan's studies?

4. The theory of positive reinforcement is that rewarded behaviors are more likely to be repeated than unrewarded behaviors. Describe a case study that could be used to demonstrate this theory.

5. Ruth wants to conduct a field study of world-class gymnasts. How could she use obtrusive observations? How could she use unobtrusive observations? Describe how she could use event sampling, individual sampling, and time sampling strategies. Develop four questions for a structured interview that Ruth could use to interview gymnasts' family members.

6. A friend's dog just had puppies, and he comments on how loving the mother dog is. Could he be using anthropomorphic thinking? Why?

7. Elaine wants to see if drivers actually use turn signals when changing lanes. She sits at a bus stop and records whether or not signals are used by each driver who changes lanes. What type of study is Elaine conducting?

8. Julian decides to do a field study by becoming a participant observer at an Alcoholics Anonymous meeting. Julian believes that most alcoholics are dangerous because of personal experience with an abusive alcoholic parent. What experimenter expectancy effects should Julian avoid?

9. Sylvia wants to examine behavior at a large, outdoor rock concert by examining physical traces. What types of artifacts should she look for, and how should she interpret them?

10. Jean is interested in understanding Washington, Lincoln, and Jackson. She finds copies of letters that each man wrote to his wife. What manifest and latent content variables might Jane use in a content analysis to better understand these men?

11. Reread "A Letter to Mom and Dad" (Box 10.3). Is Pat a male or a female? What possible experimenter expectancy effects or cultural biases may have influenced your conclusion?

11

Correlational Studies

Researchers carry out correlational studies to examine relationships among naturally occurring variables. For example, they may be interested in whether life satisfaction is related to marital status or depression is related to anxiety. Correlational studies are descriptive studies, like case studies and archival research, but their purpose is to describe relationships rather than to describe interesting phenomena.

Correlational studies are conducted for a variety of purposes. Sometimes practical or ethical considerations prevent researchers from manipulating independent variables of interest. For example, research studies on the effects of starvation on children's brain development and the long-term effects of alcoholism are conducted with measured instead of manipulated independent variables. It is not ethical to starve children or to promote alcoholism in order to study the effects of such conditions. Correlational studies also are conducted to study relationships among variables that are measured, such as various dimensions of personality. In such studies there are no clear independent and dependent variables, so there are no variables to manipulate.

EXAMPLES OF CORRELATIONAL STUDIES

Differential psychology, the study of individual and group differences, places strong reliance on correlational studies. Differential psychologists are interested in how people are different, rather than in how they are alike. They examine differences in human abilities, interests, and personalities, and they try to find the causes of differences among individuals and groups.

Box 11.1

IQs of African-American Children Adopted by European-American Families

Scarr and Weinberg (1976) studied transracial adoptions to examine genetic and experiential influences on human intelligence. During the 1960s and 1970s, the state of Minnesota was at the forefront of interracial adoptions. Scarr and Weinberg studied 101 upper-class Minnesota European-American families who had adopted an African-American child. Well-documented at the time of the study were findings that African-American children raised by their natural parents had average IQs of 85, European-American children raised by their natural parents had average IQs of 100, and European-American children adopted into upper-class European-American families had higher than average IQs, but lower IQs than the biological children in these families. The adopted African-American children followed the same pattern as adopted European-American children; they averaged 106, higher than average for the population, but lower than the biological children in their adoptive families, who averaged 117.

IQ tests were administered to all family members, and other information was obtained through interviews and from school and adoption records. A number of interesting relationships were explored, as summa-

rized in the table. Evidence supports the influence of both genetic and experiential factors on children's intelligence. Children who were adopted young, who had lived in fewer foster homes, who had been in better-quality foster homes, who were adopted by more educated and more intelligent parents, and whose biological parents were more highly educated scored higher than others. Notice that correlations with biological parents' educations are at least as high as correlations with adoptive parents' educations, a common research finding that supports the idea of genetic influences on intelligence.

CORRELATIONS WITH IQ AMONG ADOPTED CHILDREN

Variable	Correlation
Biological mother's education	.31
Biological father's education	.45
Age at adoption	−.36
Time since adoption	.30
Number of foster homes	−.36
Quality of foster homes	.38
Adoptive mother's education	.22
Adoptive father's education	.34
Adoptive mother's IQ	.18
Adoptive father's IQ	.17

Many psychological tests grew out of the work of differential psychologists who needed objective measurements of their variables, and many aspects of reliability and validity are examined in correlational studies, such as test-retest reliability and criterion-related validity. Considerable work has been conducted on intelligence, including controversial work on the impact of genetic and environmental factors. Scarr and Weinberg's (1976) study, summarized in Box 11.1, is an example of such work. Their correlational data suggest that genetics and environment influence the development of intelligence. Perhaps you can think of alternative explanations for their results.

Not all researchers who conduct correlational studies are differential psychologists. For example, Campbell, Peplau, and DeBro (1992) conducted a correlational study of condom use in heterosexual college students. This study is summarized in Box 11.2. Because of the danger of sexually transmitted disease, manipulating condom use, so that some subjects use them and others don't, would not be ethical.

Box 11.2

Condom Use Study

Campbell, Peplau, and DeBro (1992) decided to study condom use in college students because college students tend to be sexually active and at risk for sexually transmitted diseases. Each of nearly 400 unmarried, heterosexual students filled out a 16-page survey. Because of the sensitive nature of the material, each student was tested in a separate room, and surveys were collected in plain envelopes.

Included in the survey was a condom attitudes test, with 20 Likert-scale items measuring four aspects of condom use: their comfort and convenience, their effectiveness for birth control and AIDS protection, their effect on sexual sensation, and interpersonal aspects of their use. Subjects were asked to rate their agreement with statements such as "Condoms are convenient and easy to carry," "The use of a condom is an effective method of birth control," "A problem with condoms is that they reduce sexual stimulation," and "The use of a condom might be embarrassing to me or to my partner." Internal consistency reliabilities (coefficient alpha) for the four scores ranged from .60 to .76. Students also were asked to describe their experience with condoms and their intention to use condoms in the future.

A number of interesting relationships were found. For example, women generally had more positive attitudes toward condoms than men, and men were more concerned than women about the effects of condoms on sexual sensations. Chi square analyses revealed ethnic group differences in sexual experience. Asian-Americans were the least likely and European-Americans were the most likely to be sexually experienced, with African-Americans and Latinos in the middle. Condom attitude and sexual history were related to past and anticipated condom use, and some gender differences were observed in the pattern of relationships. For example, concern about interpersonal aspects of condom use was related to condom history in men, but not women.

Campbell, Peplau, and DeBro were disappointed to find the most sexually active students were less likely to report anticipated condom use with a new sexual partner. "It is both ironic and frightening that those who are most willing to take sexual risks may be the least concerned with the consequences of their risky behavior" (p. 286). Results led to a number of suggestions for public health personnel. Students believe condoms are effective, but they need to be convinced that interpersonal and sensual aspects of condoms should not preclude their use.

Other psychologists have used correlational studies to uncover relationships between stress and health. For example, Rahe (1987) developed The Recent Life Changes Questionnaire, a refinement of earlier measures of stressful events, and demonstrated its relationship to heart disease. The Questionnaire asks respondents about recent experience with 55 stressful events, and includes both pleasant and unpleasant events, such as marrying, having a child, visiting the dentist, retiring, and buying a new car. The total score involves a weighted sum of experienced stresses, with some stresses weighted more heavily than others. For example, death of a spouse earns twice as many points as marriage because research suggests it is twice as stressful. Such research is done as a correlational study because it would be unethical to stress research subjects deliberately in order to see if they develop heart disease.

Correlational research has causal ambiguity. The link between stress and heart disease is not clear. Perhaps stress affects the body directly, placing undue strain on the heart, or perhaps people under stress develop poor health habits (such as smoking, overeating, or under-exercising) that cause heart problems. On the other hand, it could be that people with heart problems develop lifestyles marked by more stress. Correlational data that allow researchers to relate stress among healthy people to subsequent heart problems provide more convincing evidence that stress precedes the heart problem.

Researchers also have found relationships between personality and health. For example, people with a Type A personality, marked by feelings of time urgency, competitiveness, and hostility, have been found to be prone to coronary heart disease. Attempts to reduce the health risk by reducing Type A behavior have had "encouraging" results, strengthening the inferred causal link between personality and disease (Suter, 1986, p. 214).

Chesler (1972), in her book, *Women and Madness,* summarized correlational studies that found relationships between gender and various aspects of mental health and treatment. For example, women are seen more often by therapists as in-patients (clients who live in mental hospitals) and as out-patients (clients who live at home), clients expressing a preference more often request a male therapist, boys are more often referred to therapists for antisocial behaviors, girls are more often referred to therapists for fears and worries, women clients are more likely to complain of nervousness and depression, and men clients are more likely to complain of substance abuse and hostility problems. Chesler interpreted these and related findings as evidence that women are sex-role stereotyped and oppressed, and that psychotherapy, like marriage, is a middle-class institution that reinforces destructive stereotypes. Feminist therapy models have been developed based on these ideas. Chesler's interpretation is not the only possible explanation of the correlational results, and many non-feminist therapies exist.

CORRELATIONS

Relationships are summarized most often by Pearson correlation coefficients. Researchers must be aware of three major factors related to correlations: linear relationships, causation, and restriction of range.

As stressed in Chapter 5, Pearson correlations indicate the direction and strength of the *linear* relationship between variables. Low correlations indicate weak linear relationships, but do not necessarily indicate that variables are not related. Variables with low correlations may have nonlinear relationships. Researchers can examine scatterplots to see if possible nonlinear relationships exist. Correlation does not imply causation. Remember from Chapter 8 that if X and Y are correlated, X may cause Y, Y may cause X, Z may cause X and Y, or X and Y may be reciprocally causative. This is a source of causal ambiguity for correlational studies and a serious threat to their internal and construct validity when causal conclusions are made. Researchers also should remember attenuation due to restriction of range. Observed correlations are reduced if the variables being examined have limited variability. This threatens research validity through its effect on statistical validity.

Alternative Statistics for Correlational Studies

Data for correlational studies may be based on observations of subjects or content analysis of archival data. Variables must be measured to produce scores that can be correlated. Correlational data frequently are obtained using tests or questionnaires. As seen in Chapter 6, many types of tests exist, such as objective and projective personality tests. The data's level of measurement affects the choice of statistical technique. Pearson correlations are used for interval or ratio data, Spearman correlations are used for ordinal data, and chi square tests are used for nominal data. Tests on Pearson correlations are quite robust, so Pearson correlations sometimes are used for ordinal data, especially if unit sizes are approximately equal.

Spearman correlations are Pearson correlations calculated on ranks. They indicate the direction and strength of the linear relationship between rank-ordered variables. Like other Pearson correlations, Spearman correlations do not imply causation, and they are attenuated due to restriction of range. Chi square analyses examine any type of relationship, so they are not only for linear relationships. Significant chi square tests do not imply causation, and they are most powerful when subjects are evenly distributed across levels. For example, if there are 120 subjects classified into three levels of a variable, the test is most powerful if there are 40 subjects at each level. (This is similar to the balanced design for *t* tests discussed in Chapter 7.)

Data must be collected from a sample, and this sample can be drawn in a number of ways, as discussed in Chapter 7. Representative samples that exhibit the full range of variability will yield the most powerful tests of the relationship because they will not suffer from attenuation due to restriction of range.

STRENGTHS AND WEAKNESSES OF CORRELATIONAL STUDIES

Researchers use correlational studies to examine relationships between variables that cannot be manipulated for practical or ethical reasons. In addition, they are used when exploring relationships between measured variables that are not classified as independent and dependent variables, such as examining tests to evaluate their reliability and validity. Correlational studies can analyze relationships in archival data, as well as newly collected data, so they may be relatively inexpensive to conduct. Results of correlational studies can suggest causal relationships, such as the relationship between Type A personality and health, and these relationships may lead to the development of therapeutic intervention programs.

Unreliable or invalid measurements, response sets, subject reactivity, and experimenter bias may lead to invalid conclusions. Researchers may forget that Pearson and Spearman correlations summarize linear relationships and may incorrectly conclude that variables with nonlinear relationships are unrelated. Correlations also are attenuated due to restriction of range, so small correlations in restricted samples provide little evidence about the relationship between variables in unrestricted samples. The biggest problem with correlational studies is that correlation does not imply causation. Researchers interested in establishing causal relationships between variables cannot prove causation with correlational data.

Survey research analyzes opinions from samples of respondents. Most of us have been interrupted by survey researchers' phone calls: "Who won the political debate last night?" "How do you like your new car?" Most of us also have received questionnaires in the mail or have been asked to respond to oral or written surveys in public places. Survey data can be analyzed to summarize group opinions, but generally survey researchers analyze relationships in their data, such as the relationship between opinions about different issues or between opinion and age, gender, or political affiliation. The major strength of survey research is that it can be used to obtain information from many respondents quickly and inexpensively. Survey researchers can obtain data from populations too large or too dispersed for field research and about opinions too current for archival research.

The basic tool for survey research is the survey or questionnaire. It is designed to collect specific information as objectively as possible. The questionnaire may be administered in writing, face-to-face interviews, or phone calls. Chapter 6 summarizes suggestions for writing clear surveys and includes a list of response sets to avoid. Some tests have built-in scales for examining response sets, such as checks based on similar or identical items to detect inconsistent response styles and **lie scales** for detecting social desirability response sets. Lie scales generally contain items such as "I never gossip" and "I always return phone calls immediately." Subjects who respond positively to many lie scale items are assumed to be misrepresenting themselves in a socially desirable way.

An appropriate sampling strategy must be developed to obtain a representative sample of the **target population**, the group of interest. The target population may be general, e.g., all adult Americans, or may be more specific, e.g., female Republicans in San Antonio. The **response rate** (proportion of completed surveys) is important because low response rates suggest nonrepresentative samples and weak external validity. For example, people with extreme attitudes may be more likely to return surveys, so the proportion of neutral attitudes in the population may be underestimated. Biased samples also may have restriction of range, so observed correlations will be attenuated, weakening statistical validity.

A classic example of biased sampling occurred in 1936. The *Literary Digest* sponsored a survey comparing preferences for Republican Alfred Landon and Democrat Franklin Delano Roosevelt. Results indicated an easy win for Landon, but Roosevelt won. This error was due to poor sampling. Subjects were selected from phone books and automobile registration records. In 1936, telephones and cars generally were owned by members of the upper classes, and these people typically voted for Republican candidates. Stratified sampling strategies may be more effective than botched attempts at random sampling.

Written Questionnaires

Written questionnaires may be distributed by mail or in person. Written surveys are convenient for researchers and for respondents. They generally take less time than interviews with the same content and can be filled out at the subject's convenience. Such surveys also may be more accurate than interviews for sensitive topics. Respondents may be more willing to reveal themselves on paper than in person to data collectors who may be judgmental, and they may perceive that their anonymity is better protected when anonymous questionnaires are collected. Nevertheless, written instruments are not suitable for subjects with low reading levels; such subjects may give inaccurate data or no data at all. Written questionnaires ensure that all subjects respond to identical questions, but this inflexibility may invalidate some answers that could have been clarified by interviewers.

Typically, two follow-up contacts are made to nonrespondents to mailed questionnaires, with a letter stressing the importance of their participation and another copy of the survey. These follow-ups are done to increase the response rate, making representative samples more likely. Survey researchers generally believe that a 50 percent return rate is "adequate," a 60 percent rate is "good," and a 70 percent rate is "very good" (Babbie, 1983, p. 226). Personally delivered surveys generally have higher response rates than mailed surveys, probably because of the social contract implied when subjects accept hand-delivered questionnaires. Mailed surveys have the advantage of being relatively inexpensive, especially for national samples. How else can you contact a national sample for the price of postage stamps?

Interviews

Face-to-face or telephone interviews allow data collectors to probe for details and to clarify questions and responses. Interviews, which commonly attain 80 to 90 percent response rates (Babbie, 1983; Evans, 1985), can be used with illiterate respondents, and they generally yield fewer neutral or omitted responses than written surveys. Interviewers who contact subjects at home or in person can assess additional characteristics that may be used to interpret results, such as the presence of books in the home or whether interviewees had problems understanding questions. They also can detect subjects who are obvious fakes, such as 80-year-olds who claim to be 35.

Interviewers must be carefully trained to avoid influencing results. For example, they may create experimenter expectancy effects by inadvertently reinforcing attitudes similar to their own or by giving biased interpretations when categorizing responses. There also may be a tendency for their interviewing style to drift as they give more surveys. They may shorten or change the wording of questions, speak more quickly, or anticipate answers without listening carefully to subjects' responses. Although the interviewers may have asked the same questions 200 times, the questions are heard for the first time by each subject.

Phone surveys, less expensive than face-to-face interviews, are becoming increasingly popular. They can provide immediate feedback on issues, such as judgments of who won political debates; this offers a major advantage over other research strategies. Phone interviews can be recorded or monitored to verify interviewers' compliance with standard procedures. Transportation costs are avoided, as compared to face-to-face interviews, and there is less concern for the safety of interviewers because they do not have to enter subjects' homes or work in unsafe areas.

Computers are playing an increasing role in phone surveys. Computer-assisted telephone interviewing may involve random number dialing by the computer (so that people with unlisted phone numbers are not omitted from the sample), and interviewers may read questions from the screen and immediately enter data into the computer. Immediate data entry allows researchers to monitor results as they come in, so they can conduct intermediate data analyses and project final results. Radio and television broadcasts sometimes conduct their own surveys, inviting audiences to share their opinions by calling phone numbers, e.g, "Do you support capital punishment? Dial 555-1207 if you support it and 555-1208 if you do not support it." Automatic recording devices count calls, and results are shared with the audience. These surveys, like those administered in magazines, may create very biased samples because of unique characteristics of the audience and of those who choose to respond. For example, a random sample of the population is unlikely to listen to a very conservative radio personality or to read *Rolling Stone*. Results may not generalize accurately to the whole population.

Strengths and Weaknesses of Survey Research

Survey researchers can obtain large, inexpensive samples of people who are widely dispersed, and all subjects respond to the same questions. Results can be collected relatively quickly, and trends can be examined using the same questionnaire and trend sampling. Representative samples allow researchers to make accurate inferences about broad populations and matters of immediate social importance. Relationships between certain responses or between responses and other characteristics (e.g., gender, ethnicity, age) can be established through correlations or chi square analyses. **Secondary analyses**, analyses of survey data collected by others, also are possible after data are encoded. For example, researchers may analyze data collected by the U.S. Census Bureau.

In survey studies, however, data are limited to subjects' responses to explicit questions (and maybe a few variables separately scored by interviewers), so survey studies lack the richness of case studies. Documented relationships are correlational, so causal conclusions are not possible; also, restriction of range may attenuate observed relationships. Response sets may invalidate results. For example, subjects may fabricate answers rather than appear ignorant about social or political issues. Survey responses, especially written responses, may be based on casual reading of the questions, so responses may not accurately represent subjects' opinions. Idiosyncratic or regional differences in language may lead some individuals or groups to misinterpret questions or response categories. For example, Crew (1983) describes a region in rural Appalachia in which "very" means "not" or "not very." If asked their health, locals report "very well" when they mean "not well." This may invalidate their responses using Likert scales that employ the word "very," such as response categories that range from "very good" to "very poor."

Data are limited to subjects who agree to be surveyed and who have the verbal skills to respond, so biased sampling may occur. The representativeness of the sample also is in question when response rates are low. Biased samples with restricted ranges will have attenuated correlations, reducing statistical validity, and results will lack external validity for the whole population.

The relationship between survey responses and actual behaviors may not be clear. For example, subjects who report they support higher taxes to fund improved educational access or better roads may vote against such initiatives in the privacy of the voting booth. An interesting study comparing survey and observational results is provided in Box 11.3. Results suggest that social desirability response sets may be especially prevalent when surveys ask about politically incorrect behaviors.

Box 11.3

Conflicting Evidence from Survey and Observational Studies

Crosby, Bromley, and Saxe (1980) reviewed the racism literature, contrasting survey and observational results. Survey results showed a decline in racism from the 1950s to the 1970s, but observational studies did not show this pattern. They speculated that survey results may have demonstrated a change in society's attitude toward politically correct thought, so results were an artifact of a social desirability response set. Unobtrusive observational studies of racism compared helping behavior, aggression, and nonverbal behaviors toward research confederates varying in ethnicity. For example, racism is suggested if European-American subjects are less likely to offer help

to African-American than European-American confederates. Various observational studies, such as comparisons of donations to Salvation Army kettles during December holidays and offers to help someone who just dropped a bag of groceries, were reviewed. They found that more prejudice occurred in anonymous situations (such as responses to a wrong phone number) than in face-to-face situations, suggesting that people exhibit racist attitudes when they believe they can get away with it. The research team concluded that "…whites today are, in fact, more prejudiced than they are wont to admit" (p. 557).

FACTOR AND PATH ANALYSIS

Two additional ways to handle correlational data are factor and path analysis. These techniques involve some advanced statistical manipulations, so only their general characteristics will be described here.

Factor Analysis

Sometimes psychologists examine patterns of correlations through factor analysis. **Factor analysis** is a technique to reduce the number of variables by combining sets of variables that appear to be measuring the same construct. New variables that are composed of a set of variables are called **factors**.

As an introduction to factor analysis, look at the correlations in Table 11.1. Table 11.1 is a **correlation matrix**, a table of correlations. Each of five tests (A, B, C, D, and E) has been correlated with the others. Entries on the main diagonal of the matrix (going from the upper left to the lower right corner) are 1.00, because these are self-correlations. Off-diagonal entries give correlations between pairs of tests. For example, Test A correlates .90 with Test B and .00 with the other three tests. Inspection of the table should convince you that Tests A and B appear to measure the same variable, which is different from what is measured by Tests C, D, and E. Similarly, Tests C, D, and E appear to be measuring the same variable, which is different from what is measured by Tests A and B. Giving every person two scores, one for Factor I (measured by Tests A and B) and one for Factor II (measured by Tests C, D, and E) reduces the number of variables from five to two. This reduction simplifies our work, because each subject has three fewer scores for us to examine.

CORRELATION MATRIX FOR TWO FACTORS **TABLE 11.1**

	A	B	C	D	E
A	1.00	.90	.00	.00	.00
B	.90	1.00	.00	.00	.00
C	.00	.00	1.00	.90	.90
D	.00	.00	.90	1.00	.90
E	.00	.00	.90	.90	1.00

This example is simple-minded because the pattern is so extreme. Researchers rarely see correlation matrices that have such clearly delineated factors. The actual conduct of a factor analysis involves a series of decisions using sophisticated computer programs, but the idea is straightforward. Factor analysis is used to reduce the number of variables that must be considered, simplifying research.

After factors are created, they are named. Suppose Test A measures algebraic reasoning, Test B measures computational skills, Test C measures vocabulary size, Test D measures verbal fluency, and Test E measures verbal reasoning. We probably would name Factor I Quantitative Skills and Factor II Verbal Skills. Researchers who conduct factor analyses name their factors by analyzing the variables that measure them.

Factor analysis has been used to explore the nature of intelligence and temperament for many years (e.g, Guilford, 1967; Guilford & Zimmerman, 1956) and has been used to create psychological tests, such as the Marital Satisfaction Questionnaire for Older Adults (Haynes et al., 1992) which measures three factors: Communication/Companionship, Sex/Affection, and Health. Goldberg (1993), after reviewing nearly fifty years of factor analytic work on personality, concluded there are five basic personality factors:

1. Extraversion
2. Agreeableness
3. Conscientiousness
4. Emotional Stability (Neuroticism)
5. Intellect

Once these dimensions are agreed on, researchers can tailor personality tests to measure them.

Path Analysis

Researchers who conduct **path analyses** test causal models with correlational data. **Causal models** specify a sequence of causes and effects. Although correlations do not imply causation, alternative causal models can be compared, and some models may fit the data better than others, suggesting they are more accurate.

To understand how we can use correlational data to test causal models, remember the classic experiments of Mendel in which he isolated the effects of dominant and recessive genes. Mendel cross-bred pea plants with various characteristics and found that the distribution of characteristics among offspring plants were consistent with his

---

FIGURE 11.1 PATH DIAGRAM FOR PREDICTING EXAM PERFORMANCE IN AN
ENGLISH CLASS

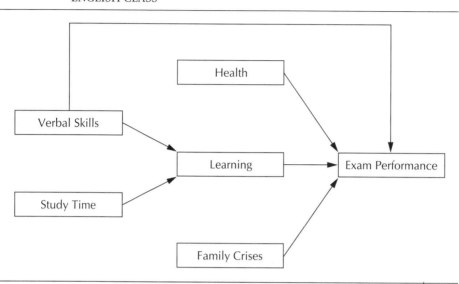

---

theoretical model. For example, if yellow flowers are dominant and white flowers are recessive, all offspring of white-flowering plants should have white flowers. Crossing a plant having only dominant yellow-flower genes with a white-flowering plant should produce only plants with yellow flowers, but crossing the resulting hybrid plants with each other should produce 25 percent white-flowering and 75 percent yellow-flowering plants. Mendel's outcomes were consistent with such predictions and were difficult to predict with alternative models, so he was able to demonstrate to the scientific community that dominant and recessive genes affect outcomes. Path analysis uses similar logic. If several models exist and one model fits the data better than any other, that model appears to be true.

Figure 11.1 is a path model for predicting exam performance in an English class. Arrows point from causes to effects, defining **causal paths**. The model postulates that verbal skills and study time cause learning and that verbal skills, learning, health, and family crises cause exam scores. Students with higher verbal skills and more study time learn more than others; and students with high verbal skills, who have learned more, who are in good health, and who are not bothered by family crises (such as being up all night with a sick child) do better on exams.

Path analysis involves evaluating the strengths of the paths using correlational data. Path strengths are indicated by regression weights. **Regression** is a statistical method for deriving equations for predicting variables. If the equation was Learning = .30(Verbal Skills) + .40(Study Time), we would predict a person's amount of learning by multiplying her Verbal Skills score by .30 and adding this to her amount of study time multiplied by .40. **The regression weights** are .30 and .40, and these weights would be **path coefficients** for the part of the model that specifies that Verbal Skills and Study Time cause learning. Notice that the model does not specify a path from Health to Learning because the creators of this model assumed these variables are not causally

CROSS-LAGGED PANEL RESULTS **FIGURE 11.2**

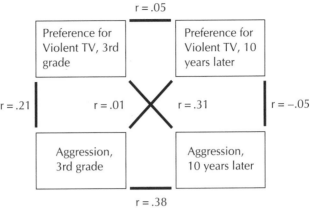

Eron, Huesmann, Lefkowitz, and Walder, 1972

related; i.e., there is a zero path coefficient when Health is used to predict Learning. Researchers could develop the regression equation for predicting Learning from Verbal Skills, Study Time, and Health. If the regression weight for Health is not significantly different from zero and if the weights for Verbal Skills and Study Time are significantly different from zero, this part of the model appears to have empirical support. Sophisticated computer programs are used to determine path coefficients and to evaluate alternative causal models. A good model will have strong paths, will not omit alternative paths that are shown strong in the data analysis, and will fit the data better than alternative models. A good introduction to path analysis, including worked examples, can be found in Bohrnstedt and Knoke (1988).

A related strategy for making causal interpretations from correlational data is to use a cross-lagged panel design. In the simplest case of a **cross-lagged panel design**, two variables hypothesized to be causally related are measured twice, with a lag between testings. The pattern of correlations suggests the direction of causation. If the two variables are A and B and they are measured at Time 1 and Time 2, we have four scores: $A1$, $B1$, $A2$, and $B2$. $A1$ is variable A measured at time 1, and so on. The correlation between $A1$ and $A2$ is the test-retest reliability of the measurement of A, and the correlation between $B1$ and $B2$ is the test-retest reliability of the measurement of B. Correlations of $A1$ with $B1$ and of $A2$ with $B2$ show the criterion-related validity of using one variable to predict the other when the two are measured simultaneously. The important pair of correlations are $A1$ with $B2$ and $B1$ with $A2$. The higher of these two numbers suggests the direction of causation. If the $A1$–$B2$ correlation is higher, A apparently causes B; but if the $B1$–$A2$ correlation is higher, B apparently causes A. The logic is that a cause should predict a subsequent effect more strongly than an effect will predict a subsequent cause.

Figure 11.2 shows results for a cross-lagged panel study conducted by Eron, Huesmann, Lefkowitz, and Walder (1972). They studied preference for violent television programming and aggression among about 200 boys measured in third grade and ten years later. Using the above paragraph as a guide, what conclusions would you reach? Aggression appears to be more stable than television violence preference (correlations of .38 and .05). Aggression and preference for television violence are positively correlated among third-graders, but not among young adults (correlations of .21 and −.05). Preference for violent television programming among boys appears to cause them to be aggressive adolescents (correlations of .31 and .01). These correlational results cannot prove this causal link, but they suggest this conclusion. Cross-lagged panel research has its critics. For example, Rogosa (1980) pointed out some technical problems with the logic of interpreting cross-lagged panel data, reinforcing the notion that correlation does not imply causation. The best way to prove causal relationships is to conduct carefully controlled experiments.

CHAPTER SUMMARY

Correlational studies examine relationships among measured variables. They are used when independent variables cannot be manipulated or when there are no clear independent and dependent variables. Differential psychologists frequently use correlational studies to better understand individual and group differences. Other psychologists also use correlational research.

Data are summarized most often using Pearson correlations. Researchers must understand that these correlations summarize only the strength of linear relationships, that correlation does not imply causation, and that correlations are attenuated due to restriction of range. Spearman correlations and chi square analyses also are used for ordinal and nominal data, respectively. Spearman correlations are Pearson correlations of rank-ordered data. Chi square tests are not restricted to linear relationships, and they are most powerful when subjects are distributed evenly across levels.

Results of correlational studies can suggest causal relationships, such as the relationship between Type A personality and health, and these relationships may lead to the development of therapeutic intervention programs. However, correlational data can never prove a causal relationship. Unreliable or invalid measurements, response sets, subject reactivity, and experimenter bias also may lead to invalid conclusions.

Survey researchers analyze opinions. Surveys are designed to measure variables objectively, and they may have built-in scales for detecting response sets. Representative samples are drawn from the target population, and researchers are more confident of unbiased results when the response rate is high. Surveys may be written or oral, and oral surveys may be conducted face-to-face or by telephone. Survey research can be used to obtain large, inexpensive samples of people who are widely dispersed, and results can be collected relatively quickly. Secondary analyses also can be conducted on data collected by others. Results generally are restricted to answers to explicit questions, and response sets and experimenter bias may influence results. Survey findings may not predict actual behaviors, especially for surveys subject to social desirability response sets.

Advanced statistical procedures for analyzing correlational data include factor and path analysis. Factor analysis reduces the number of variables by combining them into factors. Path analysis compares causal models to see which are most consistent with data. Researchers using cross-lagged panel designs examine patterns of correlations among repeated-measures data in order to reach conclusions about probable causality. Although correlation does not prove causation, some researchers use path analysis and cross-lagged panel designs to evaluate causal models.

Key Concepts

causal model
causal path
correlation matrix
cross-lagged panel design
differential psychology
factor
factor analysis
lie scales
path analysis

path coefficient
reciprocal causation
regression
regression weight
response rate
secondary analysis
survey research
target population

Review Questions

1. How do correlational studies differ from case studies and archival research?

2. Why would you use a correlational study for the following research questions? How would you conduct each study?

   a. Are suicidal thoughts related to recent stressful events?

   b. Are verbal and quantitative skills related?

3. Reread the last two sentences in the description of the condom use study (Box 11.2). Correlation does not imply causation. How might this invalidate the conclusion in the last sentence?

4. Create an original, reasonable example of two variables that might be reciprocally causative.

5. Would you use Pearson, Spearman, or chi square statistics to analyze the following relationships?

   a. The relationship between two attitude tests

   b. The relationship between IQ and height

   c. The relationship between gender and having had an appendectomy

6. Gill is studying the relationship between gender and grades at the Air Force Academy. Most students at the Academy are men. How will this affect the power of the test if a random sample of students is studied? Can you suggest a sampling strategy that would be better? Gill decides to classify grades into three levels. He can classify grades as top/middle/bottom third as or A-B/C/D-F. Which would be more powerful? Why?

7. Create two original Likert items that could be used on a lie scale.

8. Surveys are sent to a random sample of the target population, and the response rate after one month is .40. Would it be better to make follow-up contacts with nonrespondents in the original sample or to draw and contact a second random sample? Why?

9. Supporters of an initiative to create a new out-patient mental health clinic in the community want to survey voters' opinions. They plan to use interviews, but they aren't sure how to do this. What advice can you offer them?

10. Goldberg (1993) concluded there are five basic personality factors. What types of evidence should he offer to support this conclusion?

11. A research team is studying the status of senior citizens in five countries. They take thirty measures of status in each country, such as the proportion of government and religious leaders who are senior citizens, the proportion of seniors living in poverty, and the use of respectful nouns of address when addressing seniors. They want to compare the five countries, but they prefer not to analyze thirty separate variables. How might they simplify their analyses?

12. Develop a possible path analysis model for predicting income. Use at least five causal variables, and include at least one causal variable that does not have a path leading directly to income.

13. Examine Figure 11.2. How would the interpretation of causality be different if the .31 and .01 were reversed? Explain the new conclusion.

12

Quasi-Experiments

Psychologists conduct experiments to see whether changes in independent variables cause predictable changes in dependent variables. There are two types of experiments: quasi-experiments and true experiments. True experiments have random assignment of subjects to conditions and manipulated independent variables; quasi-experiments may have measured or manipulated independent variables, and they lack random assignment of subjects to conditions. The major difference between true experiments and quasi-experiments is control. Researchers have more control over true experiments, and this control generally results in increased research validity, especially statistical, construct, and internal validity. However, even quasi-experiments can lead to accurate causal conclusions if alternative explanations of results can be ruled out.

Suppose scores on a final exam are compared for two sets of students taught by teachers using different teaching methods. If researchers manipulated teaching methods and randomly assigned students to teachers, this is a true experiment. If not, this is a quasi-experiment. If teachers' teaching styles were not manipulated, the study would be a quasi-experiment. This type of quasi-experiment is a correlational study because relationships between naturally occurring variables are examined. If researchers manipulated teachers' styles, but did not randomly assign subjects to conditions, the study is a quasi-experiment because of the lack of random assignment.

If true experiments are more valid than quasi-experiments, why do researchers conduct quasi-experiments? Independent variables may not be manipulated for a number of reasons. For example, demographic characteristics cannot be manipulated. Researchers comparing women to men on

---

Box 12.1

The Effect of Shift Work on Work-Related Problems

Factories that operate around the clock require employees to work shifts. Usually the 24-hour day is divided into three shifts, such as 7 A.M. to 3 P.M., 3 P.M. to 11 P.M., and 11 P.M. to 7 A.M. Workers frequently rotate shifts, alternating between morning, evening, and night shifts. Evidence suggests that errors, accidents, and injuries occur most often among night-shift workers, probably because these shifts interfere most with normal sleep rhythms. Such interference should be less if rotation periods are longer, however, because workers can adapt gradually to changes in their sleep-wake patterns. One problem with studying this hypothesis is that researchers rarely can manipulate rotation periods for actual employees. Bell and Telman (1980) learned of a factory that planned to change shift rotation cycles, so they were able to take advantage of this natural experiment.

Subjects were 25 male assembly-line workers at a margarine factory. Each worker agreed to record errors, accidents, injuries, and health or interpersonal problems for 33 eight-hour shifts: 12 night shifts when shift changes occurred every two days, and 5 night shifts and 6 morning shifts when shift changes occurred every seven days. Workers would report problems such as broken margarine tubs, bumping into equipment, skinned knees from falls, stomach aches, and interpersonal conflicts. Records were collected at the end of each shift, and a researcher verified, from her own observations, that employee records were accurate. The study began when all employees rotated shifts in two-day intervals, and data were collected over a six-month period. All subjects recorded data during the same shifts and in this order: 12 night shifts (six two-day periods), 5 night shifts (on five consecutive days), and 6 morning shifts (on six consecutive days).

The average number of recorded problems was 16.3 during the night shift of two-day shifts, 7.4 during the night shift of seven-day shifts, and .7 during the morning shifts of seven-day shifts. Results supported Bell and Telman's hypotheses that more problems occur during night shifts when sleep patterns are disturbed and that this effect is diminished when shifts are rotated less frequently, allowing workers to adapt to different sleep-wake patterns.

---

career choice cannot randomly assign subjects to gender groups. Ethical considerations also preclude manipulation of some variables, such as blindness, miscarriages, or exposure to toxic materials.

Quasi-experiments frequently are conducted as field experiments, such as examining the effectiveness of alternative therapy models by comparing clients at clinics that practice different techniques. Clients select their own clinic, so researchers do not randomly assign them to conditions. Bell and Telman (1980; Box 12.1) conducted a quasi-experiment on the effect of shift work rotation schedules on work-related problems by taking advantage of a natural experiment: a factory that was changing its shift rotation schedule. It would have been difficult to conduct this study as a true experiment because industries are unlikely to allow researchers to manipulate shift schedules, and employees are unlikely to agree to random assignments to these schedules. Researchers conduct quasi-experiments because important independent variables can be systematically analyzed with this technique.

Quasi-experiments may be conducted to test the external validity of conclusions reached in true experiments. For example, Selye (1976) conducted animal experiments examining the effects of long-term stress. He concluded that prolonged stress causes the general adaptation syndrome, a sequence of physiological reactions that eventually damages the heart and circulatory system and suppresses the immune system, making organisms vulnerable to infection. His studies were true experiments, with random assignment of animals to conditions.

The effect of long-term stress in humans can be studied with quasi-experiments that compare people whose stress levels vary. It would be unethical to manipulate serious stress conditions among human subjects or to randomly assign people to these conditions; however, people do vary in the stressfulness of their lives and work, providing opportunities to collect quasi-experimental data. Cohen, Tyrell, and Smith (1991) documented that stress influences people's susceptibility to the common cold, suggesting a relationship between stress and immune system functioning in humans. Other researchers have demonstrated relationships between stress and other health problems, such as hypertension (Goldstein, 1981) and arthritis (Baker, 1982).

Some researchers have argued that the effect of stress depends on a number of variables, such as social support, general hardiness, and coping mechanisms (psychological ways of handling problems, such as rationalization and help-seeking); and these modifications to Selye's theory have been pursued through quasi-experiments. For example, Kobasa (1979) examined hardiness by comparing high-stress executives who have and who have not developed stress-related illness. She found that hardier executives are more committed to their jobs, enjoy challenges more, and feel more in control than less hardy executives. She sees hardiness as a personality trait that protects people from stress. The causal effect of stress depends on the hardiness of those experiencing it.

The designation of a study as correlational or quasi-experimental may be arbitrary. Generally, studies in which relationships between variables are examined using Pearson or Spearman correlations are considered correlational, and studies in which means are compared are considered quasi-experimental. Researchers interested in the relationship between parental strictness and children's respect for authority could conduct a correlational study by measuring strictness and respect in a number of families and correlating the two variables. If they classified parents into permissive, moderate, and dictatorial categories and compared the average respect scores of their children, they would be conducting a quasi-experiment. Researchers conducting the correlational study would analyze all subjects, but researchers conducting the quasi-experiment may exclude subjects who do not fit into one of the categories.

Sometimes correlational studies are considered quasi-experiments. For example, the cross-lagged panel design discussed in Chapter 11 is classified as a quasi-experiment because causal relationships are systematically examined. Studies analyzed with chi square tests may be classified either way. They are more likely to be considered experimental if independent and dependent variables are identified. Experiments are conducted to examine the causal effects of independent variables on dependent variables.

Cook and Campbell (1979), based on a series of publications by themselves and others, identified a number of quasi-experimental designs and classified them into two major groups: nonequivalent control group designs and interrupted time-series designs. **Nonequivalent control group designs** lack random assignment of subjects to conditions. **Interrupted time-series designs** involve multiple measurements across time, with at least one treatment interruption. Researchers comparing university students to community college students are conducting a nonequivalent control group study because students have not been randomly assigned to campuses. Researchers could use an interrupted time-series design to examine the effect of school level on student achievement by analyzing annual grade point averages for a group of students for several years before and after they transfer from elementary schools to secondary schools.

NONEQUIVALENT CONTROL GROUP STUDIES

Kobasa (1979) used a nonequivalent control group design to compare hardy and non-hardy executives. Each group served as a control group for the other, and she did not assign subjects to conditions. Nonequivalent control group designs are used when demographic variables are studied or when intact groups (such as classrooms or members of a club) are examined. One of the most serious problems with nonequivalent control group designs is self-selection bias. The groups probably differ in ways not specified by the independent variable, and these extraneous variables are confounded with the independent variable. For example, if Kobasa's hardy subjects exercised more than her nonhardy subjects, differences in exercise might account for health differences.

The simplest research design is the **one-group posttest-only design**, in which the dependent variable is measured after some intervention or event has occurred. If X is the intervention or event (the **treatment**) and O is the observation, this design can be symbolized by

$$X \qquad O$$

The treatment X precedes the observation, O. The use of the term "treatment" does not imply experimenter control; the treatment may be measured, rather than manipulated in quasi-experiments. This design also is called a **one-shot case study**. For example, people's attitudes toward public safety personnel may be measured after an earthquake. Cook and Campbell conclude that this design is "totally uninformative" (p. 96) because too many factors threaten its validity. One major problem is that there is no basis for comparison. Researchers cannot interpret scores because there are no pretreatment measurements. This undermines attempts to make causal inferences about the impact of treatment. Researchers might collect retrospective data about pretest scores, but the reliability and validity of these recollections may be weak; they may compare results to normative data, which might be reasonable if subjects are representative of the norm group; or they may collect multiple dependent measures that allow them to create meaningful contrasts. For example, attitudes toward fire fighters may be compared to attitudes toward police officers after a fire. Even if this comparison is significant, however, it would not provide convincing evidence that the fire experience caused residents to develop more favorable attitudes toward fire fighters; they may have had different attitudes toward fire fighters and police officers before the fire began. Cook and Campbell do not recommend this design.

Some of the above problems diminish if results are compared to a control group that has not experienced the treatment, but that is measured at the same time as the experimental group. This is the **posttest-only design with nonequivalent groups**, in which both groups are measured after one of the groups has experienced the treatment. This design can be symbolized

$$
\begin{array}{cc}
X & O \\
\hline
& O
\end{array}
$$

The dashed line separates the two groups. The experimental group experiences the treatment, X, and the control group does not. Subjects have not been randomly assigned to groups, so extraneous variable confounds threaten the validity of causal interpretations. If the experimental group is a community that experienced a fire and the control group is a community that has not experienced a fire, other differences between the groups are likely. Perhaps the communities differ in crime rate, arson history, or civic pride. Although a comparison can be made, researchers can have little confidence in the validity of causal conclusions. The causal ambiguity remains high, so this design cannot be recommended.

Kobasa's (1979) study of hardy and nonhardy executives uses the posttest-only design with nonequivalent groups, with observations of multiple dependent variables. Her nonhardy subjects had experienced health problems (X in the above diagram), and her hardy subjects had not; she compared the two groups on personality variables. Her goal was to uncover personality characteristics of hardy (healthy) executives, but differences between the groups may not have been caused by personality differences. Differences may be attributable to other factors, such as hearty constitutions (e.g., coming from healthier, long-lived families), diet, alcohol and tobacco use, and exercise. Such designs do not have high validity for causal conclusions unless additional information is collected to allow researchers to discredit alternative explanations.

The one-group posttest-only design also might be improved by adding a pretest. This is the one-group pretest-posttest design. The **one-group pretest-posttest design**, as its name implies, involves testing one group of subjects before and after the treatment. This design could be symbolized

$$O_1 \quad X \quad O_2$$

O_1 is the observation made before the treatment, and O_2 is the observation made after the treatment. For example, people experiencing psychoses may have hallucinations (perceptions that don't have a physical basis, such as hearing voices that aren't real). Medication designed to reduce hallucinations can be tested by noting the number of hallucinations among a group of psychotic clients before and after they are medicated. Although this design is an improvement over the one-group posttest-only design, many factors threaten its validity for causal conclusions, including the regression effect, subject reactivity, experimenter bias, and confounds with history. Cook and Campbell (1979) do not recommend this design.

Another alternative is to combine the last two designs. The **untreated control group pretest-posttest design** involves testing experimental and control subjects before and after the experimental subjects receive the treatment. This can be symbolized

$$
\begin{array}{ccc}
O_1 & X & O_2 \\
\hline
O_1 & & O_2
\end{array}
$$

Both groups are measured at the same times, but only one group receives the treatment. This approach avoids many of the problems associated with the previous designs, but still has causal ambiguity because subjects are not randomly assigned to groups.

This design frequently is used with waiting-list control groups. Suppose researchers are evaluating the effectiveness of some treatment, and there are more potential clients than they can treat. Untreated clients can form a **waiting-list control group**. If clients are randomly assigned to treatment and control groups, the study is a true experiment; however, if this does not occur, the study is a quasi-experiment and extraneous confounds may threaten research validity. For example, if clients with more severe problems are assigned to the treatment group, the treated and control subjects do not represent similar populations and their data cannot lead to unambiguous causal conclusions.

Other factors threaten the validity of untreated control group pretest-posttest designs. Instrumentation problems may influence results. Experimental and control groups are likely to have different pretest levels (because subjects were not randomly

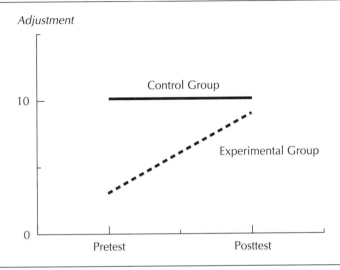

POSSIBLE OUTCOME IN AN UNTREATED CONTROL GROUP **FIGURE 12.1**
PRETEST-POSTTEST DESIGN

assigned to conditions), and it is possible that tests used to measure the dependent variable are not equally responsive to change at both levels, such as when floor or ceiling effects influence results. Regression effects also may occur. If subjects in one group are selected because they have extreme scores, they are expected to regress regardless of treatment. Experimental and control subjects' scores may be regressing to different means if they are not equivalent populations. Subjects in the two groups may differ in how they change because their experiences are different. For example, the control group may become more bored, and this boredom causes their pattern of pretest-posttest scores, an example of resentful demoralization. Confounds with history that differentially affect the two groups also may influence results. For example, treatment subjects may become aware of the suicide of another treatment subject, and this knowledge may affect their dependent variable measurements. (The last two problems would threaten the validity of this study even if it were a true experiment. However, the other problems would not be expected to influence results if subjects were randomly assigned to manipulated conditions.)

Figures 12.1 and 12.2 show some possible results for a study examining the effectiveness of a treatment designed to increase adjustment scores. In both figures the experimental group's pretest scores are lower than the control group's. If researchers were treating clients most in need of help, they would expect this pattern of pretest scores. In Figure 12.1, experimental subjects improve, and controls do not improve, a pattern consistent with the research hypothesis. There is an alternative interpretation, however; perhaps experimental subjects were selected because of extreme scores, and they are simply regressing to the population mean. Another possibility is that a ceiling effect is operating; control subjects also are improving, but the ceiling effect masks their change. The data in Figure 12.2 allow researchers to dismiss these alternative

---

FIGURE 12.2 ALTERNATIVE OUTCOME IN AN UNTREATED CONTROL GROUP
PRETEST-POSTTEST DESIGN

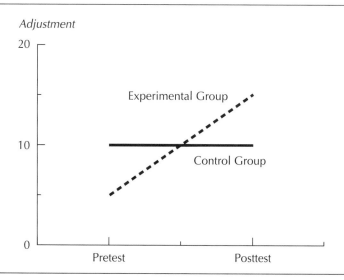

explanations. Regression is unlikely to cause experimental subjects to exceed control subjects, and ceiling effects are unlikely because experimental subjects were able to progress beyond the level of control subjects. However, neither pattern allows researchers to dismiss the possibility that confounds with history or differences attributable to control group demoralization occurred.

This design can be expanded to include multiple levels of the independent variable. A **multiple-levels pretest-posttest design** examines the influence of independent variables with more than two levels, with measurements made before and after treatment. If the independent variable has four levels, this design could be symbolized

$$O_1 \qquad X_1 \qquad O_2$$

$$O_1 \qquad X_2 \qquad O_2$$

$$O_1 \qquad X_3 \qquad O_2$$

$$O_1 \qquad X_4 \qquad O_2$$

Each of four groups is measured before and after experiencing a level of the treatment variable. For example, subjects could be given four different doses of an experimental medication. This design need not involve an untreated control group; groups sometimes serve as each other's controls. If the treatments can be ordered (e.g., from small to large doses of a medication), an orderly pattern of results, like that displayed in Figure 12.3, provides convincing evidence for treatment effectiveness. If double-blind procedures were not used, however, it is possible that subject reactivity or

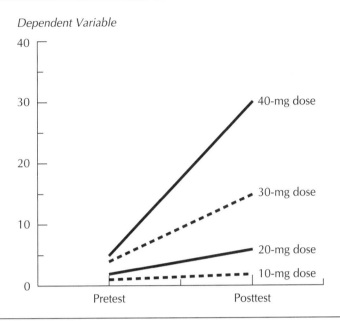

experimenter bias influenced results. For example, subjects in the low-dose group may have learned that little clinical effectiveness was expected, and subjects in other groups may have been given more encouraging prognoses.

Cook and Campbell (1979) describe a number of other nonequivalent control group designs, including designs with more than one pretest measure, with different operational definitions for pretest and posttest measures, with repeated measures of one group under treatment and no-treatment conditions, with experimental and control groups given opposite treatments (one designed to increase dependent variable scores and one designed to decrease dependent variable scores), with treatment cohorts (such as comparisons of younger and older siblings), and with treatment correlated with pretest scores (such as evaluating the effectiveness of an award program when awards are given to the most productive employees). The essential feature of all nonequivalent control group designs is the lack of random assignment of subjects to conditions. Cook and Campbell do not recommend the first three designs described here (the one-group posttest-only design, the posttest-only design with nonequivalent groups, and the one-group pretest-posttest design), but conclude that the other designs, although not as valid as true experiments, can yield results that allow researchers to eliminate many rival hypotheses.

Another variation can be added to nonequivalent control group designs with multiple groups. Subjects can be matched to create within-subject independent variables. Remember from Chapter 7 that within-subject analyses frequently are more powerful than between-group analyses. Generally this matching is accomplished by grouping subjects into **blocks** (pairs, triples, and so on) on the basis of pretest scores, but other variables (such as gender or age) may be used. If the independent variable has two levels (e.g., experimental and control groups), blocks are pairs; if the independent variable has three levels, blocks are triples, and so on. One subject in each block is in each condition. This blocking occurs after subjects have been pretested, so subjects within blocks are not randomly assigned to conditions. (If subjects within blocks are randomly assigned to conditions, the study would be a true experiment.) Once blocks have been formed, data are treated as if a block represented one subject, rather than multiple subjects. If the nonequivalent groups vary on pretest scores, some subjects may have to be dropped because they do not have equivalent subjects in other groups. This may reduce the range of examined scores and threaten research validity.

INTERRUPTED TIME-SERIES DESIGNS

Interrupted time-series designs involve multiple measurements across time, with at least one treatment interruption. This can involve repeated measurements of one group of subjects, representing an expansion of the one-group pretest-posttest design. Rather than a single observation before and after treatment, there would be multiple observations, such as

$$O_1 \qquad O_2 \qquad O_3 \qquad X \qquad O_4 \qquad O_5 \qquad O_6$$

Here three observations are made, perhaps at weekly intervals preceding and following the treatment (X). Bell and Telman (1980, Box 12.1) used this design for part of their study. They measured work problems during twelve nights when shifts were rotated every two days, then the shifts were rotated every seven days (X) and work problems were measured during five more nights. Major problems with this design are possible confounds with history. Any other event that occurred at about the same time as the shift schedule change (e.g., company layoffs of workers who had been involved in too many accidents) might cause post-treatment changes. Other problems include those associated with repeated measures, such as carryover effects, maturation, test sophistication, and instrumentation and experimenter drift. For example, Bell and Telman's subjects might have become more safety conscious because they were repeatedly recording problems, and this could have caused decreases in their reported accident rate.

Time-series data also could be collected with trend sampling from representatives of cohorts, with observations of different representatives of cohorts made at different times. Archival data may be analyzed using an interrupted time-series design. For example, data collected from college students in 1920, 1940, 1960, and 1980 could be compared to examine the effect of a treatment, such as the elimination of a foreign language requirement.

Repeated measurements made before and after an intervention allow researchers to document normal fluctuation in the dependent variable. Figure 12.4 shows average dependent variable scores for five days before an intervention and for five days after the intervention. Results suggest that score changes after the manipulation were normal

POSSIBLE RESULTS IN AN INTERRUPTED TIME-SERIES DESIGN **FIGURE 12.4**

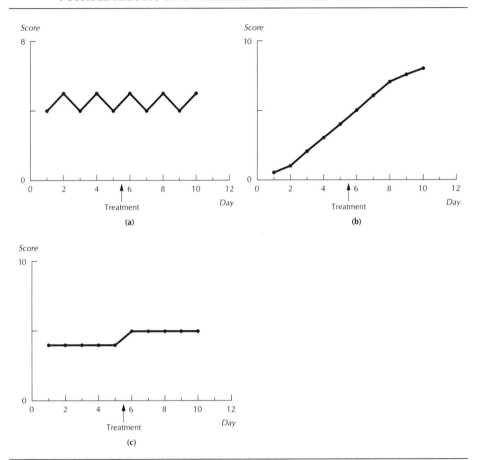

fluctuation in Figure 12.4a, were part of an ongoing trend in Figure 12.4b, and were caused by the intervention in Figure 12.4c. Only the third result suggests that the intervention caused a change in the dependent variable. If only the center two measurements were obtained, for the days immediately preceding and following the intervention, researchers could not be aware of the overall pattern and might misinterpret findings. The addition of repeated observations gives us greater confidence in causal conclusions. Nevertheless, an extraneous event that occurred at the same time as the intervention may have caused the results, even those in Figure 12.4c.

Treatments can affect dependent variables in many ways. They can affect trends, cause temporary or relatively permanent changes, or cause immediate or delayed effects. Box 12.2 illustrates some of these possible findings. Unfortunately, any of these changes could be attributed to confounds with history: other events that occurred at

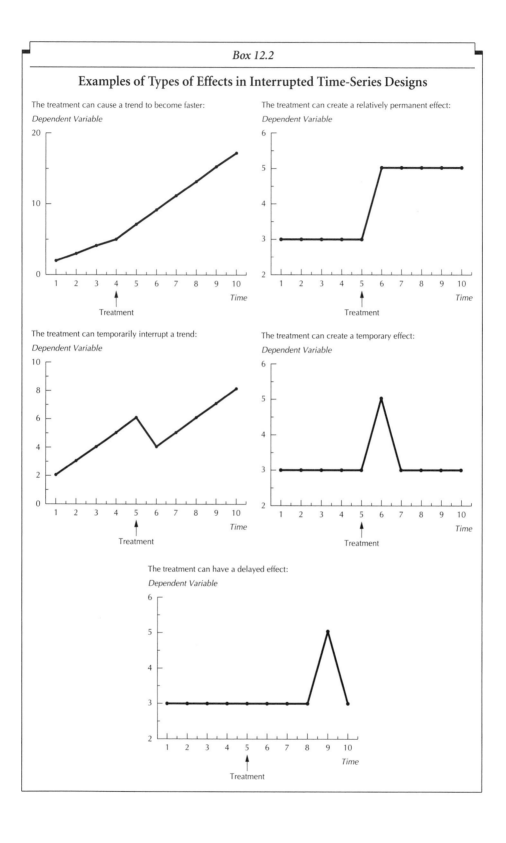

Box 12.2

Examples of Types of Effects in Interrupted Time-Series Designs

The treatment can cause a trend to become faster:

The treatment can create a relatively permanent effect:

The treatment can temporarily interrupt a trend:

The treatment can create a temporary effect:

The treatment can have a delayed effect:

about the same time as the treatment. For example, if researchers are examining the effects of store displays on purchases, and they change displays in December, then it is Christmas, rather than their treatment, that probably causes observed differences in sales. Delayed effects are particularly susceptible to such confounds because other events are more likely to appear during the longer periods required to observe effects. Other possible threats include changes in operational definitions of dependent variables over time, subject mortality, maturation (including subject fatigue), subject reactivity to repeated measurements, and nonequivalence of cohort samples when trend sampling is used. In addition, subjects may be aware that a treatment occurred, so they may respond to demand characteristics for change. Researchers who use multiple dependent variable measures may have more confidence than those using one dependent variable measure if results triangulate.

Multiple treatments can be examined, such as

$$O_1 \quad O_2 \quad X_1 \quad O_3 \quad O_4 \quad X_2 \quad O_5 \quad O_6$$

Here two observations precede the first treatment (X_1), followed by two observations, a different treatment (X_2), and two more observations. Bell and Telman (1980; Box 12.1) used this type of design when they compared the extent of problems during night shifts to the extent of problems during morning shifts. They collected data on five night shifts, followed by six morning shifts. Treatment order was confounded with time. Remember that subjects recorded their morning shift problems after 12 night shifts (during the two-day rotation cycle) and 5 night shifts (during the seven-day rotation cycle). The very act of record-keeping may have reduced their problem rate.

Different treatments may be the presence or absence of an intervention. For example, X_1 may indicate the beginning of a token economy to change prisoners' behaviors (tokens are awarded for good behaviors, and they can be exchanged for items or privileges), and X_2 may indicate the removal of the token economy. This pattern might be repeated several times, with repeated reinstatement and removal of the token economy. This would be most reasonable if treatments have temporary effects with relatively short delays, such as a study examining the effects of speed limit changes on motor vehicle accidents. Effects with long delays could not be uncovered unless times between treatments were long and filled with multiple observations, so that temporary effects are documented when they occur.

Time-series designs also can have control groups. These designs are true experiments if subjects are randomly assigned to experimental and control conditions, but are quasi-experiments if nonequivalent control groups are used. A simple interrupted time-series design with an untreated control group would look like this:

$$O_1 \quad O_2 \quad O_3 \quad X \quad O_4 \quad O_5 \quad O_6$$
$$\text{---}$$
$$O_1 \quad O_2 \quad O_3 \quad \quad O_4 \quad O_5 \quad O_6$$

Experimental and control subjects are measured six times. Confounds with history are less likely if the pattern of observations in the control group does not show the discontinuity observed in experimental subjects. Problems associated with nonequivalent groups remain, however, such as possible extraneous variable confounds due to self-selection bias. Also, history may be a problem if only one group is influenced by an event or events.

The design could be complicated further by introducing additional groups, such as groups that vary on the level of the independent variable. This could be diagrammed as follows:

$$O_1 \qquad O_2 \qquad O_3 \qquad X_1 \qquad O_4 \qquad O_5 \qquad O_6$$

$$O_1 \qquad O_2 \qquad O_3 \qquad X_2 \qquad O_4 \qquad O_5 \qquad O_6$$

$$O_1 \qquad O_2 \qquad O_3 \qquad X_3 \qquad O_4 \qquad O_5 \qquad O_6$$

$$O_1 \qquad O_2 \qquad O_3 \qquad X_4 \qquad O_4 \qquad O_5 \qquad O_6$$

Here we have four groups, each measured three times before and three times after being exposed to a level of the independent variable.

Single-Subject Designs

Sometimes researchers use **single-subject research designs**, in which an individual subject is repeatedly measured under different conditions. This is common in clinical psychology, psychiatry, and medicine. Single-subject designs involve careful examinations of one case's responses to the systematic manipulation of treatments. As with case studies of single individuals, results may not generalize to other people. A simple single-subject design involves two conditions, A and B; the dependent variable is measured as A and B occur. For example, an **ABA design** usually involves baseline readings (A), readings under a treatment condition (B), then readings under a second baseline condition. The dependent variable appears to be under experimental control if it systematically responds to the treatment. An ABA design could be used to demonstrate that a hyperactive child's activity level is reduced when behavioral techniques are applied (B), compared to normal conditions (A). If the dependent variable responds systematically to repeated alternations, as shown in Figure 12.5, the evidence becomes increasingly convincing. For example, a positive pattern for an ABA design may have been caused by chance; perhaps the hyperactive child was sick or tired during the B phase. If, however, the pattern persists under an ABAB design, an ABBA design, or an ABABA design, such confounds are less likely. These designs are appropriate to examine treatments with temporary effects, so the dependent variable responds to repeated manipulation. Sometimes ABA and related designs are conducted with groups of subjects, and data are analyzed for the whole group.

Additional complications can be added to the design, such as multiple dependent variables, with treatments targeting specific dependent variables sequentially introduced, as illustrated in Figure 12.6. In this example, parents have rewarded a child for keeping her room clean and for doing the dishes. The pattern suggests that rewards caused changes in the targeted behaviors.

STRENGTHS AND WEAKNESSES OF QUASI-EXPERIMENTS

Quasi-experiments without manipulated variables are correlational studies, so they share the strengths and weaknesses of correlational designs. They can be used to

ABAB DESIGN RESULTS **FIGURE 12.5**

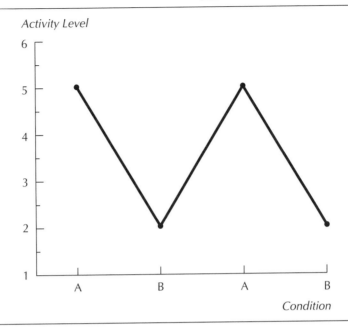

INTERRUPTED TIME SERIES DESIGN WITH TWO **FIGURE 12.6**
DEPENDENT VARIABLES

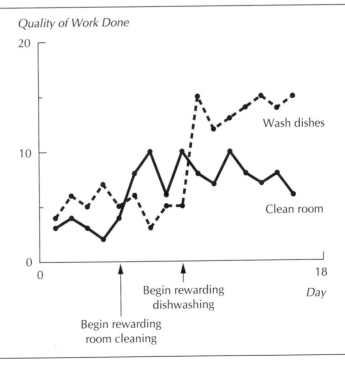

evaluate the effect of naturally occurring independent variables, but extraneous variables may be confounded with the independent variable, including extraneous variables related to self-selection bias. Quasi-experiments with manipulated independent variables, but without random assignment of subjects to conditions, may control the independent variable more carefully, but causal conclusions are threatened by possible preexisting group differences. Unreliable or invalid measurements, subject reactivity, and experimenter expectancy effects may undermine researchers' conclusions. Subject reactivity may be particularly strong in repeated measures designs that require subject cooperation through a series of assessments over a long time period. Longitudinal designs also may suffer from subject mortality.

CHAPTER SUMMARY

Psychologists conduct experiments to examine the effects of independent variables on dependent variables. True experiments have random assignment of subjects to conditions and manipulated independent variables, and quasi-experiments lack random assignment of subjects to conditions. Quasi-experiments with measured independent variables are correlational studies. Quasi-experiments may be conducted as field experiments, and they may be used to examine the external validity of conclusions reached in true experiments.

Cook and Campbell (1979) classified quasi-experimental designs into two groups: nonequivalent control group designs and interrupted time-series designs. Cook and Campbell do not recommend the following three designs: the one-group posttest-only design, the posttest-only design with nonequivalent groups, and the one-group pretest-posttest design. Instead, they suggest designs with stronger potential validity. Interrupted time-series designs can involve one or more groups. Because multiple dependent variable measurements precede and follow treatments, researchers who use these designs are better able to eliminate causal explanations involving confounds with history. Time-series designs are sometimes applied to single research subjects, such as the ABA design in which a subject is measured under different conditions. Although quasi-experiments offer some opportunities for causal conclusions, they generally suffer from validity threats due to nonrandom assignment of subjects to conditions, confounds with history, and confounds associated with repeated measurements.

Key Concepts

ABA (ABAB, ABBA, ABABA, etc.) design
blocks
interrupted time-series designs
multiple levels pretest-posttest design
nonequivalent control group design
one-group posttest-only design
one-group pretest-posttest design
one-shot case study

posttest-only design with nonequivalent
    groups
single-subject research design
treatment
untreated control group pretest-posttest
    design
waiting-list control group

Review Questions

1. Are the following experiments quasi-experiments or true experiments? Briefly explain each answer.

    a. Researchers randomly assign subjects to one of three conditions. Each subject is told of potential adoptive parents. For one-third of the subjects the potential parents are married, for one-third the potential parents are unmarried persons living together, and for one-third the potential parent is an unmarried person living alone. Subjects are asked to rate their recommendation for adoption approval. All prospective parents are described identically with respect to education, income, career, and health history.

    b. Joan studies the effectiveness of diet on a depressed child. For six weeks, diet is alternated weekly from high protein to high carbohydrate, and ratings of the child's depression are recorded.

    c. SAT scores for African-American, Asian-American, and Latino test takers are compared.

    d. Condom sales at drugstores near sports arenas are analyzed weekly for six weeks preceding and for six weeks following the announcement that a major sports figure has AIDS.

2. Identify the independent and dependent variables in each of the studies in Question 1. Name at least one reasonable extraneous variable that is confounded with the independent variable in each study. How might these confounds influence results?

3. Ronald found that people who rationalize failures are more optimistic than people who internalize failures. (Rationalizers blame failures on temporary or external factors; internalizers blame themselves for failures.) He induced failures in all subjects by giving them false feedback on an algebra test, telling them they scored far below average; then he had them explain their failure (to classify them as rationalizers or internalizers) and predict their score on the next test (to see if they are optimistic or pessimistic about future performance). Identify the independent and dependent variables. Was this an experiment or a quasi-experiment? Why? What aspects of this study may threaten its validity?

4. What are Kobasa's (1979) independent and dependent variables? Did she postulate that her independent variable caused changes in her dependent variables? Explain your answer.

5. Joan doesn't understand why the data in Figure 12.2 are more convincing about causal conclusions than the data in Figure 12.1. Explain this to her.

6. Bell and Telman's (1980; Box 12.1) evidence concerning night and morning shift accident rates is confounded with time. How could their study be improved to reduce this confound?

7. Box 12.2 shows a number of different effect patterns. Describe original, realistic examples of variables that might have the illustrated relationships.

13

True Experiments

True experiments are the most effective ways to reach unambiguous causal conclusions about research hypotheses. In previous chapters, we looked at descriptive studies, correlational studies, and quasi-experiments. Although these alternative strategies can be used to make causal conclusions, the conclusions generally are suspect because alternative explanations of results cannot be dismissed. For example, Bell and Telman's (1980; Box 12.1) study of the effect of shift schedule changes may have had problems due to confounds with history, maturation, or instrument drift. (The subjects were their own "instruments" because they recorded problems that occurred in each examined shift.)

True experiments involve researcher control of subject assignment and conditions, so they are more likely to provide convincing evidence for causal relationships. Researchers systematically manipulate independent variables and expect to produce and to measure systematic differences in dependent variables. Extraneous variables are controlled or eliminated. Subjects are randomly assigned to treatment conditions, and control groups are used to eliminate possible confounds. A simple, elegant logic underlies true experiments. Researchers manipulate independent variables and observe effects on dependent variables while holding everything else constant.

THREATS TO RESEARCH VALIDITY

The essence of true experiments is **control,** and various controls are instituted to eliminate rival explanations. Extraneous variable confounds that plague nonequivalent control group studies are controlled through random assignment of subjects to conditions. This randomization makes it unlikely that experimental and control groups are different at the beginning of the study. Conditions are manipulated, and researchers carefully control their timing and content. Extraneous variables that might affect dependent variables are controlled by holding them constant or by including them as variables in the design. This control adds precision to the study, increasing statistical, internal, and construct validity. Let's reconsider some of the threats to research validity described in Chapters 8 and 9 to better understand the planning of valid experiments.

Threats to Statistical Validity

Experiments have statistical validity if statistical evidence leads to accurate conclusions about relationships. Type I errors (rejecting accurate null hypotheses) and Type II errors (not rejecting false null hypotheses) are unlikely if analyses are conducted with low alpha and high power. Researchers conducting true experiments can design studies to maximize power. Chapter 7 summarizes ways to increase power, such as using large effect sizes, large sample sizes, one-tailed tests, balanced designs, and precision. Unlike quasi-experiments conducted with measured independent variables, effect sizes often are under experimental control. Experimenters control the number of subjects and their conditions, so balanced designs can be implemented. Research hypotheses are based on specific theoretical predictions, so one-tailed tests often are possible. Experimenters can control many factors that influence statistical validity.

Statistical validity also is threatened by fishing (conducting many tests without explicit hypotheses). Fishing is less likely in true experiments because research is designed to evaluate specific research hypotheses. Another problem that can threaten statistical validity is restriction of range. This problem is less subject to experimenter control in correlational studies and quasi-experiments than in true experiments. Researchers conducting true experiments control independent variables, so they force levels to vary. They carefully manipulate independent variables to create treatment differences.

Threats to Internal Validity

Experiments have internal validity if identified independent variables actually cause changes in dependent variables. The causal ambiguity inherent in correlational studies and quasi-experiments with nonmanipulated independent variables does not threaten true experiments, because in true experiments independent variables are manipulated. Self-selection bias and regression, which are major problems for nonequivalent control group studies, are avoided by random assignment of subjects to conditions. Demand characteristics can be reduced by conducting double-blind research, and treatment contamination may be eliminated by scheduling manipulations and data collection so that subjects in different conditions are unlikely to interact.

Subject demoralization and compensation might occur, but these problems are less likely if subjects in all conditions are engaged in reasonable activities. Subject reactions to data collectors can be eliminated by holding characteristics of data collectors constant (e.g., having one researcher collect all the data) or by balancing their influence. For example, if there are two data collectors, each can collect half the data in each condition. In addition, experimenters can depersonalize the data collection process by using unobtrusive measurements or by using recorded instructions and objective data collection instruments. Control groups are used to account for the Hawthorne effect. Subjects can be screened and instructions can be given to reduce threats by good or bad subjects, and evaluation apprehension can be reduced if researchers stress anonymity, confidentiality, and privacy, and if they present materials in nonthreatening ways.

Repeated measures data are subject to a number of threats, such as test sophistication, memory and practice effects, pretest sensitization, and maturation. Within-subject variables can be examined through matching subjects, and between-group variables can be used if other threats cannot be eliminated. Extraneous variables introduced by other interested parties are eliminated by carefully controlling conditions.

Some threats to internal validity may remain. Differential mortality can threaten experimental conclusions if subjects are less likely to continue under some conditions. Experimenters may be able to replace lost subjects, but this complication threatens the positive effect of random assignment. For example, if randomly assigned subjects who have needle phobias drop out of experimental conditions that requires needles, but do not drop out of conditions in which drugs (or placebos) are orally administered, extraneous variable confounds are introduced. Experimenters could solve this by giving all subjects injections, by giving all subjects pills, or by including the type of administration as another variable in the study. If differential mortality has occurred, researchers can statistically control for group differences.

Threats associated with historical confounds can be eliminated by the use of randomly assigned control groups, but a threat remains if groups are differentially exposed to this history. For example, subjects in quiet experimental conditions may be more aware of happenings in adjacent rooms than subjects in noisy conditions. This problem could be solved by testing all subjects in soundproofed rooms.

Rosenthal and his colleagues have identified a number of ways that researchers can bias research results, such as modeling effects and experimenter expectancy effects (see Box 8.3). These biases are less likely if conditions are carefully controlled. Experimenters can monitor data collectors to ensure that subtle, unplanned differences among treatment conditions do not exist and that data collectors do not drift from planned procedures. Double-blind strategies also help to reduce the impact of subject reactivity and experimenter bias.

Threats to Construct Validity

Experiments have construct validity if independent variables correspond to hypothetical causal variables and dependent variables correspond to hypothetical effects, as specified by the theory being evaluated. Pilot studies can be conducted to verify that experimental conditions are well conceived, and manipulation checks may be included in pilot or actual studies. Pilot studies also can be used to verify that instrumentation is effective, so that floor and ceiling effects and instrument drift do not bias results. Experimenters may use multiple manipulations, avoiding the mono-operation bias, and multiple dependent variables in order to verify that results are consistent across different operational definitions of the independent and dependent variables. Investigator paradigm effects may "blind" researchers to alternative interpretations and models. Probably the best protection against this effect is a willingness to consider alternative paradigms and to contrast predictions made from different theories.

Threats to External Validity

The basis for external validity is replication, and any factors that cause replication failures threaten external validity. Experiments should yield consistent results across subjects, settings, times, and operational definitions of variables. Editors generally prefer to reserve journal space for studies that extend results, rather than studies that are exact replications. Results can be extended by adding variables, by eliminating rival explanations, or by verifying that conclusions are consistent when different populations or different operational definitions are examined.

TYPES OF EXPERIMENTAL DESIGNS

Experiments are designed to provide unambiguous tests of research hypotheses concerning causal relationships. The complexity of the design depends on the complexity of the hypotheses to be examined and the possible threats that must be controlled.

The simplest true experiment has one independent variable and one dependent variable. The **posttest-only control group design** has random assignment of subjects to experimental and control groups, and subjects have been measured after experimental subjects are exposed to the treatment. It can be diagrammed as follows:

$$X \qquad O$$
$$\text{------------}$$
$$O$$

Although the diagram is the same as the diagram for the quasi-experimental posttest-only design with nonequivalent groups, this design is different because of random assignment of subjects to conditions.

A variation on this design is to have two treatment conditions, with each serving as a control for the other. This would be diagrammed as

$$X_1 \qquad O$$
$$\text{-------------}$$
$$X_2 \qquad O$$

Subjects would be randomly assigned to one of the two conditions (X_1 and X_2). For example, Schachter and Singer (1962) conducted a classic study on the effects of the social environment on responses to adrenalin, a central nervous system stimulant. All subjects were treated identically, with one exception. Each subject was given a "vitamin" injection of adrenalin, then was asked to wait with another subject in the waiting room. Unknown to subjects, the other person was a **stooge**, a colleague of the researcher, who either simulated depression or elation. The independent variable was the emotional state of the stooge, and the dependent variable was the emotional state of the subject. Results indicated that social environments affect psychological reactions; subjects mimicked the mood of their stooge. This is a true experiment because subjects were randomly assigned to conditions and all extraneous variables were carefully

---

Box 13.1

When Will People Help?

Darley and Latane (1968) hypothesized that diffusion of responsibility is one reason for bystander apathy. People who believe they are the only ones responsible for helping are more likely to help than people who are in situations with shared responsibility. Contrast an emergency room team, with each professional responsible for specific aspects of the treatment (taking blood pressure, binding wounds, etc.), with a disorganized group of people who happen upon a car accident, each assuming that someone else has called for emergency assistance. It is as if each person is expecting everyone else to help, and the result is that no one offers assistance.

College student volunteers were asked to participate in a discussion with other students on personal problems associated with college life. They were told that discussions would be held over an intercom system to protect their privacy. Students would hear each other but would not see each other. Each microphone was switched on and off in sequence, and discussion members introduced themselves in turn and talked about personal problems. Unknown to the actual subjects, only one real subject participated in each group; the rest were tape recordings of simulated participants. The independent variable was the size of the group (two, three, or six people), and participants were randomly assigned to one of the three conditions.

Shortly into his discussion, one of the simulated participants mentioned that he had problems with seizures. Later he began gasping for air, feigned a seizure, and asked for help. The dependent variables were whether or not the subject tried to offer help and how long it took for this help to be offered. As with the Kitty Genovese murder, subjects knew whether other people were aware of the emergency, but they did not know if others had already helped. If subjects did not respond in six minutes, the experiment was terminated.

When there were fewer people listening and less diffusion of responsibility, subjects were more likely to offer help, and help was offered more quickly. In about two minutes all the subjects in the two-person discussion had tried to help, but nearly 40 percent of subjects in the six-person groups did not report the problem within six minutes. When asked if their decision to help was affected by knowledge of the presence of other bystanders, all subjects responded negatively. Apparently diffused responsibility influences behaviors at an unconscious level.

Subjects who did not report the seizure were not uncaring. Many showed obvious signs of nervous discomfort when the study was terminated, asking if the man was all right. Darley and Latane concluded that these subjects wanted to help, but were unable to resolve the conflict with overreacting and ruining the experiment, so they became more uncomfortable than subjects who resolved the conflict by reporting the emergency.

---

controlled. The only difference between the two groups was the independent variable, the way the stooges acted.

Box 13.1 describes another classic study using this design. Psychologists' interest in bystander apathy was aroused in 1964, when Kitty Genovese, a New York woman, was killed outside her apartment house. She screamed and fought her attacker for half an hour, and at least 38 neighbors witnessed the scene. Yet no one called the police until after her death. Darley and Latane (1968) conducted a true experiment. Conditions were carefully controlled and standardized by using tape recordings, and subjects were randomly assigned to experimental conditions.

	TIME	
Group	Before film	After film
Control group	20	15
Experimental group	20	15

AVERAGE ATTITUDES TOWARD PROMISCUOUS SEX **TABLE 13.1**

The Darley and Latane experiment was one of many studies that examined situational variables that affect bystander apathy. In some situations most people will help, and in other situations almost no one will help. For example, most people won't interfere in marital quarrels, so they are more likely to ignore male-female violence if they interpret the couple as being married, rather than strangers to each other (Shotland & Straw, 1976). Darley and Latane's study involved subjects who did know each other. In a similar study, Latane and Rodin (1969) found that people are more likely to help a stranger when in groups of friends than when in groups of strangers. Perhaps coordinating help and the potential embarrassment of overreacting to a situation are less threatening when one is among friends. How the subject interprets the relationship within quarreling couples and the degree of friendship among those who might offer help are moderator variables. **Moderator variables** influence the relationship between independent and dependent variables. We develop more accurate causal models as we extend research to include examination of possible moderator variables. You have met the concept of moderator variable before. Kobasa (1979), in her study of personality characteristics associated with hardy executives, suggested that personality factors served as moderator variables affecting the relationship between stress and health.

The laboratory nature of the Darley and Latane study may have made generalizations to the real world suspect, but results were replicated in other situations, such as simulated emergencies in public places. Limitations were also uncovered by other work that demonstrated the influence of moderator variables. One experiment does not reveal the whole picture; taken together, however, the accumulated literature allows us to understand complex causal relationships.

True experiments also can involve repeated measurements, as in quasi-experimental pretest-posttest and interrupted time-series designs. In contrast to quasi-experiments, however, true experiments include control groups and random assignment of subjects to conditions. For example, suppose two groups of subjects are measured twice on their attitudes toward promiscuous sex. In between the testings, the control group watches a ten-minute film on basket weaving, and the experimental group watches a ten-minute film on sexually transmitted diseases. Table 13.1 gives some possible mean scores, with higher scores indicating greater acceptance of promiscuous sex. To the disappointment of those who made the film on diseases, results do not support its effectiveness, because both experimental and control subjects had decreased scores on the posttest. Perhaps simply taking the pretest led all subjects to reexamine their values. Had this study been conducted without a control group (as a one-group pretest-posttest design), the researchers might have reached a different, erroneous conclusion that the film was effective in changing attitudes. Inclusion of

---

Box 13.2

Pain Tolerance During Pregnancy

Gintzler (1980) hypothesized that women's bodies prepare for the discomfort of labor and delivery by increasing endorphin production. Endorphins are chemicals, such as morphine, that block pain and produce euphoria. Rather than test his hypothesis with human subjects, Gintzler decided to study another mammal, the rat.

Pain tolerance in rats can be measured as the amount of stimulation required to induce an escape behavior. Narcotic antagonists, chemicals that prevent the utilization of endorphins, can be used to block the receptors that normally would be occupied by endorphins. If endorphins have caused increased pain tolerance, animals given naltrexone, one of these antagonists, should have lower pain tolerance than animals not given this drug.

Gintzler examined 14 pregnant and 14 nonpregnant female rats. Each rat was tested for pain tolerance over a 16-day period, and half the rats in each group were given naltrexone. Tests were begun 16 days before parturition (delivery) for the pregnant rats. In addition, the two groups not given naltrexone

were tested for 41 days after parturition. Pain tolerance was measured by subjecting each animal's feet to a series of shocks of increasing intensity. The jump threshold is the amount of stimulation needed for the animal to jump to avoid the shock. Pain tolerance is high if animals do not jump until higher-level shocks are administered, and pain tolerance is low if animals jump for lower-level shocks.

Figures 1 and 2 display Gintzler's main findings. Group 1 contained pregnant rats tested from days −16 (16 days before parturition) to +41 (41 days after parturition), and Group 2 contained nonpregnant rats tested at the same times as Group 1. Group 3 contained pregnant rats tested from day −16 to day −1, with naltrexone; and Group 4 contained nonpregnant rats tested at the same times as Group 3, with naltrexone.

Analyses of the data summarized in Figure 1 revealed a significant main effect for pregnancy (pregnant rats had significantly higher jump thresholds), a significant main effect for day of testing (jump thresholds were higher around the time of parturition),

the control group eliminated the confound of being sensitized to sexual issues when taking the pretest, leading to a more accurate conclusion. Because subjects are randomly assigned to conditions, extraneous variable confounds associated with nonequivalent control groups are avoided.

Box 13.2 describes an experiment involving an interrupted time-series design with control groups. Notice how Gintzler used four different conditions to account for possible confounds, so that causal conclusions about the effects of endorphins could be made. Group 2 was used to control for confounds due to history; Group 3 was used to demonstrate that eliminating the effect of endorphins eliminated the pattern of jump threshholds found in Group 1; and Group 4 was used to demonstrate that the naltrexone specifically affected pain tolerance. Had Gintzler studied only the first two groups, he would have been conducting a quasi-experiment using an interrupted time-series design with a nonequivalent control group. The additional control groups allowed him to demonstrate that the endorphins associated with pregnancy cause changes in pain thresholds.

and a significant interaction (jump thresholds showed variability across time only among pregnant rats). Analyses of the data summarized in Figure 2 revealed no significant group differences and no significant jump threshold variation across time.

Taken together, results indicate that pain tolerance increases as parturition time approaches, peaking just before parturition and shortly after. Rats given the naltrexone showed no variation in jump threshold, indicating that eliminating the effect of the endorphin eliminates the changes in jump threshold. Therefore, the changes observed in Group 1 are caused by changes in endorphin level, confirming Gintzler's hypothesis. Nature apparently provides pregnant females some natural protection from the pain of delivery.

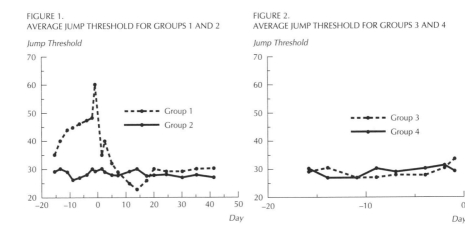

FIGURE 1.
AVERAGE JUMP THRESHOLD FOR GROUPS 1 AND 2

FIGURE 2.
AVERAGE JUMP THRESHOLD FOR GROUPS 3 AND 4

If subjects will be exposed to multiple treatments, researchers need to counterbalance treatment order. For example, suppose an ABA-style design will be used. True experiments include control groups. If each subject is examined four times, twice under baseline (A) conditions and twice under treatment (B) conditions, six groups could be randomly created, with treatments in counterbalanced orders: ABAB, BABA, ABBA, BAAB, AABB, and BBAA. Data could be analyzed to examine order effects and to eliminate any biases introduced by them.

Blocking was described in Chapter 12, and it can occur in true experiments, too. Once blocks are formed, however, subjects within blocks are randomly assigned to conditions, so these are called randomized-block designs. **Randomized-block designs** involve grouping matched subjects into blocks and randomly assigning one subject from each block to each condition. Block size is determined by the number of levels of the independent variable or the number of cells in the design if all variables will be within-subject. For example, we could examine the effect of brightness (3 levels) and hue (4 levels) on latency of response (how long before subjects respond to the image) using a 3×4 factorial design with different subjects in each of the 12 conditions, using a 3×4 repeated-measures design (with each subject measured in each cell), or using a 3×4 repeated-measures design (with randomized blocks). We would form blocks of 12 subjects who are matched on speed of pattern recognition or some other variable known to affect the dependent variable, randomly assigning one subject to each of the twelve conditions. Alternatively, we could create a mixed design by forming blocks of three or four subjects and treating brightness or hue as a within-subject variable and the other as a between-groups variable. These randomized block designs allow experimenters to take advantage of the power of within-subject variables but avoid validity threats associated with repeated-measures designs.

ANALYZING EXPERIMENTAL DATA

There are a number of ways to analyze experimental data. Analysis of variance can be used to examine group differences in posttest scores when posttest-only or pretest-posttest data are available.

Let's consider a simple design with one independent variable that has three levels. Figure 13.1 gives possible data for this design. A one-way analysis of variance or a one-way repeated-measures analysis of variance could be used to analyze these data. Researchers would use the one-way analysis of variance if the independent variable is between-groups, and they would use the one-way repeated-measures analysis of variance if the independent variable is within-subject because subjects have been blocked or repeatedly measured. Figure 13.1a is for a between-groups independent variable; Figure 13.1b shows the same data organized into blocks by matching subjects. The one-way analysis of variance on the data in Figure 13.1a was not significant, but the one-way repeated-measures analysis of variance on the blocked data in Figure 13.1b was significant, $F(2, 4) = 294.00$, $p < .001$.

These data were intentionally created with strongly correlated columns. As pointed out in Chapter 7, strongly correlated data make within-subject data analyses more powerful than between-group analyses. Although treatment means (21.67, 28.67, and 14.67) were the same in both designs, the one-way analysis of variance was not powerful enough to reveal significant results. As shown below, the F test used to analyze hypotheses in one-way analyses of variance involves the ratio of two variances: one that estimates error variance *plus* variance attributable to the independent variable, and one that estimates error variance.

$$F = \frac{\text{Error Variance} + \text{Variance due to the Independent Variable}}{\text{Error Variance}}$$

This ratio should be about 1.0 if the independent variable did not systematically influence the dependent variable, and it should be greater than 1.0 if the independent variable *did* systematically influence the dependent variable. The null hypothesis of no treatment effect is rejected when the observed value of the F statistic is in the upper tail of the F distribution, which is a one-tailed test.

One-way analysis of variance and one-way repeated-measures analysis of variance use the same numerator but different denominators. **Error variance** is variability in the dependent variable not accounted for by the design. The variances in the three cells of Figure 13.1a measure error variance in this design because variability

POSSIBLE DATA FOR A STUDY OF ONE INDEPENDENT VARIABLE **FIGURE 13.1**
WITH THREE LEVELS

(a) Unblocked data

	Level 1	Level 2	Level 3
	25	32	19
	10	18	3
	30	36	22
Means	21.67	28.67	14.67

(b) Blocked data

Block	Level 1	Level 2	Level 3	Block mean
1	25	32	19	25.33
2	10	18	3	10.33
3	30	36	22	29.33
Means	21.67	28.67	14.67	

among subjects in the same condition represents unexplained variability: that is, variability not accounted for by the independent variable. (Everyone in the same condition experiences the same experimental treatment, so different results cannot be attributed to differences in how subjects were treated in the study.) By blocking, we reduced the error term because some of the variation among subjects in the same treatment condition can be attributed to differences among blocks. Notice that block means are quite variable; they ranged from 10.33 to 29.33. When we take these differences into account, we reduce the error variance estimate, increasing the F ratio and creating a more powerful test. If there are relatively large differences among block means, and relatively small differences among scores within blocks, blocking reduces the denominator of the F ratio, creating more powerful tests. The error variance estimates for the data in Figure 13.1 were 100.67 for the between-groups design and .50 for the within-subject design, a considerable reduction in the denominator of the F ratio for the blocked design. This reduction occurred when variance due to differences among blocks was eliminated from the error variance estimate.

One-way designs examine the effect of one independent variable. Two-way designs examine the effects of two independent variables. As discussed in Chapter 5, a two-way analysis of variance involves three tests: a test for the main effect of the first independent variable, a test for the main effect of the second independent variable, and a test for the interaction of the two independent variables. Interactions occur when the effect of one independent variable depends on the level of the other independent variable. In effect, each variable is a moderator variable that influences the effects of the other variable. Three F ratios are calculated, and each represents the ratio of two variance estimates. As before, null hypotheses are rejected for large values of the test statistic. Factorial, repeated-measures, or mixed-design analyses of variance may be conducted, depending on the nature of the independent variables (between-groups or within-subject).

Figure 13.2 shows possible cell means for a two-way analysis of variance examining the effects of gender and age on self-esteem. Group means were calculated under the assumption that the same number of subjects are in each cell. For purposes of discussion, assume that a group difference of at least 5.0 is statistically significant. (For actual studies, the significance probability of the F ratio determines whether differences are statistically significant.) These hypothetical means represent different patterns of possible results.

Data in Figure 13.2a show a main effect for gender (because means for boys and girls are 10 units apart), a main effect for age (because the means for the three age groups differ by 5 units), and no interaction (because the effect of gender is the same at each age level). Data in Figure 13.2b show no main effects (male and female means and means for the three age groups do not differ by at least 5 units), but they do show an interaction (girls score higher among the youngest subjects, boys score higher among the oldest subjects, and gender has no effect in the middle age group). Data in Figure 13.2c show a main effect for gender (male and female means are 20 units apart), no main effect for age (the three means do not differ by at least 5), and an interaction (the effect of gender is stronger among children in the middle age group than in the other two age groups). Data in Figure 13.2d show main effects (male and female means are 5 units apart, and age group means vary by 5 to 10 units) and no interaction (the effect of gender is the same at each age level).

Interactions are easier to visualize by graphing results. Figure 13.3 graphs the data displayed in Figure 13.2. Interactions occur when the lines in the graph are significantly not parallel. The interactions described above are obvious on these graphs. The lines in Figure 13.3a and d are parallel, demonstrating no interaction; the lines in the other two figures are not parallel, demonstrating interactions. Notice that the nonparallel lines need not intersect, as shown in Figure 13.3c; and the parallel lines need not be straight, as shown in Figure 13.3d.

Main effects must be interpreted with caution when interactions are found. The lack of significant main effects for the data in Figure 13.2b does not imply that gender and age have no effect on self-esteem. They do not have main effects, but they do affect self-esteem through their interaction. The girls in Figure 13.2c have an average self-esteem score that is 30 points higher than the boys' average, but this difference is only 10 points among the youngest and oldest children and is 40 points among the children in the middle age group. Researchers cannot conclude that girls always average 30 points higher than boys.

An interaction also influences the test for main effects if the number of subjects in each cell is different. For example, if there were 90 girls and 10 boys in each cell of the study, the girls would contribute more scores to the averages, affecting the age group means. Means of the age groups for the data in Figure 13.2b would become 14, 10, and 6, respectively. This would cause a significant main effect for age (because the 6 and 14 are more than 5 units apart). Balanced designs are more powerful and do not have this problem, so they should be used whenever possible.

Analyses using factorial analyses of variance of posttest scores do not make use of pretest information. This generally is not a problem in true experiments, because

POSSIBLE MEANS FOR TWO-WAY DESIGNS **FIGURE 13.2**

(a)

Age

Gender	0–10	11–15	16–25	Mean
Male	15	20	25	20
Female	5	10	15	10
Mean	10	15	20	

(b)

Age

Gender	0–10	11–15	16–25	Mean
Male	5	10	15	10
Female	15	10	5	10
Mean	10	10	10	

(c)

Age

Gender	0–10	11–15	16–25	Mean
Male	20	5	20	15
Female	30	45	30	35
Mean	25	25	25	

(d)

Age

Gender	0–10	11–15	16–25	Mean
Male	10	20	15	15
Female	5	15	10	10
Mean	7.5	17.5	12.5	

FIGURE 13.3 INTERACTION GRAPHS FOR THE DATA IN FIGURE 13.2

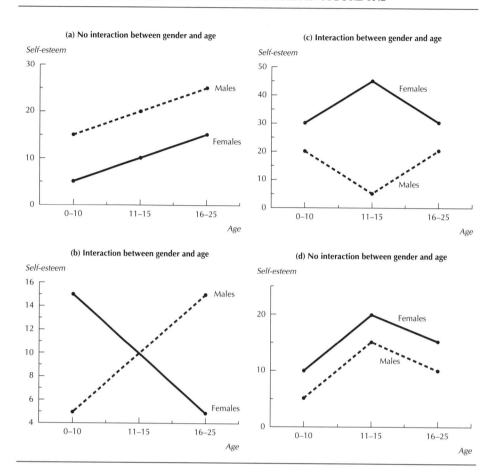

pretest differences are unlikely. Blocking is one way to take pretest scores into account in quasi-experiments or in true experiments with differential mortality that results in group differences. Alternatively, time (pre- vs. post-intervention) may be included as a within-subject variable in a mixed-design analysis of variance. Two other strategies exist: analysis of change scores and analysis of covariance. Researchers could calculate a **change score** for each subject (the difference between pretest and posttest scores), then conduct an analysis of variance on change scores. Experimental subjects would be expected to have larger change scores than control subjects. This finding would be equivalent to an interaction between time and condition in the mixed-design analysis.

Analysis of covariance is a type of analysis of variance that statistically controls for extraneous variables by treating them as covariates. Analysis of covariance uses regression techniques to predict what posttest scores would be if no treatment effects occurred, then asks if treatments systematically created differences between observed and predicted scores. **Covariates** are used in the regression equations to predict posttest scores, and pretest scores can be used as covariates. A complete discussion of analysis of change scores and analysis of covariance is beyond the level of this book, but you should be aware that the different approaches to data analysis may result in different conclusions. Cook and Campbell (1979) provide a good discussion of these alternative data analysis strategies, and they describe occasions under which each is best.

Significant main effects and interactions lead researchers to conclude that groups differ, but the pattern may not be clear. For example, if three means are compared and there is a significant difference among them, it could be that two are alike and one is different, or it could be that all three are different from each other. Additional analyses are made to explore the pattern or to make specific comparisons stated in research hypotheses. Sometimes only these specific comparisons are examined, and the analysis of variance is not conducted. For example, each of a set of experimental group means may be individually compared to a control group mean. Remember from earlier discussions of "fishing" that conducting multiple tests threatens statistical validity. However, there are statistical techniques that control Type I errors when making multiple comparisons. Each test is less powerful, but researchers are unlikely to reject the null hypotheses when relationships do not exist. Consult any textbook that covers analysis of variance for a review of these procedures (e.g., Keppel, 1982).

Significant interactions also may lead to a set of analyses to understand the pattern. For example, Gintzler (1980; Box 13.2) found a significant interaction between pregnancy and day of testing. Follow-up analyses were used to demonstrate that the pattern was consistent with predictions: jump thresholds were not significantly related to day of testing among nonpregnant subjects, but they were significantly related to day of testing among pregnant subjects. Gintzler examined simple effects. **Simple effects** are significant if levels of an independent variable have significantly different means when we analyze subjects at a specific level of another independent variable. He examined the simple effect of day of testing for pregnant rats and the simple effect of day of testing for nonpregnant rats.

Researchers working with time-series data often must analyze masses of information. The diagrams presented in Chapter 12 demonstrated simple patterns that were unaffected by random variation. Actual data rarely are so clear; they more typically resemble Figure 13.4. Visual inspection is insufficient to determine if the dis-

FIGURE 13.4 POSSIBLE TIME-SERIES DATA

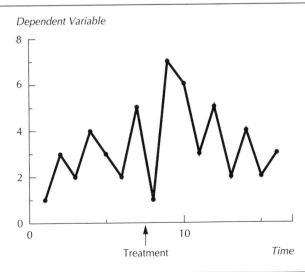

Box 13.3

Can People Learn to Behave Randomly?

Many studies have found that people cannot behave randomly. For example, Bakan (1960) asked subjects to list a set of outcomes that could occur if they randomly tossed a fair coin 300 times. Subjects listed a series of heads (H) and tails (T); however, their lists were not random sequences. A head is just as likely to be followed by a head as a tail, and a sequence of two or three consecutive heads is just as likely as any other two- or three-toss sequence (the probability of HH is the same as the probability of HT, TH, or TT; and the probability of HHH is the same as the probability of HHT, HTH, THH, TTH, THT, HTT, or TTT). Examination of the lists generated by Bakan's subjects revealed major violations of these random principles; some series occurred too often and others occurred too infrequently.

These findings suggest that people cannot behave randomly. Researchers familiar with these studies argued that the lack of an ability to behave randomly is a trait (permanent characteristic) of humans, and they offered a variety of explanations. They suggested that people are inherently unable to perform randomly because they have limited memory capacity, they are unable to disregard previous answers, or they are unable to discriminate random from nonrandom series. Alternatively, Neuringer (1986) suggested that behaving randomly may be a skill, similar to playing tennis; and this skill should improve with appropriate feedback and practice. He conducted a study to examine his theory that the ability to create random sequences is a skill, rather than a trait.

Neuringer's subjects were seven undergraduate, paid volunteers. They were asked to type a random sequence of "1s" and "2s" into a computer; after a baseline was established, they were provided feedback on accuracy after every trial (a sequence of 100 numbers). There are many ways to judge randomness (e.g., you can examine two-character, three-character, or four-character sequences). Five statistical indicators of different aspects of nonrandomness were used, and feedback on the statistics were added across a series of feedback trials. Early trials received only one feedback statistic; trials at the end received all five feedback statistics. Neuringer offered a $15 bonus if randomness was achieved, and interpretative feedback (e.g., "You are

---

ruption in the pattern was random fluctuation or an effect of the treatment. Special techniques and computer programs for analyzing time-series data exist, but they are beyond the scope of this book. Interested readers should consult sources dedicated to this topic (e.g., Brockwell & Davis, 1987).

Data from time-series designs may be analyzed by subject, rather than by group. Box 13.3 summarizes two studies by Neuringer (1986). The first study involved seven subjects; the second involved four subjects. This pair of studies illustrates Mook's (1983; Box 9.1) comments that experiments are designed to demonstrate what "can" happen. Neuringer was motivated to demonstrate that people can learn to behave randomly because he disagreed with previous conclusions that random behavior was impossible (e.g., Bakan, 1960). All subjects were trained until their responses met criteria that defined them as random; and additional analyses, using different criteria for randomness, were conducted for each subject's data. Neuringer's use of multiple criteria allowed him to eliminate alternative explanations that his subjects only learned to meet the training criteria and did not learn to behave randomly.

alternating 1s and 2s too frequently.") was provided during training trials. Data analyses revealed that all seven students were nonrandom during baseline, and all seven students were able to generate random sequences at the end of the experiment, when randomness was judged using the five statistical indicators. Subjects learned at different rates and required from 171 to 483 trials before producing random sequences.

Neuringer then repeated procedures with four high-school subjects, providing feedback using ten statistical indicators and minimizing experimenter interpretations and guidance. Results were the same; subjects were nonrandom during baseline recordings and became random with feedback, according to the ten indicators used during training. In addition, Neuringer analyzed their responses using eight different statistical indicators of randomness and found that two of the four subjects satisfied all eighteen criteria; the other two satisfied all but two criteria. This suggests that subjects were learning to behave randomly, rather than learning to satisfy only those criteria applied during training. Some additional tests involving the 6,000 responses each subject provided during his or her last 60 trials did, however, indicate significant nonrandomness when some criteria were applied, so no subject was perfectly random.

Neuringer's evidence supported his hypothesis that the ability to perform randomly is a skill, rather than a trait, because subjects were able to learn to meet criteria that earlier researchers claimed were beyond human capacity. He also concluded that further research would be necessary to demonstrate that subjects could learn to meet alternative mastery criteria and to investigate the effectiveness of using longer or shorter trials, different types of rewards, and different learning models (e.g., distributed vs. massed practice). He suggested that people have an "internal source of variability" (p. 74) that is subject to reinforcement. From this perspective, we behave nonrandomly because we have been reinforced for systematic behaviors; but we can learn to generate random behaviors when reinforcement contingencies support this outcome.

Neuringer did not use control groups, so his studies are quasi-experiments using interrupted time-series designs. They are good examples of quasi-experiments that do not suffer from interpretive problems due to the lack of control groups. Earlier researchers consistently established the lack of random behavior under conditions similar to those he examined. Experiments are designed to control for factors that might create ambiguous findings. Probably no one would argue that untrained subjects in his studies would have begun to respond more randomly after participating in hundreds of trials. (More likely, subjects would refuse to continue after the first 50 or 60 trials.) Neuringer's article was published in the *Journal of Experimental Psychology*, suggesting that his studies, regardless of their classification, satisfied rigorous scrutiny.

Neuringer's studies are interesting in another way. His goal was to present counterevidence to the theoretical basis for trait conceptions about random behavior. If the trait concept requires the assumption that people are incapable of responding randomly, then any clear demonstration of a person who can generate random behavior threatens the theory. In effect, each of his eleven subjects was an individual case study, and any of his subjects provided evidence to threaten the notion that random behavior is impossible. What is most important is whether studies provide unambiguous answers to research questions, and although Neuringer's studies were quasi-experiments, most people would agree that he accomplished his goal.

RESEARCH DESIGN

Research is both science and art. Like artists, researchers create models of reality: theories that postulate hypothetical constructs and causal ties among them. As scientists, they design appropriate descriptive, correlational, or experimental studies. As they select research strategies, they take into account threats to statistical, internal, construct, and external validity. They also consider practical constraints, such as the costs of conducting long-term longitudinal research. True experiments are the epitome of the scientific method because they can be used to reach unambiguous, valid conclusions about causal relationships. Nevertheless, case studies may describe phenomena that are not easily explained by current theories, archival research may be the only practical route for examining historical phenomena, and correlational studies and quasi-experiments may be the only ethical strategies for exploring relationships among some variables in human subjects, such as the effects of drug addiction during pregnancy. Psychologists use a variety of research strategies because each can provide important information.

Research may be theory-based or issue-based, and issue-based researchers generally are most interested in the immediate external validity of their findings. Although correlations do not prove causation, correlational data may suggest solutions to pressing problems. The discipline, as a whole, grows as researchers using different strategies and different operational definitions of variables seek the truth. There is constant interchange between researchers with different goals. Many researchers conduct both theoretical and applied research, and applied research often involves extending theoretical research into the field. In the last chapter of this book, we will discuss applied research. Applied researchers use all of the research strategies described in this book.

CHAPTER SUMMARY

True experiments are the most effective strategy for reaching unambiguous causal conclusions. Subjects are randomly assigned to manipulated conditions, and control groups are added to allow researchers to eliminate rival hypotheses. The key element of true experiments is control. Control allows researchers to design experiments that have high validity. Most of the common threats to statistical, internal, and construct validity can be handled through careful experimental design, and external validity can be examined through replication.

True experiments may look like quasi-experiments, but subjects are randomly assigned to conditions, and the timing and content of conditions are under experimenter control. Complex theories can be developed by examining possible moderator variables, and randomized blocks can be used to have the power of within-subject data analyses without introducing threats associated with repeated measurements.

Analysis of variance frequently is used to analyze experimental data, and there are techniques to control Type I errors when making comparisons among treatments or when examining simple effects. Analyses also may be done on change scores. Analysis of covariance can be used to statistically control for pretest scores or extraneous variable confounds. Time-series data are analyzed with special techniques, and each subject may be analyzed separately.

Research is both science and art. Researchers create and test theories, and they design research strategies that balance the need for valid conclusions with practical constraints. No single study can prove a theory, but taken together, results from multiple studies can lead to more accurate descriptions of reality.

Key Concepts

analysis of covariance	moderator variable
change score	posttest-only control group design
control	randomized-block design
covariate	simple effect
error variance	stooge

Review Questions

1. Sylvia wants to examine the effect of categorization on memory. Some subjects are asked to learn a list of words selected to represent three categories (foods, household objects, and vehicles), and other subjects are asked to learn a list of unrelated words. Each subject is given five minutes to study the list, then is asked to write all words that can be remembered. What controls should Sylvia use to protect the statistical, internal, and construct validity of her experiment?

2. Design an experiment to test the theory that frustration causes aggression. What controls are you using to protect your study from threats to statistical, internal, and construct validity?

3. What moderator variables may affect the relationship in your frustration-aggression study? How might you conduct experiments to demonstrate their influence?

4. Must researchers randomly select subjects from the population to conduct true experiments? Why or why not?

5. Walter and Sarah draw a sample of 400 people from three regions. Walter compares incomes of people in the three geographical regions using a one-way analysis of variance. Sarah uses the same data, but uses a two-way analysis of variance to examine the effects of geographical region and gender on income. Who is more likely to find a main effect for geographical region? Explain your answer. (*Hint*: Walter and Sarah will have the same numerator in the F ratio used to test the main effect of geographical region. The error term in the denominator of the F ratios is based on the variance within each cell of the design. Walter's study has three cells; Sarah's has six cells. Who should have a smaller error term for the denominator of the F statistic?)

6. New and returning basketball players practice shooting for three months before the season begins. They are tested three times to determine how many baskets they can make out of fifteen attempts. New team members average 6 baskets when they begin training, 10 baskets halfway through training, and 14 baskets at the end of training. Returning team members average 12 baskets at the beginning of training, 13 baskets halfway through training, and 14 baskets at the end of training. Assume that half the team is new and half is returning. Do there appear to be any main effects or an interaction? Plot the data to examine the possible interaction, as illustrated in Figure 13.3.

7. Jamie conducts a memory experiment and compares three groups of subjects. Subjects learn lists of unrelated words, lists of words that rhyme, or lists of words that belong to the same category (household objects). Jamie discovers that her three groups of subjects differ in age. How might she use analysis of covariance to statistically control for age? Explain the logic of this technique.

8. Describe the nature of the interaction illustrated in Figure 1 of Box 13.2.

9. Why was Darley and Latane's study (Box 13.1) a true experiment, and why were Neuringer's studies (Box 13.3) quasi-experiments?

14

Applied Research

Psychologists conduct applied research to meet practical needs. They design and test aircraft cockpits for maximum safety and efficiency; they develop and examine employment screening tests and programs for people with disabilities; they empirically evaluate the effectiveness of therapy for mental disorders; they evaluate alternative designs for low-income housing; and they design and evaluate programs to treat substance abusers. Psychologists working in research laboratories have conducted research to reduce motion sickness in space, to understand the effects of brainwashing on prisoners of war, and to evaluate the effectiveness of anti-depressant medication. Applied psychologists remain mindful of the scientific, empirical, and theoretical bases for their work, and they conduct research using all the techniques summarized in previous chapters. There is a symbiotic relationship between basic and applied research; they complement each other and frequently intersect.

APPLIED AND BASIC RESEARCH

Applied research, like any research, involves careful identification of the problem, review of the related literature, and development of explicit research hypotheses, operational definitions of variables, sampling schemes, data collection strategies, and analyses. Applied researchers recognize the fact that their research may have immediate impact on people and organizations, so adherence to strict scientific and ethical standards is crucial.

The major difference between applied and basic research is the motivation of researchers. Applied researchers' primary objective is to solve practical problems, and basic researchers' primary objective is to contribute to our theoretical understanding of some phenomenon. The distinction is not always clear, and many studies serve both functions. For example, neuropsychologists conducting research on medication for mental disorders are interested in developing theoretical models for brain functioning and in finding cures for problems that wreck people's lives. The theoretical and applied aspects of their research are developed simultaneously, and developments in either arena provide information for the other. Similarly, theoretical research on the causes of juvenile delinquency and the development of delinquency prevention programs progress together (Zigler, Taussig, & Black, 1992), as do theoretical research on memory and the evaluation of eyewitness testimony (Loftus, 1992).

Applied researchers may conduct studies to describe, to predict, or to evaluate phenomena. Case studies of individuals or organizations and survey research of populations may yield useful descriptive information for parole boards, public administrators, and businesses. Applied research that identifies high-risk children or unmet community needs predicts future problems if appropriate counter-measures aren't developed; in the business world, personnel psychologists predict which candidates best fit positions. Applied researchers may evaluate the effectiveness of public interest campaigns or treatment strategies for mental illness.

Two areas of applied research that have received considerable attention and development are human factors and evaluation research. Many other applied specialties exist, such as educational, industrial, clinical, and forensic psychology, but we cannot discuss all of them here. Instead, we will describe two fields to give you some insight into the variety of applied research studies. Human factors researchers investigate the relationship between people and the technology that serves them. Evaluation researchers provide information useful to those who fund community programs and agencies, so that more effective programs are developed and supported and less effective programs are modified or eliminated. As these two examples of applied research demonstrate, applied psychologists often contribute to multidisciplinary teams that may include medical doctors, engineers, statisticians, and social workers. Strict lines dividing scientific specialties may melt as team members investigate common problems, and new cross-disciplinary specialties may develop as necessary skills cross divisional boundaries.

HUMAN FACTORS RESEARCH

Every day we interact with technology. We turn light switches on and off, we drive vehicles, and we type at computer keyboards. Incorrectly placed or wired switches, vehicles that are difficult or inconvenient to control, and keyboards that require awkward positioning of the wrists can inconvenience our lives and threaten our well-being. For example, people who do repetitive motions with equipment, such as typists and assembly-line workers, may develop inflammations in their shoulders, elbows, or wrists because of inadequate human factors engineering of the tools they use. **Human factors researchers** investigate strategies to optimize interactions between people and technology. Some human factors researchers are non-psychologists, such as industrial engineers and computer scientists, but most are trained in psychology (Parsons, 1984).

Human factors researchers examine **systems** composed of humans, machinery, and the environment in which they meet; then they apply the results of their research to maximize the effectiveness and safety of these systems. This may be accomplished by training or more carefully selecting the people, by redesigning the machinery, or by improving the environment in which the interaction takes place. For example, potential pilots are selected for visual skills, eye-hand coordination, and the ability to function under stress, and they are trained in simulators and under careful supervision before they actually fly by themselves. The cockpit controls are carefully designed to be convenient, with understandable gauges and with protective safeguards in place. The cockpit environment is designed to control temperature and air pressure, with comfortable positioning and ease of access. The system, as a whole, is designed to function well. Technological accidents, such as the Three Mile Island nuclear plant malfunction in 1979, are not necessarily attributable to human error when a systems perspective is applied. Human factors researchers work to anticipate possible systems problems, and they attempt to design systems with sufficient safeguards to compensate for potential errors.

Humans make errors, and human factors researchers study errors to improve systems. Kantowitz and Sorkin (1983) describe five types of human errors: errors of omission, errors of commission, errors due to extraneous acts, sequential errors, and time errors. **Errors of omission** occur when necessary steps are not completed, such as forgetting to tighten a gas cap. **Errors of commission** occur when steps are performed incorrectly, such as increasing the flow from a faucet when intending to turn it off. **Errors due to extraneous acts** occur when people are distracted by some factor outside the system, such as daydreaming. **Sequential errors** involve the right processes, but in the wrong order, such as typing "hte" instead of "the." **Time errors** involve incorrect pacing of work, such as burning cookies by leaving them in the oven too long.

Human factors researchers break down system processes into steps, evaluating potential errors in each step. For example, in order to brush your teeth you must locate toothpaste, toothbrush, and a water supply; open the toothpaste; place toothpaste on your brush; and so on. This system generally involves very simple tools (a toothbrush, a tube of toothpaste, and a faucet), but errors are possible at each step. For example, you could try to squeeze the toothpaste without removing the cap (an error of omission), you could miss the toothbrush and spill toothpaste on the floor (an error of commission), you could accidently skip brushing your bottom teeth because you are distracted by a conversation (an error due to an extraneous act), you could rinse the paste off the toothbrush before you brush your teeth (a sequential error), or you could brush too quickly and miss a food deposit in your mouth (a time error). Systems are changed to reduce the likelihood of errors and to minimize their impact. For example, hinged toothpaste caps improve the system by reducing the probability that caps are lost or incorrectly returned to tubes. Human factors researchers generally examine systems more complex than toothbrushing. Imagine the potential for error in a large electrical switching facility or in the operation of a jumbo jet.

Some human factors researchers emphasize engineering psychology, an application of experimental psychology to human factors problems. **Engineering psychologists** develop theoretical understandings of the limits of human abilities and how these limits relate to systems design. They conduct research to understand the capabilities and limitations of human thinking. After these limits are understood, alternative systems can be compared or developed based on their suitability for promoting what people do well and compensating for human failings. For example, if you write ideas better than you spell, you can write papers on a computer and make frequent use of the spelling checker in your word processing software. Your software will help you to produce papers that contain your ideas but are relatively free of spelling errors.

In general, engineering psychologists find that humans are better than machines at recognizing complex patterns, improvising entirely new solutions, generalizing theories from specific observations, and making subjective judgments; machines are better than humans at performing highly repetitive tasks over long periods of time, sensing stimuli outside of human sensory abilities (e.g., high-pitched sounds), counting or measuring physical characteristics, and detecting well-specified, infrequent stimuli (Kantowitz & Sorkin, 1983). It is not surprising that modern medical labs are becoming increasingly automated, relying more and more on machines for routine analytical procedures and for the preparation of detailed information for human examination (such as brain scans done through magnetic resonance imaging). As computers become increasingly sophisticated, the relative limitations of humans and machines require continuing evaluation.

Major decisions about the allocation of tasks to humans or machines must take into account the limits of all elements in the system. As Kantowitz and Sorkin (1983) point out, however, the design of an effective system involves more than juggling the relative skills of humans and machines. Humans who are overwhelmed or understimulated will not perform optimally. As they emphasize, "The first commandment of human factors is 'Honor Thy User'" (p. 13) by creating systems that offer humans dignified, productive, interesting, comfortable, safe interactions with technology.

Environments also are important. **Environmental psychologists** examine relationships between people and their environments, and they may study human factors problems or general effects of environments on people's lives. They examine the effects of air pollution, urban stress, crowding, and architectural designs on people. If they specialize in human factors, they ask questions about environments in which people interact with technology. At what illumination, temperature, vibration level, noise level, and density do humans and machines function well? Should workers stand, sit, or be supported by platforms? Should they be isolated in private cubicles or should they be housed in open environments?

Human factors researchers may conduct basic research to develop theoretical models for human behavior, or they may have a more directly applied focus within a particular industry. Wickens (1984) describes five general strategies for human factors research: observations of working real-world systems, field studies of systems in operation under controlled conditions, simulations, laboratory experiments, and mathematical models. As he points out, these categories form a realism continuum, with on-site observations embedded in the real world and mathematical modeling farthest removed from the real world. Each research strategy can lead to important contributions to systems development. For example, mathematical models are applied for the design of car braking systems, laboratory experiments verify that aspects of the model hold true, simulations are used as prototype pieces of equipment are developed, equipment installed on experimental cars is tested by skilled drivers on test tracks, and systems installed in production cars are tested on actual roads. Human factors researchers design these studies, evaluate their results, and work to produce finished systems that are safe and effective. Errors generally are most costly to correct in working real-world systems, as manufacturers faced with equipment recalls can testify.

Sometimes seemingly insignificant details can lead to systems failure. For example, a computer company was field-testing a new medical computer system. A nurse volunteered to test the system, punched a few keys, then refused to continue. The term "fatal error" was flashing on the screen, indicating that the system had encountered a software error. In the context of a medical facility, however, the term "fatal error" had a much different connotation. The need for real-world systems testing is clear.

Human factors researchers need to develop theoretical understandings of human performance, so they frequently are trained as experimental psychologists with specializations in **human information processing** (how people respond to incoming sensory information, such as lights and sounds). How are sensory inputs processed, how are they combined with memories, how are decisions made, and how are responses executed? Human sensory processing, memory, attention, motivation, decision-making, and reaction times are examined. Mathematical models may be developed. For example, **signal detection theorists** (who analyze the probabilities that various environmental stimuli will be detected) have developed mathematical models that allow them to understand and to predict how factors interact to create more detectable stimuli (such as warning lights that signal an overheated engine). Much of this work is basic, theoretical research, but human factors researchers eventually apply their theories to solve practical problems.

The field of human factors research has developed into an interdisciplinary approach to systems design, with psychologists, physiologists, engineers, and others contributing to solutions. Human factors research is an exciting area for theoretical and applied research on complex interactions between people and an ever-evolving technology. The principles of good research described in earlier chapters, tied to specializations in fields such as information processing, allow psychologists to make important human factors contributions.

EVALUATION RESEARCH

Evaluation research uses social science methodology to plan, to monitor, and to evaluate the impact and efficiency of human service programs. Evaluation researchers examine programs that teach, train, treat, counsel, assist, or serve clients in some way. These programs do not produce a product that is evaluated easily. Human service programs' product is service. Simple counts of how many clients come and go are insufficient evidence of program effectiveness. Evaluators need to ascertain the quality of the services and their impact on clients' lives. Well-meaning social agencies that don't help clients are a luxury we can't afford, and improvements are unlikely if program quality is not evaluated routinely.

Evaluators publish reviews of their work to disseminate information on important findings and new techniques. Journals dedicated to evaluation have been established, such as *Evaluation and Program Planning, Evaluation News,* and *Evaluation Quarterly;* evaluation studies are reported in books on social issues (e.g., Powell, 1988), and some large-scale evaluations have been published as books, such as *Sesame Street Revisited* (Cook et al., 1975) and *As the Twig Is Bent: Lasting Effects of Preschool Programs* (Consortium for Longitudinal Studies, 1983). Reviews allow evaluators to anticipate problems, to compare outcomes with other studies, and to locate instrumentation or techniques previously found useful. Meta-analyses of the evaluation literature may become increasingly useful to program planners, such as meta-analyses of

---

Box 14.1

Meta-Analysis of the Effectiveness of Child and Adolescent Therapy

Weisz, Weiss, and Donenberg (1992) compared the effectiveness of child and adolescent therapy in two types of studies: studies in which therapy is conducted under carefully controlled laboratory conditions, and studies in which therapy is conducted in the field under real-life conditions.

Therapy with children and adolescents is big business. About 2.5 million juveniles are treated each year, at a cost of over $1.5 billion. Children are treated for many problems, including aggression, withdrawal, hyperactivity, impulsivity, delinquency, underachievement, anxiety, depression, phobias, obesity, headaches, and enuresis.

Weisz and his colleagues examined more than 200 impact studies documenting the effectiveness of treatment on over 12,000 children. Most of these studies were conducted by researchers examining carefully controlled therapy programs in laboratory clinics; only a few involved children treated at regular clinics. These types of clinics differ in a number of ways. Laboratory clinics generally recruit subjects with specific disorders (such as phobias), randomly assign subjects to condition, carefully train and monitor therapists, and focus therapy on specific problems. Practicing clinics' clients are self-referred (or are indirectly referred by schools or doctors), have heterogeneous and multiple problems,

are rarely assigned to conditions using a random process, and are treated by therapists with heavy caseloads, less direct supervision, and eclectic approaches.

Several meta-analyses on the effectiveness of therapy on juveniles, based predominantly on published studies conducted at research clinics, find effect sizes of about .80, similar to effect sizes found for adult therapy clients. Weisz and his colleagues reviewed the few practicing clinic studies, however, and found little or no significant effects for treatment. Follow-up analyses of untreated and treated children show little or no difference in their adjustment or need for further therapy services.

Because so few studies are conducted in practicing clinics, Weisz and his colleagues call for increased cooperation between researchers and practitioners, so that studies on the impact of therapy are made in real-life settings with real-life clients. They conclude that research on the effectiveness of therapy with juveniles in research clinics does not generalize to practicing clinics. The bulk of the research demonstrates that children and adolescents can be helped by therapy, but limited evidence based on research in practicing clinics suggests that most of the children actually treated by clinic therapists do not benefit from this experience.

---

the effectiveness of Head Start programs, the influence of teachers' expectations on children's cognitive development, and the effectiveness of job training programs (Light, 1987). Box 14.1 describes a meta-analysis with important implications for the delivery of psychological services to children.

Evaluators traditionally have been trained in one or more of the social sciences, such as psychology or sociology. However, a specialized science of evaluation, with its own theories and strategies, may be evolving (Scriven, 1987). Specific legal and ethical principles for their work have been developed (Thurston, Ory, Mayberry, & Branskamp,1987) that include consideration of issues such as libel and slander.

In-House and Outside Evaluators

Evaluators may be in-house or outside the organization. **In-house evaluators** are permanent employees of the organization. They may be experts in the services being provided, but they may have conflicts of interest when they make evaluations. They may have been instrumental in establishing programs, their incomes may depend on positive evaluations, they may be subject to political pressure from their employers, and they may have personal ties to employees that cloud their judgments. **Outside evaluators** are consultants hired to conduct the evaluation. They may avoid many of the conflicts faced by in-house evaluators, but their incomes may depend on maintaining good relationships with those who hire them. Experienced outside evaluators may come in with fresh ideas and with broad perspectives on human services delivery.

Because of their continuing association with the organization, in-house evaluators can immediately monitor changes in service delivery, and they can maintain continuous records. On the other hand, management may pay closer attention to outside consultants because of their perceived objectivity and expertise. Accreditation programs, such as those for schools and hospitals, require periodic outside evaluation. Subsequent evaluators explicitly examine responses to prior evaluations. Proposed and ongoing public programs are unlikely to be funded unless they include regular outside evaluations.

Formative and Summative Evaluations

Two basic types of evaluations are made: formative evaluations and summative evaluations. **Formative evaluations** are designed to improve program quality. **Summative evaluations** are designed to form global judgments on program quality. Formative evaluations may identify unmet needs or weak links in the operation. Summative evaluation may lead to changes in funding or program discontinuation.

Types of Evaluations

Evaluation can be useful at any stage of a program's existence. Needs assessments are conducted before programs are created. Evaluability assessments are conducted on existing programs when evaluations are planned; program monitoring occurs as programs are established and periodically checked; program impact studies examine the effectiveness of programs; and efficiency analysis is used to see if benefits justify costs and to compare costs of alternative programs.

Needs Assessment

Needs assessments identify unmet needs, describe the scope of needs, and identify program objectives. Social programs are expensive, and funds are limited. Objective needs assessments allow social planners to evaluate which programs are most needed. Failed programs that neglected appropriate needs assessments include urban renewal programs that destroyed inexpensive housing and replaced it with unwanted multistory apartment buildings, AIDS identification programs targeting doctors who did not collect necessary sexual history information, and media programs that swamped screening clinics with hypochondriacs (Rossi & Freeman, 1985). Pressman and

Wildavsky (1973), in *Implementation: Or How Great Expectations in Washington Are Dashed in Oakland*, describe a failed multi-million-dollar job creation program that could have benefitted from better needs assessment and planning.

Evaluators conducting needs assessments define target populations and the extent of required services. Representatives of social agencies (e.g., clinics, schools, hospitals), community and civic groups (e.g., PTA organizations, religious organizations, social clubs, local community leaders), and community residents may be surveyed. Those in need of service are identified. For example, evaluators may conclude that 15 percent of the community's senior citizens have alcohol-related problems that are not met by current social programs. Results may indicate which areas of the city are most in need of services and special aspects of those areas, such as problems with transportation or English. Recommendations are made explicit, such as establishing a senior alcohol treatment center in a specific neighborhood with buses to transport seniors from other neighborhoods, bilingual alcohol treatment specialists, nutritionists, and social workers. Social planners can decide whether the program should be established and what its level of funding should be, based on objective evidence provided in the needs assessment.

Needs assessment may involve comparisons of alternative solutions to identified problems. Should new programs be created or should preexisting programs be modified? Should the public or private sector be involved? Should clients be transported to central facilities or should satellite programs be established in different neighborhoods? Prioritizing needs allows evaluators to compare alternative solutions. A particular solution may meet one need well, but not others. Points can be assigned to each possible solution for each objective, with more points available for high-priority objectives; sums of points can be used to rank-order alternative programs. For example, if high priority is placed on ease of access, satellite clinics would receive more points than centralized clinics; but if clinics require expensive medical equipment that is too costly to be placed at separate clinics, centralized clinics would receive higher ratings.

Evaluators may suggest model programs for primary, secondary, or tertiary prevention of social problems. **Primary prevention** is preventing a problem before it occurs, such as conducting sex education programs that encourage students to avoid sexually transmitted diseases and adolescent pregnancies. **Secondary prevention** provides immediate treatment for problems, such as nutritional counseling for pregnant teenagers. **Tertiary prevention** targets long-term complications of problems, such as providing job training to the chronically unemployed. Target populations and objectives for these approaches are different.

Needs assessments may lead to suggestions for pilot studies or partial implementation of new programs. Careful evaluation of the operations and effectiveness of these experimental programs can lead to redefining objectives and rethinking implementation strategies. For example, before Sesame Street was aired, sample formats were tested on children to see which presentations best captured their attention (Reeves, 1970).

Evaluability Assessment

Sometimes an evaluability assessment is conducted before evaluations of preexisting programs are begun. **Evaluability assessments** are conducted to identify program objectives, to describe program components, to outline appropriate evaluation strategies, and to secure the cooperation of relevant parties. One possible outcome of the evaluability assessment is to postpone the evaluation study. For example, careful refinement of program objectives may lead to changes in the program that must be implemented before they can be evaluated.

Evaluators identify **stakeholders**, people whose lives are affected by the program. Stakeholders include program personnel, clients, sponsors, and community representatives. Each stakeholder group may view the program and its objectives differently. For example, sponsors and personnel for job training programs may see their work as tertiary prevention of unemployment, but clients may see their involvement as a temporary job, with no long-term consequences. Some may view prisons as punishment; others may view them as rehabilitation agencies or as temporary housing to keep criminals off the street. Sex education programs may be used for primary prevention of unwanted pregnancy or disease, or they may be designed to reduce sexual violence or exploitation. Based on the input of stakeholders, researchers develop specific objectives that are to be evaluated. Stakeholder groups should agree to these objectives, so that cooperation with the evaluation is more likely. If stakeholders cannot agree, the evaluator already has identified a major problem.

Objectives should be explicit and measurable. For example, an objective may be to offer three one-hour parenting classes to new adolescent mothers at the local county hospital. This can be evaluated. By comparison, the objective of "promoting parenting knowledge" is too amorphous to be evaluated clearly. The anticipated impact of the intervention also is specified, such as stating that the parenting classes should significantly improve weight gain in the infants of mothers who participate compared to a control group of mothers who don't participate, and that fewer medical emergencies requiring emergency room visits should occur in participating families. These objectives can be examined to analyze the intervention's effects. Generally, multiple objectives are defined, so the breadth and extent of program impact are determined.

Evaluators cannot simply borrow criteria used in previous evaluations or found in old documents. As Rossi and Freeman (1985) emphasize, "evaluators conduct their work in a continually changing milieu" (p. 33). Political shifts, changes in stakeholder populations, previous findings, and social changes may create major shifts in objectives and priorities for human service programs. In addition, as psychologists learn more about interventions, clinicians are judged by escalating quality standards in diagnosis and treatment. Objectives and techniques defined in earlier evaluations need periodic updating. This suggests that evaluability assessments should be incorporated routinely into evaluation efforts.

Program Monitoring

Program monitoring assesses how well programs conform to planned specifications. One reason for program failure is that original plans were never implemented. Program monitors examine the means for service delivery, based on plans designed by program creators or established in the evaluability assessment. They verify that physical specifications (e.g., 1500 square feet of office space and four buses that work), personnel specifications (e.g., licensed therapists, bilingual staff, bus drivers), and other specifications (e.g., location, access for the handicapped, hours of operation) are met. In addition, client characteristics are monitored. If the program was developed to serve alcoholic seniors, but the clients are predominantly drug-abusing adolescents, the program is not meeting planned specifications. Usually, monitors record the gender, age, and ethnicity of clients; the referral source; the nature of the problem; and provided services. Unexpected findings, such as too few clients in one gender or ethnic group, may lead to enhanced efforts to meet the needs of these populations. For example, Robertson (1984) reports "**creaming**" in job-training programs: providing disproportionate services to clients who are least disadvantaged.

Program monitoring generally provides formative information. Discrepancies between plans and observations are objectively documented, so directors can adjust the program or its objectives. For example, program monitors may discover that too few therapy hours are available in the evening, that too few clients have been recruited, or that necessary equipment has not been purchased. Outcome objectives may be adjusted if program monitors find that insufficient funds have been provided for needed equipment and personnel. Summative evaluations may lead to the recognition of poorly managed or ill-conceived programs that need major restructuring or cancellation.

Program Impact

Program impact studies are conducted to examine how well programs have met their objectives. Program monitoring examines the process; program impact studies examine the products. Evaluators examine the overall impact of programs on clients and on communities. Possible side effects, both positive and negative, are examined. For example, extensive followups of preschool intervention programs suggest they are useful for primary prevention of juvenile delinquency (Zigler, Taussig, & Black, 1992). A treatment center for substance abusers may help some clients eliminate drug habits but may lead to increased neighborhood littering or car accidents because of increased traffic around the center. Although not planned, these negative side effects may influence community acceptance of treatment facilities.

Research is conducted to measure and evaluate objectives. For example, Kagan, Kearsley, and Zelazo (1977) compared the development of infants who spent each weekday for their first two-and-a-half years in a quality day-care program to a control group of matched infants not in day care. To the relief of parents with children in day care, the groups were very similar in cognitive and social development.

Untreated control groups (sometimes created from waiting lists) may be examined, and samples or entire populations of stakeholders may be surveyed, tested, or interviewed. Data may include physical characteristics, behavioral observations, and test or survey results. Archival records in case files or government documents may be examined. Reliability and validity issues are important in order that objectives be measured accurately and meaningfully, and response rates are important because low rates suggest biased samples. Program impact studies may require longitudinal designs to examine long-term effects. For example, evaluators may examine the proportion of alcohol recovery program graduates who are sober one month, six months, and one year after participation.

Accountability is the key word for program impact studies. We hold service providers accountable for the services they provide. Medical doctors, therapists, courts, and directors of primary prevention programs are expected to accomplish their established goals and to cooperate with evaluators to secure evidence of these accomplishments.

Evaluators conducting program impact studies look at overall program functioning, but they also may analyze individual service providers. **Individual performance appraisals** of the effectiveness of individuals within the organization may be time-consuming but necessary for key personnel, such as managers or therapists. For example, an evaluator may discover that two of the four therapists at a clinic see 80 percent of the clients and conduct 90 percent of effective treatments. This information probably would be more useful than a global conclusion that the program was effective with 60 percent of clients. As with global program evaluation, individual performance appraisals must be done after criteria for judging performance have been well defined. Various stakeholders may contribute to prioritizing objectives. Employees who are informed of these criteria when they are hired should not be surprised when they are held accountable for meeting them later. The blame for a poor individual performance appraisal may be shared by managers who have structured nonsupportive work environments. Formative evaluation of individuals should be designed to improve performance, and this may be a function of both the individuals and the situations in which they work.

Efficiency Analysis

Efficiency analysis examines cost-benefit or cost-effectiveness ratios and may contrast results from alternative programs. **Cost-benefit ratios** are costs per unit of benefit when benefits are expressed in dollars. For example, a federal commission established to reduce government paperwork had benefits that outweighed costs by a factor of 350 to 1 (Abelson, 1977). Every dollar invested in the commission saved the federal government $350 in paperwork, with an annual savings of about $10 billion. The benefits of social programs often cannot be designated in monetary units. **Cost-effectiveness ratios** are costs per unit of benefit when benefits are not expressed in dollars. For example, the costs per pupil for educational programs are cost-effectiveness ratios.

Alternative programs can be compared. Evaluators may find that group counseling is more cost-effective than individual counseling or that "lay" counselors are more cost-effective than psychiatrists for treating alcoholics. Long-term costs also may be considered. For example, investing a small amount in free immunization programs may save millions of dollars in potential medical costs, and investing moderate amounts in programs to help high-risk families may save millions of dollars in potential welfare, criminal, or other social costs.

Simple cost-effectiveness ratios may not describe the whole picture. For example, two mental hospitals may have quite different costs per patient, but the cheaper one is not necessarily more efficient. The cheaper one may have improperly trained staff and little effective treatment. Efficiency analysts may look at the relative effectiveness of the two hospitals by comparing the average cost per significantly improved patient, and they may calculate separate ratios for patients with different diagnoses.

Sometimes opportunity costs are examined. Decisions to implement one program often mean that other programs cannot exist; the **opportunity cost** is what is sacrificed to maintain the program being evaluated. For example, treating babies with severe birth defects may exhaust budgets that could be used to treat more babies with milder defects. Providing huge scholarships to a few students may preclude offering moderate assistance to many students. On a personal level, full-time college students

---

Box 14.2

Curriculum-Based Suicide Prevention Programs for Adolescents

Garland and Zigler (1993) reviewed the accumulated literature on adolescent suicide and the effectiveness of selected prevention programs, including curriculum-based programs. Psychologists and the general public are concerned over increases in the suicide rate among children. About 2300 juveniles took their lives in 1988, approximately a 200-percent increase since 1960. Experts estimate that from 50 to 200 children attempt suicide for each one who is successful, although the percentage of suicide attempts actually intended to cause death is not clear.

Research indicates that almost all adolescents who commit suicide suffer from psychiatric problems, especially affective disorders (e.g., bipolar illness and depression), conduct or antisocial personality disorders, and substance abuse. The actual suicide often is preceded by a crisis, such as an arrest or rejection by an intimate friend.

Curriculum-based intervention programs have become increasingly popular and are mandated by some states. They may be offered as one-shot experiences (such as two-hour voluntary programs) or may be integrated into required high school courses. According to Garland and Zigler, almost all curriculum-based programs use a stress model, rather than a mental illness model; they present suicide as a reaction to crisis and deny or underplay its relationship to mental health. "The curricula often explicitly state that people who commit suicide are *not* mentally ill and that everyone is vulnerable to suicidal behavior" (p. 174). Program developers argue that this approach destigmatizes suicide, so that at-risk children will not be afraid to come forward for help.

Garland and Zigler are concerned about this approach because the destigmatization of suicide may undermine taboos against it. Teenagers may come to believe that suicide is a normal response to adolescent life crises. In addition, programs may exaggerate the incidence of suicide to increase student concern; but this may make suicide appear even more normal, acceptable, and common. Strong evidence on suicide clusters and copy-cat suicides suggests that troubled adolescents mimic others who commit suicide, so presenting case histories of relatively healthy individuals who sought this option can backfire. The case history approach "may have a paradoxical effect in that students may closely identify with the problems portrayed

---

suffer opportunity costs by delaying entry into careers. After graduation they have to compete with people who already have more work experience, and they may delay home buying and child rearing until educational loans are repaid. These are opportunity costs associated with attending college.

Cost-effectiveness ratios may not be stable. For example, a clinic that costs $200 per client each day for the 20 clients in residence may cost $250 per client each day if expanded to serve 40 clients. Added space, staff, and management requirements may grow faster than the client list. On the other hand, underutilized programs may be able to absorb clients with little additional cost, so their cost-effectiveness ratios will improve with expansion. Obviously the type of client served affects costs. We cannot hold intensive care units to the same costs per patient as ambulatory units. Evaluators and consumers of their reports must make wise comparisons that are fair to all programs.

by the case examples and may come to see suicide as the logical solution to their own problem" (p. 175). Suicide ideation is common and occurs in over half of high school and college students; but there is a large difference between suicide ideation and actual suicide that the stress model does not highlight.

Garland and Zigler also are concerned that curriculum-based models for suicide prevention may target the wrong audience. Attendance at voluntary meetings and normal school activities is less likely among adolescents most at-risk for suicide. At best, this approach would be inefficient. At-risk adolescents may be indirectly, rather than directly served by the program if they are identified and referred by friends who do participate.

Most curriculum-based programs have never been evaluated, and most published evaluations lack control groups. Garland and Zigler located two well-conducted large-scale evaluation studies. Results suggest no effect on rates of suicide ideation or attempted suicide and minimal effectiveness in changing knowledge and attitudes; some results indicate that boys become more hopeless and less adaptive after participation.

Garland and Zigler recognize their conclusions are based on limited information, but they argue that the stress model underlying curriculum-based strategies leads to the dissemination of misinformation and may cause harm. They suggest a number of alternative strategies that might be more effective, including primary prevention programs that reduce risk factors for suicide (e.g., delinquency, substance abuse, truancy, and pregnancy), that teach teenagers coping strategies and facts about mental illness, and that provide family support (including before-school and after-school programs). They also suggest expanded training for teachers and for health and mental health professionals on suicide and referral procedures; restricting firearm access for teenagers; encouraging the media to recognize their contributions to copy-cat suicides; identifying and serving high-risk teenagers (such as classmates of children who have committed suicide); expanding suicide prevention hotline services for adolescents; and developing closer, cooperative relationships among researchers, program developers, and policymakers interested in affecting adolescent mental health.

Expanded Cooperation

Weisz, Weiss, and Donenberg (1992; Box 14.1) and many others (e.g., Garland and Zigler; Box 14.2) have argued the need for expanded cooperation among researchers, program developers, and policymakers. Evaluation efforts provide these links at all stages of program development, from needs assessment to efficiency analysis. Evaluation efforts are standard components of experimental programs supported by government funds; they are increasingly required for all human services programs. Human services programs are too expensive and too important to be established and run without evidence supporting their effectiveness and without reference to our accumulated knowledge about strategies that have been proven effective elsewhere.

Box 14.3

Advice to Evaluators

1. Don't be arrogant. You need the cooperation of all stakeholders, and they have other things to do with their time.
2. Be patient. Program changes take time.
3. Be fair. Administrators, sponsors, staff, and clients may have different priorities for efficiency, outcomes, and service. Take all these perspectives into account.
4. Be practical. Program stakeholders need practical advice. Theoretical suggestions may be of little value unless tied to reasonable, practical solutions.
5. Be reasonable. It may be impossible to do a five-year longitudinal follow-up study on the budget and time set for the evaluation. Define and evaluate important, reasonable goals.
6. Select your variables carefully. Stakeholders may refuse to provide thousands of pieces of information, and you may not have time to analyze everything you could possibly examine.
7. Avoid jargon. Technical jargon appropriate for journal articles or professional meetings generally is inappropriate for evaluation reports. Remember your audience, and write so they will understand your report. Your best ideas may have no impact if the consumers of your report can't understand them.

8. Help people learn from problems. Every complex enterprise has problems, and no person or organization is perfect. Your attitude should recognize this. Focus on opportunities for improvement.
9. Evaluate yourself. If your recommendations are ignored, how might you conduct the evaluation or present your findings differently to improve your effectiveness next time?
10. Give positive feedback. Don't just emphasize the negative. Explicitly recognize positive achievements and outstanding performances.
11. Be wise. Careers and professional reputations of personnel and sponsors and the lives of clients may be affected by your report. Your evaluation may alienate and create rigid resistance in the very people you most want to help. Your evaluation should have positive impact.
12. Do the right thing. Glowing evaluations of ineffective programs or incompetent staff are inappropriate. Part of the job of being an evaluator is the obligation to "take the heat" when honest, negative evaluations are needed.

Points 1 through 9 are adapted from Posavac & Carey (1989, pp. 321–323).

Advice to Evaluators

It is clear that professional evaluators perform important and difficult research, and it is easy to see why Rossi and Freeman (1985) argue that evaluation is both art and science. Posavac and Carey (1989), based on much experience in evaluation, offer sage advice to evaluators (Box 14.3). Much of this advice would be useful to any psychologist conducting research.

CHAPTER SUMMARY

The major difference between basic and applied research is the motivation of researchers. Basic research is designed to contribute to our theoretical understanding of some phenomenon, and applied research is designed to solve practical problems. The distinction is not always clear; developments in either area provide information for the other. Two examples of applied research are human factors research and evaluation research.

Human factors researchers investigate strategies to optimize interactions between people and technology. They examine systems composed of people, machinery, and the environment in which they meet, and they develop ways to maximize the effectiveness and safety of these systems. They analyze systems for potential errors, and they design safeguards to prevent catastrophes. Engineering psychologists examine the limits of human functioning and design systems with these limits in mind. Environmental psychologists contribute to human factors work by designing optimum environments for people and machines. Human factors researchers use a variety of strategies that range from real-world experiments to mathematical modeling. Some human factors researchers have a foundation in human information processing, and they examine factors that affect how people respond to stimuli, such as sensory processing, memory, attention, motivation, decision making, and reaction times.

Evaluation researchers use social science methodology to plan, to monitor, and to evaluate the impact and efficiency of human service programs. Evaluators may be in-house or outside professionals, and they may conduct formative or summative evaluations. They conduct needs assessments to identify unmet needs, describe the scope of needs, and identify program objectives. Alternative solutions to problems may be contrasted, and models for primary, secondary, and tertiary prevention may be considered.

Evaluability assessments are conducted before evaluations of ongoing programs to identify program objectives, to describe program components, to outline appropriate evaluation strategies, and to secure the cooperation of stakeholders. The objectives of human services programs may change over time, so they should be reevaluated periodically. Program monitoring assesses how well programs conform to planned specifications. Program monitors examine the delivery process, not the product. They verify that needed equipment and personnel are available and that appropriate clients are being served.

Program impact studies examine how well the program has met its objectives and possible side effects of the program. Impact research may involve the analysis of control groups, and all major stakeholder populations are examined. Evaluators may assess the global program and also may conduct individual performance appraisals of key personnel. Efficiency analysis examines cost-benefit ratios (dollars spent per dollars saved) or cost-efficiency ratios (cost per unit of benefit) and may contrast alternative programs. Opportunity costs also may be evaluated, and researchers recognize that efficiency ratios may not be stable if programs are changed.

Evaluation efforts link researchers, program developers, and policymakers at all stages of program development, from needs assessment to efficiency analysis. Evaluation is both art and science. Evaluators should avoid arrogance and should be patient, fair, practical, reasonable, and wise. Their evaluations should be honest and should have a positive effect.

Key Concepts

cost-benefit ratio	individual performance appraisal
cost-effectiveness ratio	needs assessment
creaming	opportunity cost
efficiency analysis	outside evaluator
engineering psychology	primary prevention
environmental psychology	program impact study
error due to extraneous act	program monitoring
error of commission	secondary prevention
error of omission	sequential error
evaluability assessment	signal detection theory
evaluation research	stakeholder
formative evaluation	summative evaluation
human factors research	systems
human information processing	tertiary prevention
in-house evaluator	time error

Review Questions

1. Under contract to a manufacturer of diet pills, an experimental psychologist examines the side effects of prolonged ingestion of the pills. Is this applied or basic research? Could it be both?

2. The psychology department office is a system. Analyze your department's office from a systems perspective. Suppose this system is creating next semester's class schedule. What types of errors could be made? How might the system be changed to correct these errors before the schedule is distributed?

3. You are an engineering psychologist hired by the Brown Printing Company to analyze their Christmas card production. What tasks would you assign to people and what tasks would you assign to machines? Why?

4. Wickens (1984) described five general strategies for human factors research. Describe the development of a new line of hair brushes for left-handed people. Use at least three of the five strategies.

5. Universities are required to conduct periodic evaluations of their effectiveness, including evaluation visits from accreditation program staff. The accreditation program may fully accredit the campus, may give provisional accreditation with a scheduled reevaluation, or may withdraw a campus's accreditation. Imagine that you are an outside evaluator charged with evaluation of your department. Describe the formative and summative evaluations that you would conduct.

6. The director of a local mental health clinic has training in evaluation and proposes to save money by conducting an evaluation of the clinic. What are the positive and negative aspects of this suggestion?

7. Patricia has been invited to chair a citizen's advisory panel to conduct a needs assessment for a program to reduce smoking in high school students. What analyses should her panel conduct? What primary, secondary, and tertiary prevention strategies should they consider?

8. Jesse is hired to conduct an evaluability assessment of the campus' student counseling center. What are his major tasks?

9. A county agency funds a residential program for adolescents convicted of a first offense for gang-related activities. The program was created to rehabilitate these teenagers, to keep them in school and out of gangs. A program monitoring study is to be conducted in three months, and a program impact study is to be conducted in one year. Describe appropriate research strategies for these studies.

10. Jerod is hired to conduct an efficiency analysis of IRS auditors. How might he conduct this study using a cost-benefit ratio?

11. Ruby is hired to conduct an efficiency analysis of the juvenile probation program that works with children who are given early release from confinement. How might she conduct this study using a cost-effectiveness ratio?

12. A clinic decides to buy, rather than rent, a computer to maintain client records. What are the opportunity costs associated with this decision?

13. Colin is hired to do summative evaluations of six neighborhood day-care centers serving low-income families. Results from his analyses will be used to eliminate one center or to reduce funding for all centers because budget cuts are necessary. Colin asks for your advice. What specific advice do you offer him?

References

Abelson, P. H. (1977). Commission on federal paperwork. *Science, 197,* 1237.

Adair, J. G., Dushenko, T. W., & Lindsay, R. C. (1985). Ethical regulations and their impact on research practice. *American Psychologist, 40,* 59–72.

Addison, W. E. (1986). Agonistic behavior in preschool children: A comparison of same-sex versus opposite-sex interactions. *Bulletin of the Psychonomic Society, 24,* 44–46.

Allen, M. J., & Gutierrez, D. M. (1989). University students' support for heterosexual women with AIDS. *Psychological Reports, 65,* 171–176.

Allen, M. J., & Yen, W. M. (1979). *Introduction to measurement theory.* Monterey, CA: Brooks/Cole.

American Psychiatric Association. (1980). *Diagnostic and statistical manual of mental disorders* (3rd ed.). Washington, DC: Author.

American Psychological Association. (1987). *Casebook on ethical principles of psychologists.* Washington, DC: Author.

American Psychological Association. (1990). Ethical principles of psychologists. *American Psychologist, 45,* 390–395.

American Psychological Association. (1994). *Publication Manual of the American Psychological Association* (4th ed.). Washington, DC: Author.

Babbie, E. (1983). *The practice of social research* (3rd ed.). Belmont, CA: Wadsworth.

Bak, P., & Chen, K. (1991, January). Self-organized criticality. *Scientific American,* pp. 46–53.

Bakan, P. (1960). The capacity for generating information by randomization. *Quarterly Journal of Experimental Psychology, 18,* 119–129.

Baker, G. H. B. (1982). Life events before the onset of rheumatoid arthritis. *Psychotherapy and Psychosomatics, 38,* 173–177.

Barber, T. X. (1976). *Pitfalls in human research: Ten pivotal points.* NY: Pergamon Press.

Baumeister, R. F. (1988). Should we stop studying sex differences altogether? *American Psychologist, 43,* 1092–1095.

Baumrind, D. (1971). Principles of ethical conduct in the treatment of subjects: Reactions to the draft report of the committee on ethical standards in psychological research. *American Psychologist, 26,* 887–896.

Baumrind, D. (1985). Research using intentional deception. *American Psychologist, 40,* 165–174.

Beck, A. T., Steer, R. A., & Garbin, M. G. (1988). Psychometric properties of the Beck Depression Inventory: Twenty-five years of evaluation. *Clinical Psychology Review, 8,* 77–100.

Bell, C. R., & Telman, N. (1980). Errors, accidents, and injuries on rotating shift-work: A field study. *International Review of Applied Psychology, 29,* 271–291.

Benn, S., and Gay, J. (1992). A course on the rights of children. *Teaching of Psychology, 19,* 226–228.

Berkowitz, L. & Donnerstein, E. (1982). External validity is more than skin deep: Some answers to criticism of laboratory experiments. *American Psychologist, 37,* 245–257.

Bohrnstedt, G. W., & Knoke, D. (1988). *Statistics for social data analysis* (2nd ed.). Itasca, IL: Peacock.

Brockwell, P. J., & Davis, R. A. (1987). *Time series: Theory and methods.* New York: Springer.

Brown, M. P., Silvas, T., & Allen, M. J. (1993, April). Effects of religion, religiosity, and gender on attitudes toward AIDS. Paper presented at the joint meeting of the Western Psychological Association and Rocky Mountain Psychological Association, Phoenix, AZ.

Campbell, S. M., Peplau, L. A., & DeBro, S. C. (1992). Women, men, and condoms: Attitudes and experiences of heterosexual college students. *Psychology of Women Quarterly, 16,* 273–288.

Ceci, S. J., Peters, D., & Plotkin, J. (1985). Human subjects review, personal values, and the regulation of social science research. *American Psychologist, 40,* 994–1002.

Chesler, P. (1972). *Women and madness.* NY: Doubleday.

Code of Federal Regulations. (1983), *Title 45,* Part 46, Section 46.101 to Section 46.409.

Cohen, J. (1977). *Statistical power analysis for behavioral sciences* (Rev. ed.) New York: Academic Press.

Cohen, S., Tyrell, D. A., & Smith, A. P. (1991). Psychological stress and susceptibility to the common cold. *New England Journal of Medicine, 325,* 606–612.

Committee on Lesbian and Gay Concerns. (1991). Avoiding heterosexual bias in language. *American Psychologist, 46,* 973–974.

Consortium for Longitudinal Studies (Ed.). (1983). *As the twig is bent: Lasting effects of preschool programs.* Hillsdale, NJ: Erlbaum.

Cook, T. D., Appleton, H., Connor, R. F., Shaffer, A., Tamkin, G., & Weber, S. J. (1975). *Sesame Street revisited.* NY: Russell Sage.

Cook, T. D., & Campbell, D. T. (1979). *Quasi-Experimentation: Design and analysis issues for field settings.* Boston: Houghton Mifflin.

Crew, K. (1983). How much is "very"? In E. Babbie, *The practice of social research* (3rd ed., p. 230). Belmont, CA: Wadsworth.

Crosby, F., Bromley, S., & Saxe, L. (1980). Recent unobtrusive studies of black and white discrimination and prejudice: A literature review. *Psychological Bulletin, 87,* 546–563.

Croyle, R. T., & Cooper, J. (1983). Dissonance arousal: Physiological evidence. *Journal of Personality and Social Psychology, 45,* 782–791.

Darley, J., & Latane, B. (1968). Bystander intervention in emergencies: Diffusion of responsibility. *Journal of Personality and Social Psychology, 8,* 377–383.

Denmark, F., Russo, N. F., Frieze, I. H., & Sechzer, J. A. (1988). Guidelines for avoiding sexism in research: A report of the Ad Hoc Committee on Nonsexist Research. *American Psychologist, 43,* 582–585.

Denzin, N. K. (1984). Ideographic/nomethetic psychology. In R. J. Corsini (Ed.), *Encyclopedia of psychology* (Vol. 2, pp. 182–183). NY: Wiley.

Eagly, A. H. (1978). Sex differences in influenceability. *Psychological Bulletin, 85,* 86–116.

Eagly, A. H. (1987). Reporting sex differences. *American Psychologist, 42,* 756–757.

Easterbrook, G. (1991, July 29). The sincerest flattery. *Newsweek,* pp. 45–46.

Eron, L. D., Huesman, L. R., Lefkowitz, M. M., & Walder, L. O. (1972). Does television violence cause aggression? *American Psychologist, 27,* 253–263.

Etaugh, C. (1980). Effects of nonmaternal care on children: Research evidence and popular views. *American Psychologist, 35,* 309–319.

Evans, J. D. (1985). *Invitation to psychological research.* New York: Holt, Rinehart, Winston.

Faust, D. (1984). *The limits of scientific reasoning.* Minneapolis: University of Minnesota Press.

Feild, H. S., & Barnett, N. J. (1978). Students vs. "real" people as jurors. *Journal of Social Psychology, 104,* 287–293.

Festinger, L. (1957). *A theory of cognitive dissonance.* Stanford, CA: Stanford University Press.

Festinger, L., & Carlsmith, J. M. (1959). Cognitive consequences of forced compliance. *Journal of Abnormal and Social Psychology, 58,* 203–210.

Festinger, L., Riecken, H., & Schachter, S. (1956). *When prophecy fails.* Minneapolis: University of Minnesota Press.

Fossey, D. (1972). Living with mountain gorillas. In T. B. Allen (Ed.), *The marvels of animal behavior.* Washington, DC: National Geographic Society.

Frederick, C. J. (1969). Suicide notes: A survey and evaluation. *Bulletin of Sociology, 3,* 17–26.

Friedman, M. (1980). *Overcoming fear of success.* NY: Seaview.

Friedman, M. (1985). *Overcoming fear of success* (Tape No. 20284). Brooklyn, NY: Psychology Today Tapes.

Friedman, M. P., & Wilson, R. W. (1975). Application of unobtrusive measures to the study of textbook usage by college students. *Journal of Applied Psychology, 60,* 659–662.

Galla, J. P., Frison, J. D., Jeffrey, L. R., & Gaer, E. P. (1981). Effect of experimenter's gender on responses to a sex-role attitude questionnaire. *Psychological Reports, 49,* 935–940.

Galton, F. (1872). Statistical inquiries into the efficacy of prayer. *Fortnightly Review, 12,* 125–135.

Gamson, W. A., Fireman, B., & Rytina, S. (1982). *Encounters with unjust authority.* Homewood, IL: Dorsey Press.

Garland, A. F., & Zigler, E. (1993). Adolescent suicide prevention: Current research and social policy implications. *American Psychologist, 48,* 169–182.

Gibaldi, J. & Achert, W. S. (1988). *MLA handbook for writers of research papers* (3rd ed.). New York: MLA.

Gintzler, A. R. (1980). Endorphin-mediated increases in pain threshold during pregnancy. *Science, 210,* 193–195.

Gleitman, H. (1991). *Psychology* (3rd ed.). NY: W. W. Norton.

Goldberg, L. R. (1993). The structure of phenotypic personality traits. *American Psychologist, 48,* 26–34.

Goldberg, P. A. (1968). Are women prejudiced against women? *Transaction, 5,* 28–30.

Goldberg, P. A. (1976). A personal journal. In M. P. Golden (Ed.), *The research experience* (pp. 153–156). Itasca, IL: Peacock.

Golden M. P. (Ed.). (1976). *The research experience.* Itasca, IL: Peacock.

Goldstein, J. B. (1981). Assessment of hypertension. In C. K. Prokop & L. A. Bradley (Eds.). *Medical psychology.* New York: Academic Press.

Goodall, J. (1986). *The chimpanzees of Gombe: Patterns of behavior.* Cambridge, MFA: Harvard University Press.

Gould, S. J. (1981). *The mismeasure of man.* NY: W. W. Norton.

Guilford, J. P. (1967). *The nature of human intelligence.* NY: McGraw Hill.

Guilford, J. P., & Zimmerman, W. S. (1956). Fourteen dimensions of temperament. *Psychological Monographs, 70,* No. 10.

Hale, J. L. (1987). Plagiarism in classroom settings. *Communication Research Reports, 4*(2), 66–70.

Haney, C., Banks, C., & Zimbardo, P. (1973). Interpersonal dynamics in a simulated prison. *International Journal of Criminology and Penology, 1,* 69–87.

Harrington, A. (1987). *Medicine, mind, and the double brain: A study in nineteenth-century thought.* Princeton, NJ: Princeton University Press.

Haynes, S. N., Floyd, F. J., Lemsky, C., Rogers, E., Winemiller, D., Heilman, N., Werle, M., Murphy, T., & Cardone, L. (1992). The Marital Satisfaction Questionnaire for Older Persons. *Psychological Assessment, 4,* 473–482.

Henry, L. (1993, January 31). Super Sunday puts more women at risk. *The Bakersfield Californian,* p. A4.

Herek, G. M., Kimmel, D. C., Amaro, H., & Melton, G. G. (1991). Avoiding heterosexist bias in psychological research. *American Psychologist, 46,* 957–963.

Holmes, D. S. (1976a). Debriefing after psychological experiments I: Effectiveness of post-deception dehoaxing. *American Psychologist, 31,* 858–867.

Holmes, D. S. (1976b). Debriefing after psychological experiments II: Effectiveness of post-deception desensitizing. *American Psychologist, 31,* 868–875.

Holmes, D. S., & Bennett, D. H. (1974). Experiments to answer questions raised by the use of deception in psychological research. *Journal of Personality and Social Psychology, 35,* 358–367.

Horner, M. (1969). Fail: Bright women. *Psychology Today, 3*(6), 36.

Hyde, J. S. (1991). *Half the human experience: The psychology of women* (4th ed.). Lexington, MA: Heath.

Kagan, J., Kearsley, R. B., & Zelazo, P. R. (1977). The effects of infant care on psychological development. *Education Quarterly, 1,* 109–142.

Kagan, J., Reznick, J. S., & Snidman, N. (1988). Biological bases of childhood shyness. *Science, 240,* 167–171.

Kantowitz, B. H., & Sorkin, R. D. (1983). *Human factors: Understanding people-system relationships.* NY: Wiley

Kaplan, R. M., & Saccuzzo, D. P. (1989). *Psychological testing: Principles, applications, and issues* (2nd ed.). Pacific Grove, CA: Brooks/Cole.

Keith-Spiegel, P., & Koocher, G. P. (1985). *Ethics in psychology: Professional standards and cases.* New York: Random House.

Kemmick, D. L., & Cardwell, J. D. (1980). Interfaith comparison of multidimensional measures of religiosity. In J. D. Cardwell (Ed.), *The social context of religiosity* (pp. 47–60). Lanham, MD: University Press of America.

Keppel, G. (1982). *Design and analysis: A researcher's handbook* (2nd ed.) Englewood Cliffs, NJ: Prentice-Hall.

Kobasa, S. C. (1979). Stressful life events, personality, and health: An inquiry into hardiness. *Journal of Personality and Social Psychology, 37,* 1–11.

Koenig, H. G., Kvale, J. N., & Ferrel, C. (1988). Religion and well-being in later life. *The Gerontological Society of America, 28*(1), 18–28.

Kraemer, H. C., & Thiemann, S. (1987). *How many subjects?* Beverly Hills, CA: Sage.

Latane, B., & Rodin, J. (1969). A lady in distress: Inhibiting effects of friends and strangers on bystander intervention. *Journal of Experimental and Social Psychology, 5,* 189–202.

Levine, E. K. (1982). Old people are not all alike: Social class, ethnicity/race, and sex are bases for important differences. In J. E. Sieber (Ed.), *The ethics of social research: Surveys and experiments.* New York: Springer-Verlag.

Light, R. J. (1987). Six evaluation issues that synthesis can resolve better than single studies. In D. S. Cordray and M. W. Lipsey (Eds.), *Evaluation Studies Review Annual: Volume 11* (pp. 703–719). Newbury Park, CA: Sage.

Loftus, E. F. (1992). When a lie becomes memory's truth: Memory distortion after exposure to misinformation. *Current Directions in Psychological Science, 1,* 121–123.

Lyons, J. A., & Serbin, L. A. (1986). Observer bias in scoring boys' and girls' aggression. *Sex Roles, 14,* 301–314.

Mednick, M. T. (1989). On the politics of psychological constructs: Stop the bandwagon, I want to get off. *American Psychologist, 44,* 1118–1123.

Milgram, S. (1963). Behavioral study of obedience. *Journal of Abnormal and Social Psychology, 67,* 371–378.

Milgram, S. (1964a). Group pressure and action against a person. *Journal of Abnormal and Social Psychology, 69,* 137–143.

Milgram, S. (1964b). Issues in the study of obedience: A reply to Baumrind. *American Psychologist, 19,* 848–852.

Milgram, S. (1965a). Liberating effects of group pressure. *Journal of Personality and Social Psychology, 1,* 127–134.

Milgram, S. (1965b). Some conditions of obedience and disobedience to authority. *Human Relations, 18,* 57–76.

Miller, A. G. (1972). Role-playing: An alternative to deception? *American Psychologist, 27,* 623–636.

Miller, N. E. (1985). The value of behavioral research on animals. *American Psychologist, 40,* 423–440.

Miller, N. E. (1992). Introducing and teaching much-needed understanding of the scientific process. *American Psychologist, 47,* 848–850.

Monahan, L., Kuhn, D., & Shaver, P. (1974). Intrapsychic versus cultural explanations of the "fear of success" motive. *Journal of Personality and Social Psychology, 29,* 60–64.

Mook, D. G. (1983). In defense of external invalidity. *American Psychologist, 38,* 379–387.

Morin, S. F., & Rothblum, E. D. (1991). Removing stigma: Fifteen years of progress. *American Psychologist, 46,* 947–949.

Mullen, B., & Rosenthal, R. (1985). *BASIC meta-analysis: Procedures and programs.* Hillsdale, NJ: Lawrence Erlbaum.

Nash, S. C. (1979). Sex role as a mediator of intellectual functioning. In M. A. Wittig & A. C. Petersen (Eds.), *Sex-related differences in cognitive functioning: Developmental issues* (pp. 263–302). NY: Academic Press.

Neale, J. M., & Liebert, R. M. (1969). Reinforcement therapy using aides and patients as behavioral technicians: A case report of a mute patient. *Perceptual and Motor Skills, 28,* 835–839.

Neuringer, A. (1986). Can people behave "randomly?": The role of feedback. *Journal of Experimental Psychology: General, 115,* 62–75.

Newsom, C., Favell, J. E., & Rincover, A. (1983). Side effects of punishment. In S. Axelrod & J. Apsche (Eds.), *The effects of punishment on human behavior.* New York: Academic Press.

Orne, M. T. (1959). The nature of hypnosis: Artifact and essence. *Journal of Abnormal and Social Psychology, 58,* 277–299.

Orne, M. T. (1962). On the social psychology of the psychological experiment with particular reference to demand characteristics and their implications. *American Psychologist, 17,* 776–783.

Orne, M. T., & Scheibe, K. E. (1964). The contribution of nondeprivation factors in the production of sensory deprivation effects: The psychology of the "panic button." *Journal of Abnormal and Social Psychology, 68,* 3–12.

Osgood, C. E., & Tannenbaum, P. H. (1955). The principle of congruence in the prediction of attitude change. *Psychological Bulletin, 62,* 42–55.

Paludi, M. A. (1984). Psychometric properties and underlying assumptions of four objective measures of fear of success. *Sex Roles, 10,* 311–316.

Parsons, H. M. (1974). What happened at Hawthorne? *Science, 183,* 439–440.

Parsons, H. M. (1984). Human factors. In R. J. Corsini (Ed.), *Encyclopedia of psychology* (Vol. 2, pp. 149–150). NY: Wiley.

Peters, T. J., & Waterman, R. H. (1982). *In search of excellence: Lessons from America's best-run companies.* NY: Harper & Row.

Pfungst, O. (1911). *Clever Hans (The horse of Mr. Von Osten).* NY: Henry Holt. (Reissued 1965 by Holt, New York).

Phillips, D. P. (1977). Motor vehicle fatalities increase just after publicized suicide stories. *Science, 196,* 1464–1465.

Polyson, J., Levinson, M., & Miller, H. (1982). Writing styles: A survey of psychology journal editors. *American Psychologist, 37,* 335–338.

Posavac, E. J., & Carey, R. G. (1989). *Program evaluation: Methods and case studies* (3rd ed.). Englewood Cliffs, NJ: Prentice-Hall.

Powell, D. (Ed.) (1988). *Parent education as early childhood intervention: Emerging directions in theory, research and practice.* Norwood, NJ: Ablex.

Pressman, J., & Wildavsky, A. (1973). *Implementation: Or how great expectations in Washington are dashed in Oakland.* Berkeley, CA: University of California Press.

Rahe, R. H. (1987). Recent life changes, emotions, and behaviors in coronary heart disease. In A. Baum & J. E. Singer (Eds.), *Handbook of psychology and health: Vol. 5 Stress* (pp. 229–254). Hillsdale, NJ: Lawrence Erlbaum Associates.

Reeves, B. F. (1970). *The first year of Sesame Street: The formative research.* NY: Children's Television Workshop.

Reuder, M. E. (1984). Phrenology. In R. J. Corsini (Ed.), *Encyclopedia of psychology* (Vol. 3, pp. 39–40). NY: Wiley.

Ring, K., Wallston, K., & Corey, M. (1970). Mode of debriefing as a factor affecting subjective reaction to a Milgram-type obedience experiment: An ethical inquiry. *Representative Research in Social Psychology, 1,* 67–88.

Riordin, C. A., & Marlin, N. A. (1987). Some good news about some bad practices. *American Psychologist, 42,* 104–106.

Robertson, D. B. (1984). Program implementation versus program design. *Policy Studies Review, 3,* 391–405.

Robinson, G. H. (1984). Weber's law. In R. J. Corsini (Ed.), *Encyclopedia of psychology* (Vol. 3, p. 466). NY: Wiley.

Roethlisberger, F. J., & Dickson, W. J. (1939). *Management and the worker.* Cambridge, Mass: Harvard University Press.

Rogosa, D. (1980). A critique of cross-lagged correlation. *Psychological Bulletin, 88,* 245–258.

Romanczyk, R., Kent, R. N., Diament, C., & O'Leary, K. D. (1973). Measuring the reliability of observational data: A reactive process. *Journal of Applied Behavior Analysis, 6,* 175–184.

Rosenhan, D. (1973). On being sane in insane places. *Science, 179,* 250–258.

Rosenthal, R. (1966). *Experimenter effects in behavioral research.* NY: Appleton-Century-Crofts.

Rosenthal, R. (1984). *Meta-analytical procedures for social research.* Applied Social Research Methods Series, Vol. 6. Beverly Hills, CA: Sage.

Rosenthal, R., & Rosnow, R. L. (1991). *Essentials of behavioral research: Methods and data analysis* (2nd ed.). NY: McGraw Hill.

Rosnow, R. L., & Suls, J. M. (1970). Reactive effects of pretesting in attitude research. *Journal of Personality and Social Psychology, 15,* 338–343.

Rossi, P. H., & Freeman, H. E. (1985). *Evaluation: A systematic approach* (3rd ed.). Beverly Hills, CA: Sage.

Rubin, Z. (1970). Measurement of romantic love. *Journal of Personality and Social Psychology, 16,* 256–273.

Rubin, Z. (1973). Designing honest experiments. *American Psychologist, 28,* 445–448.

Rubin, Z. (1976). On studying love: Notes on the researcher-subject relationship. In M. P. Golden (Ed.), *The research experience* (pp. 508–513). Itasca, IL: Peacock.

Sacks, O. (1985). *The man who mistook his wife for a hat.* New York: Summit Books.

Scarr, S. (1988). Race and gender as psychological variables: Social and ethical issues. *American Psychologist, 43,* 56–59.

Scarr, S., & Weinberg, R. A. (1976). IQ test performance of black children adopted by white families. *American Psychologist, 31,* 726–739.

Schachter, S., & Singer, J. E. (1962). Cognitive, social, and physiological determinants of emotional state. *Psychological Review, 69,* 379–399.

Schieber, F. (1988). Vision assessment technology and screening older drivers: past practices and emerging techniques. In National Research Council (Eds.), *Transportation in an aging society,* Vol. 2 (pp. 270–293). Washington, D.C.: Transportation Research Board.

Schwartz, S. (1986). *Classic studies in psychology.* Palo Alto, CA: Mayfield.

Scriven, M. (1987). New frontiers of evaluation. In D. S. Cordray and M. W. Lipsey (Eds.), *Evaluation Studies Review Annual: Volume 11* (pp. 93–130). Newbury Park, CA: Sage.

Selye, H. (1976). *The stress of life.* New York : McGraw-Hill.

Shotland, R. L., & Straw, M. (1976). Bystander response to an assault: When a man attacks a woman. *Journal of Personality and Social Psychology, 34,* 990–999.

Silverman, I. (1975). Nonreactive methods and the law. *American Psychologist, 30,* 764–769.

Smith, M. L., & Glass, G. V. (1977). Meta-analysis of psychotherapy outcome studies. *American Psychologist, 32,* 752–760.

Spector, P. E. (1992). *Summated rating scale construction: An introduction.* Beverly Hills, CA: Sage.

Sperry, R. W. (1968). Hemisphere deconnection and unity in conscious awareness. *American Psychologist, 23,* 723–733.

Stoloff, M. L., & Couch, J. V. (Eds.). (1992). *Computer use in psychology* (3rd ed.). Washington, DC: American Psychological Association.

Summary report of journal operations, 1991. (1992). *American Psychologist, 47,* 968.

Suter, S. (1986). *Health psychophysiology: Mind-body interactions in wellness and illness.* Hillsdale, NJ: Lawrence Erlbaum.

Thigpen, C. H., & Cleckley, H. (1954). *The three faces of Eve.* Kingsport, TN: Kingsport Press.

Thorndike, E. (1911). *Animal intelligence.* New York: Macmillan.

Thurston, P. W., Ory, J. C., Mayberry, P. W., & Branskamp, L. A. (1987). In D. S. Cordray and M. W. Lipsey (Eds.), *Evaluation Studies Review Annual: Volume 11* (pp. 262–274). Newbury Park, CA: Sage.

Tresemer, D. (1977). *Fear of success.* NY: Plenum.

Watson, J. B., & Rayner, R. (1920). Conditioned emotional reactions. *Journal of Experimental Psychology, 3,* 1–14.

Wedding, D., & Corsini, R. J. (1989). *Case studies in psychotherapy.* Itasca, IL: Peacock.

Weisz, J. R., Weiss, B., & Donenberg, G. R. (1992). The lab versus the clinic: Effects of child and adolescent psychotherapy. *American Psychologist, 47,* 1578–1585.

Wickens, C. D. (1984). *Engineering psychology and human performance.* Columbus, OH: Merrill.

Wilson, C., & Marcus, D. K. (1992). Teaching anatomy of the sheep brain: A laboratory exercise with Play Doh. *Teaching of Psychology, 19,* 223–225.

Winter, D. G. (1987). Leader appeal, leader performance, and the motive profiles of leaders and followers: A study of American presidents and elections. *Journal of Personality and Social Psychology, 52,* 196–202.

Yalom, I. D. (1989). *Love's executioner.* NY: Basic Books.

Zigler, E., Taussig, C., & Black, K. (1992). Early childhood intervention: A promising preventative for juvenile delinquency. *American Psychologist, 47,* 997–1006.

Zimbardo, P. G. (1969). The human choice: Individuation, reason, and order versus deindividuation, impulse, and chaos. In W. J. Arnold & D. Levine (Eds.), *Nebraska symposium on motivation* (Vol. 17). Lincoln, NE: University of Nebraska Press.

Zinsser, H. (1960). *Rats, lice and history.* NY: Bantam Books.

Zuckerman, M. (1990). Some dubious premises in research and theory on racial differences. *American Psychologist, 45,* 1297–1303.

Zuckerman, M., & Wheeler, L. (1975). To dispel fantasies about the fantasy-based measure of fear of success. *Psychological Bulletin, 82,* 932–946.

Index